FIRST IN THE FIELD

The History of the World's First Cricket League
The Birmingham and District Cricket League
Formed 1888

Alex E. Davis

K.A.F. BREWIN BOOKS

First published by K.A.F. Brewin Books, Studley, Warwickshire.
in March 1988

DEDICATION

To my wife Chris, a lover of the game
of cricket whose support has made
completion of this work possible.

ISBN No. 0 947731 34 2

©   Alex Davis 1988

Typeset in Press Roman
Made and Printed in Great Britain
by Supaprint (Redditch)Ltd.
Redditch, Worcs.

FOREWORD
BY CHARLES H. PALMER, C.B.E.

It was to a wide audience at the 1983 International Cricket Conference that I had a welcome opportunity to refer with pride to my long association with the Birmingham League.

Discussion was in full spate on the New Zealand v. Australia One Day International match in 1981 when the Australian Captain Greg Chappel sank to prominence by ordering his brother Trevor to bowl the last ball of the match along the ground to prevent any possibility of a six to tie. Proposals had subsequently been made to ban underarm bowling completely. In resisting this total ban in all cricket I spoke of when I was 14 and fortunate to be playing for Old Hill Second XI with Bill Hollies (father of Eric), when he was bowling his underarm spinners — fascinating cricket for player and spectator alike. It was, incidentally, 1933 — underarm at Old Hill and bodyline in Australia!

I was proud to refer to this because ever since those early days I have retained an affectionate respect for the Club and League in which, with the particular encouragement of my family, I formed my first impressions outside school of good standards of cricket and behaviour.

Now the Birmingham League has reached its Centenary and the consequent pride and pleasure I have is, of course, shared by so many cricketers, administrators and supporters. There will be many who, like me, will be grateful for the friendships made and, we hope, retained and strengthened through our League cricket.

A browse through this book will revive personal memories of such friendships and of much good cricket and dedicated service. The record of so many fine names makes me feel immensely privileged to have been asked to write this foreword. We must all be grateful to author Alex Davis and all who have assisted him in this labour of love. I confidently recommend this history which will speak splendidly for itself.

Charles Palmer

Sep 9 87

REFERENCES AND ACKNOWLEDGEMENTS

Principal References

Newspapers

Birmingham Post
Birmingham Mail
Birmingham Gazette
Sports Argus
Express and Star
Kidderminster Shuttle
Smethwick Telephone
Walsall Observer
Athletic News

Books

Wisden
Cricket in the Leagues by John Kay
The Story of Warwickshire Cricket by Leslie Duckworth
S.F. Barnes: Master Bowler by Leslie Duckworth
The Complete History of Walsall Cricket Club 1833—
1909 by Benjamin Evans
The Gorway Story by E.J.A. Cook
Moseley's Early Years (1855—1895) by Bill Stanton
Who's Who of Cricketers by Philip Bailey, Philip Thorn,
Peter Wynne-Thomas
Scorebooks and Minute Books

Acknowledgements

Mr. Patrick Baird and the Staff of the Local Studies Department of Birmingham Reference Library who made available 100 years of microfilm newspaper tapes.

Birmingham Post and Mail for permission to produce items and photographs.

Authors of all publications listed in References.

To my fellow scorers in the League and the League and Club Officers who have sorted out and checked information.

To many individuals who have offered material and given permission for it to be reproduced.

To Roy Abell for the Illustrations of the Grounds.

To Alan Richardson for his help with photographs.

To Mrs. V. Day, M.L. Simms and Ken Hayes for help in compilation.
David Ratcliffe for encouragement and support.
John Reeves for collating the playing records, making contributions to the text and for general support throughout the research.

My wife, Chris, and daughter, Anne, who have wrestled with my handwriting to type the draft. To my son, Michael, who has assisted with the reading of the proofs and the preparation of the Index.

To all the above and the many others who have given encouragement, my sincere thanks.

CONTENTS

Page

PREAMBLE

This book has been prepared to coincide with the Celebrations of the League's Centenary in 1988.

The idea of a written history was first mooted in 1951. Austin Gethin was invited in 1953 to undertake the task. Austin had played for Kidderminster for many years and he and his father W.G. Gethin contributed articles on the League for the Sports Argus. Austin, however, declined and the League then inserted an advertisement in the Birmingham Sports Argus 'Historian Required'.

No historian came forward and the matter lapsed until Mr. Gerald Humphries, also of Kidderminster, made a start in the late 1970's. Gerald did a considerable amount of work based on a comprehensive set of press cuttings collected from 1923 to 1960 by A.W. Gethin and R.I. Scorer. Gerald died in 1983 and the project was delayed until I responded to an appeal by David Bryant during his term as President in 1985. The work of Gerald Humphries was made available to me and has been of considerable assistance, particularly covering the period 1923 to 1949 when Gerald wrote an account of each game played and collected information on some of the players of his time.

A specification for the preparation of a history was set out in Minutes of 1951:—

"From time to time, suggestions are mooted for a Hand Book, or a History of the League — nebulous indeed, but giving cause for reflection. Your Committee discussed this matter pretty fully and while it is of the opinion that a History of the League over its long and famous life would be an admirable contribution to the game, its compilation presents a task of monumental proportions not to be entered into lightly.

Such compilation must be the perfect production, authoritative, all embracing and in keeping with the League tradition of dignity.

The Advisory Committee therefore at this stage, leaves the suggestion with the Clubs themselves. Those who have kept journals (and indeed it is known that some have a more or less complete history) will be better placed than others. It will be appreciated however, that a League History, must be all embracing and therefore many Clubs will require time for search and full discussion before the matter can be looked upon as a practical proposition to be considered by the League".

I have endeavoured to meet this specification and leave the reader to be the judge of whether these ideals of the Advisory Committee have been met.

Every effort has been made to ensure that the details given are correct but since the majority of the information has been extracted from micro film archives of newspapers some mistakes may well have arisen. I shall be pleased to receive any corrections or additional material so that a true and comprehensive archive of information can be left for the use of future generations.

Alex E. Davis.

ORIGINS OF CLUBS

1. Aston — In 1888 an independent Local Board area on eastern fringe of Birmingham, became Borough of Aston Manor in 1903 and incorporated into Greater Birmingham in 1911.

2. Coventry — Cathedral City — 18 miles east of Birmingham.
   Main industry automobile engineering.

3. Dudley — Town — 10 miles west of Birmingham — main industries in 1888 mining and heavy engineering, now chiefly light engineering.

4. Duport — Firm making beds and kitchen furniture located close to Dudley Port railway station near Dudley.

5. Handsworth — Originally an Urban District 4 miles north-west of City Centre of Birmingham — incorporated into Greater Birmingham in 1911.

6. Kidderminster — Town — 17 miles south-west of Birmingham — main industry — carpet making.

7. Mitchells & Butlers — Large brewery firm in Cape Hill 2 miles west of Birmingham City Centre.

8. Moseley — Part of Urban District of Kings Norton and Northfield on southern fringe of Birmingham incorporated in Greater Birmingham in 1911 — 2½ miles from City Centre.

9. Old Hill — Was part of Municipal Borough of Rowley Regis now the Metropolitan Borough of Sandwell on western fringe of Greater Birmingham — 7 miles from City Centre. Was in Staffordshire now in West Midlands.

10. Salters — Firm located between Smethwick and West Bromwich making steel springs.

11. Small Heath — Suburb one mile east of City Centre.

12. Smethwick — Urban District in 1894 — 3 miles north west of Birmingham centre now part of Metropolitan Borough of Sandwell. Main industry — engineering.

13. Stourbridge — Town — 14 miles south west of Birmingham — main industry glassware. Now part of Metropolitan Borough of Dudley.

14. Warwickshire — County Cricket Club with Headquarters at Edgbaston, Birmingham.

15. Walsall — Town — 9 miles north west of Birmingham — famous for leather goods, saddles and harness.

16.	Wednesbury	8 miles north west of Birmingham main industry steel tubes and general engineering.
17.	West Bromwich	Town — 5 miles north west of Birmingham — main industry — engineering. NB. Club gets its name from name of town and from Earl of Dartmouth on whose land the Club played.
18.	Worcestershire	County Cricket Club with headquarters at Worcester.
19.	Worcester	Cathedral City, 29 miles south west of Birmingham main industries manufacturing of china and porcelain.
20.	Aldridge	Originally an Urban District incorporated into Metropolitan District of Walsall in 1974. Main industries, brick making and sand and gravel workings.

THE BIRMINGHAM CRICKET ASSOCIATION

'The Tower of Babel'

The middle of the nineteenth century saw a great surge in interest in team sports, particularly in cricket and in both codes of football. This growth probably had its stimulus from the grouping of large centres of population looking for a group identity and interest.

These centres were still within walking distance of green fields which surrounded the cities, towns and villages. In addition, city and town councils and philanthropic employers, such as Mitchells, were allocating areas for recreation, so spaces were available for group sports.

Further stimulus for interest in cricket was generated by the matches played by the touring All England XI and United England XI sides which created great interest and a desire to participate in the game.

Cricket and football teams sprang up everywhere, with individual challenge matches developing into annual fixtures.

The establishment of the comprehensive local railway system opened up the possibilities of travel beyond that of the horse drawn transport of the day. This facilitated the possibility of fulfilling fixtures at some distance even after work was finished on Saturday lunchtimes, thus opening up the enjoyment to a wider range of the working classes than had normally taken part in team events.

Football, with its immediate action and competitive element soon became organised into associations and cup competitions but cricket was arranged in a much more casual manner, the relaxed tempo of the game being matched by an equally offhand approach by some of the sides in respect of their arrangements.

At the end of 1879, Mr. Harry Brettell, a former Town Clerk of Dudley, conceived the idea that having regard to the success of the Birmingham County Football Association in organising football, a similar body could bring more efficiency into the organisation of cricket. Early in the following year, at his initiative, a number of clubs formed the "Birmingham and District Cricket Association".

This Association tried to bring some control into the organisation and stimulation of cricket interest in the area and with Mr William Ansell, a Headmaster at a Birmingham School, as secretary, the Association became a considerable force contributing to the eventual founding of the Warwickshire County Cricket Club.

Many of the clubs had little sense of any corporate identity with, or responsibility to the Association, and little was achieved to improve the casual approach to organisation of local cricket. Contemporary accounts of those days record teams not turning up,

MITCHELLS' BREWERY CRICKET CLUB,
WINNERS OF THE
BIRMINGHAM & DISTRICT CRICKET CHALLENGE CUP 1887.

H.G. Bainbridge, Esq. (Vice-President), E.T. Grant, Esq. (Hon.
Treasurer), J.E. Chambers, Esq. (Vice-President) W.McCowan, Esq.
(Vice-President)
D. Ray, H. Sproson (Scorer), C. Allen (Capt.), Jno. M. Lones (Hon.
Sec.), J. Cresswell,
S.G. Morgan, A. Law, T. Rollings, G. Payton, H. Widdowson,
T. Hawkins, H. Vaughton, T. Stevenson.

turning up short of players, no positive starting times, grounds not prepared, players and teams leaving early, lack of discipline on the field and constant disputing of club umpires' decisions.

The problems were aggravated by the decision of the Association to run a Cup Competition, anathema to conventional cricket lovers then, as it is today. It was this competition which was eventually to signal the demise of the Association and the formation of the League. The Cup Competition was a constant source of acrimony, the final curtain providing high drama.

Smethwick, who had already won two of the cups outright, were to play Mitchells in the 1887 Final. The games were played over two innings (limited over or time matches were unthinkable in those days) and two days were set aside to achieve a result.

After the two days the game ended in a draw, after some dispute the Association, ruled that the game should be replayed and continue until a result was achieved. It was a two innings game and after four days Mitchells claimed victory on the grounds that Smethwick had lost nine wickets in their second innings and the last Smethwick player was not available to bat and time for the day had not been reached. Smethwick claimed that time had been reached and claimed victory on the fifth day, because when they and the Umpires went out on to the field Mitchells had not turned up! The scores were Mitchells 167 and 259; Smethwick 233 and 182—9. An eventual acrimonious General Meeting, likened to the 'Tower of Babel', awarded the game to Mitchells, although even this was disputed. Clubs resigned from the Association, which lost its influence and faded out.

It was against this background that the League derived its origins when keen cricketers in leading Clubs, led by Mr. H. Grosvenor Hill, decided that the game should be put on a proper footing with order, responsibility and discipline, and moves were made to establish the Organisation which, one hundred years later, still carries the title "The Birmingham and District Cricket League".

Walsall

4

1888 — THE LEAGUE IS FORMED

The initiative for calling a meeting to form the League was taken by Messrs. F.E. Rowe and E.T. Grant of Mitchells, who sent out a circular to leading clubs inviting them to a meeting to discuss the desirability of forming a cricket league to take the place of the Cricket Association.

This historic meeting was held on Friday 30 November, 1888, at the Queen's Arms Hotel, Easy Row, Birmingham, and was attended by the following clubs and representatives: —

Mitchells C.C.	Messrs F.E. Rowe & E.T. Grant
Salters C.C.	Messrs. Harold & Spender
Aston Unity C.C.	Mr. C.R. Durban
Walsall C.C.	Mr. F.T. Cozens
West Bromwich Dartmouth C.C.	Mr. H.W. Phillips
Handsworth Wood C.C.	Mr. H.B.G. Hill

Mr. William Ansell, who was by this time Honorary Secretary of Warwickshire County Cricket Club, was in the Chair.

The opinion of those present was that a competition for the mere honour of first place among local clubs would create more interest among cricketers and the public than the previous cup competition without creating unpleasant rivalry. The number of Clubs to be admitted was to be limited to ensure the best standards were obtained and to enable League clubs to leave a few Saturdays open to continue friendly games.

Mr. Ansell for Warwickshire and Mr. Charles Durban for Aston Unity were not in a position to pledge their Clubs' full concurrence without consulting their Committees and, as Kings Heath C.C. and Smethwick C.C. were not represented, it was ultimately resolved "That this meeting considers it desirable to form a cricket league for the Birmingham District and the representatives present undertake to bring the question before their own Committees and report thereon at a meeting to be held on Friday 14 December, 1888". Mr. Rowe was appointed temporary Honorary Secretary.

This second meeting held at the same venue was attended by representatives of Mitchells C.C., Kings Heath C.C., Aston Unity C.C., Walsall C.C., West Bromwich Dartmouth C.C., Salters C.C., and the Warwickshire County Cricket Club, Mr. W. Ansell again presiding.

The representatives of the County Club reported that the County Club had decided not to join, the County Committee expressing the view that such a League would not be conducive to the interests of the Warwickshire Club. At that time, Warwickshire were not one of the eight first class counties, but were competing in the Second Class Counties' Competition. (It is interesting to note

5

Presidents of the
BIRMINGHAM & DISTRICT CRICKET LEAGUE
F.T. Cozens, 1888-1930. J.A. Lones,1932-1934, 1945, 1951
C. Herbert Smith. 1935-1936. W.J. Phair, 1931.

that nine years later in an article Lord Harris declared that he was worried about the effect on County Clubs due to the attractions offered by League Clubs to professionals and the public).

Smethwick, although not represented, had intimated they were not in favour of the scheme (perhaps the sores were still open from the cup final of the previous year) and this lack of support created some doubt as to the desirability of proceeding. The support of Kings Heath was, however, encouraging because they had always been hostile to the Cup Competition and had never competed.

After a long discussion, it was agreed that "The Birmingham and District Cricket League" should be formed and worked as an experiment for one season comprising Aston Unity C.C., Handsworth Wood C.C., Kings Heath C.C., Mitchells C.C., Salters C.C., Walsall C.C., and West Bromwich Dartmouth C.C.

The formation of the League was welcomed by an article in the 'Birmingham Mail' in the following terms:

"After the various fiascos and unpleasantness in connection with the local Cricket Cup Competition the news of the formation of a Birmingham and District League should come as a boon and a blessing to cricketers who like to take their cricket in a rational manner and without the feverish anxiety which appears to attach itself to cup ties."

Two committed and active cricketers, Mr F.T. Cozens (Walsall) and Mr. H. Grosvenor Hill (Handsworth Wood) were elected President and Honorary Secretary, respectively, and under the leadership of these two dynamic personalities, the League soon became established as the leading competition in the area.

The first set of Rules (see the Appendix) was drawn up by Mr. Sam Durban of Aston Unity. So wise were his ideas that the same rules exist today with additions and alterations incorporated by the Clubs to suit the changing conditions. These Rules have always been concise and precise without seeking to close every loophole so that throughout the history of the League it has been the 'spirit' rather than the 'letter' which has always governed the determination of the few points of dispute that have arisen.

The successful operation of the League has been this willingness of Clubs to accept and put the League interests before their own.

The Objects of the League as set out in the first rules were:—

'The objects of this League shall be to promote the best interests of Local Cricket and Club Matches, consistent with loyal support to County Cricket'.

These objects have been faithfully observed by League Administrators as successive generations of local cricketers and enthusiasts have derived enjoyment from the games and many Test and County players have obtained their first experience of high standard competitive cricket.

Mitchells & Butlers

8

THE CLUBS (1888—1987)

Of the seven founder members, Aston Unity, Handsworth Wood, Kings Heath, Mitchells, Salters, Walsall and West Bromwich Dartmouth, three: Aston Unity, Walsall and West Bromwich, have continued their membership without a break or change of title throughout the life of the League.

Kings Heath who moved from their Billesley Ground to the Reddings, Moseley, and joined up with members of the Moseley Cricket Club, changed their name to Moseley after the first season to maintain unbroken membership of the League. A Kings Heath side was subsequently reformed as a separate club and returned to Billesley but has never re-entered the League.

Mitchells (Mitchells and Butlers following the amalgamation of the two brewery firms in 1898) left the League after the 1892 season. This followed friction arising from the playing of ineligible players which had culminated in the club's having points deducted and from a dispute about the standard of their wicket. They were re-admitted for the 1896 season since when they have been strong supporters of the League, on both the playing and administrative sides.

Salters, who played in Roebuck Lane, West Bromwich resigned after one season. Handsworth Wood performed creditably until they lost their ground at Browne's Green to developers after the 1914—18 war. They struggled on during the 1919 season by playing at the County Ground, Edgbaston, but when they could offer no permanent playing ground, by a majority of only one vote, Old Hill were elected in their place. Shortly afterwards, the Handsworth Wood Club was wound up. The parting from the League was without rancour and Handsworth Wood handed to the League their cash balance to supplement a League Benevolent Fund.

Following their decision not to join the League on its inauguration, Smethwick later entered a new Midland League. When a number of their players left the club to join a reformed Birmingham C.C. an application by a new Smethwick Committee to join the League for the 1891 season was welcomed and they too have since maintained unbroken membership.

In the early 1890's, the League had a number of seasons of consolidation and adjustment as Clubs found their level in this new style of competition. Wednesbury C.C. were elected for the 1890 season, playing as they do now on their ground in Wood Green Road, but had difficulty matching the standards set by the other clubs and after struggling for four seasons they resigned. Small Heath C.C. joined for the 1892 season but they too struggled and left after three seasons. They played in Small Heath Park and their wicket was described as second only to that at the County Ground. A visitor to

9

the ground commented at the time on the delightful aspect with adjoining fields alive with cricketers and a most excellent tea at one penny a cup!

The Warwickshire County Cricket Club entered their Club and Ground side for season 1894 but on being admitted into the County Championship for season 1895 they withdrew their League side. Their one season in the League had not been altogether satisfactory since from week to week their side was dependent on County calls and varied from extremely strong to very weak, resulting in an imbalance in the competition.

The centre of gravity of the clubs in membership shifted towards the west with the inclusion of Dudley C.C. in 1893, Stourbridge C.C. in 1894 and Kidderminster C.C. in 1895. These clubs have brought a strong Worcestershire flavour to the League's activities and by 1896, the League comprised ten clubs and, with the exception of the Handsworth Wood/Old Hill change in season 1920 the constitution remained the same until 1975.

This settled state of affairs caused many to consider that the League operated a 'closed shop' practice. Examination of the League Minutes shows that this is not so for in the 1930's, and again in the 1950's, the League made moves to attract other clubs. To keep the fixtures balanced, the League endeavoured to attract two clubs with reserve teams and, although applications were received, the League were unable to find two sides who could be admitted without the League's compromising on the standards of grounds, accommodation, or reserve strength, so no changes were made.

In 1974 the Warwickshire and Worcestershire County Cricket Clubs applied to join. Welcome as this was as a tribute to the strength and standing of the League, the Member Clubs gave the proposition considerable thought since compromises had to be accepted in the League Rules to accommodate two virtually professional sides. Although the applications were accepted there are still some club members not wholly in favour of the admission of the professional sides, which can vary in strength depending on the County's other commitments.

Warwickshire entered a side in each Division, Worcestershire entered a side in the First Division with Duport C.C. filling the Second Division place. The League extended the playing season for 1975 to accommodate the extra games.

After two seasons Worcestershire, who did not have a large staff of professionals, found it impossible to field a properly balanced side every week so Duport C.C. undertook to fill their place for season 1977 in addition to their Division Two commitment. Duport attempted to strengthen their side but were unable to provide consistently strong competition in the First Division and with cutbacks in the support from the Works Sports Club they withdrew both sides to be replaced by Worcester City C.C. for season 1982.

Dudley were forced to resign at the end of the 1985 season. In the middle of May of that season a forty foot hole appeared on the square! The ground was in an area subject to subsidence caused by old limestone workings. In the 1950's parts of the adjacent football field had been affected and for some seasons the terracing in front of the cricket pavilion had been cordoned off as unsafe. When the large hole appeared the whole ground was declared unsafe.

Subsequent investigations revealed a large cavern under the ground and Dudley Council had to face the problems posed by a ten million pound estimate of the cost of infilling the old workings. Dudley completed the season by playing all matches on opponents' or borrowed grounds. The Club were unable to obtain an alternative playing area and their place in the League was taken by Coventry and North Warwickshire C.C., winners of the Midland Club Cricket Championship in 1980 and 1983, 4 and 5 seasons.

It is interesting to note that Coventry and North Warwickshire had applied for League membership in 1920 when Handsworth Wood left. The application was then rejected because of the distance to travel.

The Second Division of the League was formed in 1893 comprising second elevens of the sides in the First Division, except in 1975–1976 when Duport played in place of Worcestershire.

At the instigation of John Huband, of Stourbridge, and Barrie Middleton of Walsall, a Third Division was formed. This Division was started in 1977 with the aim of encouraging younger players by giving them good disciplined League cricket in company with experienced players who were willing to move on from First or Second Division cricket and act as player/coaches.

In the first season eight League clubs entered teams and were joined for 1980 and 1981 by Holy Trinity. In 1983 Aldridge joined and now all League clubs are represented except Warwickshire. Aldridge have joined as Associate Members of the League.

Mr. F.T. Cozens (Walsall)
One of the founders of the League and President for 42 years.
(1888—1930)

1889—1914 THE FIRST YEARS

Administration

The general administration of the League was vested in the hands of the Hon. Secretary and Treasurer with matters of dispute referred to the League Clubs who usually met first at The Colonnade Hotel and from 1901 at The Exchange Restaurant both in the city centre.

It is interesting to note in a minute of 1896 that it was ruled that the Hon. Secretary alone should give information to the press on League Rulings and Decisions a wise ruling when one considers the various sources and interests in such a widespread organisation. It is a ruling which it has subsequently been necessary to remind members of from time to time when the press have been eager to publicise some differences of opinion.

Commencing in 1897 the League fixtures were prepared by 'The Fletcher System'. Mr. Fletcher devised a system of arranging fixtures which provided for clubs to be allocated fixtures by a ballot system. For some years Mr. Fletcher personally attended the League Meeting when the fixtures were arranged and received a fee for his services.

In 1898 it was ruled that results of matches were to be forwarded to be received by the Hon. Secretary by Tuesday following the game. Clubs failing to do so were to be fined 5/-. Later in 1907 the League introduced Result Cards and in 1909 Clubs were required to have a copy of League Rules posted in their Pavilions.

By 1896 an Annual Dinner was a feature of the League activities, tickets 2/6. After the presentation of the trophies and speeches entertainment was usually provided by 'entertainers', a soprano, baritone or tenor and an accompanist — hardly likely to be popular today!

In 1909 Grosvenor Hill retired as Honorary Secretary and Treasurer and was succeeded by C. Herbert Smith.

Engagement of Professionals

The inaugural League Rules made provision for each club to sign and play three professionals. The definition of a professional embraced any player who received remuneration in connection with the game as player, coach, groundsman or net bowler, or any player receiving a benefit without permission of the League. When the Warwickshire Club and Ground side joined for 1894 they were allowed to register six professionals providing only three played in any one match.

It is difficult to imagine how clubs could afford to pay for such service although most did. The main exceptions were Handsworth Wood who registered their groundsman Barton and Moseley who had support from County side amateurs.

In 1896 it was further ruled that no League club should approach professionals of another League club without first consulting that club.

Applications by professionals to be reinstated as amateurs posed thorny problems and after four such applications had been received in the 1899 season the League ruled that no further reinstatements would be considered under any circumstances. This was a more rigorous ruling than the then current M.C.C. ruling. This decision was to be the subject of much debate in the League Councils over many years.

The number of professionals was reduced to two per club in 1897 and to one in 1900, as clubs found it difficult to pay their way.

A ruling in 1908 precluded professionals from playing in the Second Division. The attitude to the distinction between amateurs and professionals which prevailed in cricket at the turn of the century can be gauged from a report of a 'tragic blunder at Lords' when the scorecards were printed with W.G. Quaife given the title Esq! Fortunately, the report goes on to say, the mistake was found before the cards had been issued and new ones were printed.

Two League rulings of 1909 and 1912 are also of interest. The first ruled that the son of Mitchells and Butlers groundsman could play as an amateur since he was not paid. The 1912 ruling was ingenious in that money received as a benefit for an accident occurring at cricket did not mar amateur status since it went to the doctor!

Boundaries

In 1896 the League ruled there should be uniformity on boundaries on all grounds; namely all balls in play passing to or over the boundary should count four. Previously each ground had had its own regulations. This rule was amended in line with the changes in the M.C.C. Laws in 1910 for 6 to be scored for all hits over the boundary. Prior to this the ball had to be hit out of the ground for a six.

Playing Time

From 1897 season games were started at 2.30 p.m. instead of 2.45, finishing at 7.30 p.m. instead of 7.15.

Until 1913 clubs were allowed a fifteen minute margin for unpunctuality before the opposing captain could claim an extra quarter of an hour.

Points

Initially 2 points for a win and one point for a draw were awarded but from 1911 to stimulate urge for victory the award was changed to 3 for a win 1½ for a tie and 1 for a draw.

Overs

5 balls constituted an over until 1901 season when 6 balls was standardised to conform to changes legalised in 1900 by the M.C.C.

Match Balls

A new ball for each innings was not a requirement in these early days. The provision of new balls conformed with M.C.C.Laws, whereby, until 1907, a new ball could not be claimed until 200 runs had been scored off the old one and then only if the old one was, in the opinion of the umpire, unsatisfactory. From 1907 a new ball could be claimed after 200 runs had been scored.

The Playing Scene — The Inaugural Season

The first match to be played in the League, and indeed what is thought to be the first cricket match in the World to be played under League Rules, took place on Saturday May 4th 1889 between Handsworth Wood and Aston Unity, the scorecard reading:—

Handsworth Wood C.C. v Aston Unity C.C.
played at Browne's Green, Handsworth Wood.
Saturday May 4th 1889

Innings of Aston Unity C.C.

H.J. Pallett	c	Eagles	b	Featherstone	12
C.R. Durban	c	Everett	b	Featherstone	0
H. Widdowson	c	Sylvester	b	Stevenson	13
C. Vale	c	H.B.G.Hill	b	Stevenson	26
Lancelott	c	Eagles	b	Stevenson	6
E. Durban			b	Featherstone	1
Grew			b	Eagles	0
S. Durban	c	Everett	b	Featherstone	0
I. Perkins				not out	13
E.J. Leake	c	Sylvester	b	Stevenson	0
H. Packer			b	H.B.G. Hill	2
				Extras	2
				Total	75

Featherstone	4 w
F. Stevenson	4 w
H.B.G. Hill	1 w
Eagles	1 w

Innings of Handsworth Wood C.C.

J. Carter	st	Packer	b	Pallett	40
F. Stevenson	c	Packer	b	Pallett	0
H.B.G. Hill	c	Grew	b	Leake	8
Featherstone	st	Packer	b	Pallett	8
J.E. Hill		c and b		Leake	2
R.S. Everett	st	Packer	b	Pallett	11
Hardy		Hit Wicket	b	Pallett	1
Dr. T.E. Hill			b	Pallett	6
Sylvester		Lbw	b	Pallett	0
Eagles		not out			1
I. Pemberton			b	Pallett	0
				Extras	4
				Total	81

H.J. Pallett	8 w
E.J. Leake	2 w

Handsworth Wood were recorded as having won by 6 runs. Until 1945 games had to be played out and the wins by number of wickets lost when opponents score had been passed was not always recorded.   H.B.G. Hill was the Honorary Secretary of the League and the Hills and the Durbans were to be stalwarts of the League's early years.   Followers of Warwickshire will recognise H.B.G. Hill, J.E. Hill and H.J. Pallett as members of the early County sides.

The first century in the League was scored by Alf Law of Mitchells, who was also a County player.   He scored 104 not out against Kings Heath on 1st June 1889.   The first hat-trick was performed by C. Vale of Aston Unity, also against Kings Heath, on 18 May.   On 25 May the first tied match occurred when Walsall and Handsworth Wood both scored 95.

Aston Unity were to become the First League Champions. The final League Table reading: —

	P	W	D	L	Pts
Aston Unity	12	8	3	1	19
Mitchells	12	6	4	2	16
Handsworth Wood	12	4	5	3	13
Salters	12	4	5	3	13
West Bromwich Dartmouth	12	3	4	5	10
Kings Heath	12	1	5	6	7
Walsall	12	1	4	7	6

The League was welcomed locally as a great success showing clearly the form of the local clubs.   The early starting times, better punctuality and system of independent umpires had, it was felt, done much to improve the sport and although the League had introduced keener cricket than in the ordinary inter club games the causes for unpleasantness created by the old cup competition had been removed.

The Playing Scene 1890—1914

Aston Unity were a strong force before the Great War, winning seven titles and only slipping out of the top half of the table on three occasions.   Handsworth Wood who initially claimed to be the best all amateur club in the Midlands finished top five times and in the top four in the first eighteen seasons, but fell away after dropping to bottom place in 1907.   Even allowing for this dominance by Aston Unity and Handsworth Wood during these 24 years, the championship was won by seven of the ten clubs and on five occasions the title was shared.   In 1910 three clubs, Aston Unity, Kidderminster and Mitchells and Butlers shared top spot, with Moseley only one point behind.

The players in the League in these early seasons read like a Warwickshire XI; Billy Bird, Alf Law, John Devey and Harry Pallett with Aston Unity, Edward Pereira with Dudley, Grosvenor Hill, Ernest Hill, Alfred Glover, Tom Fishwick and Walter Quaife with Handsworth Wood, Fred Collishaw with Mitchells, James Byrne, William Quaife, Edwin Diver with Moseley, James Whitehead with Small Heath and Jack Shilton and Walter Richards with Salters.

Even after Warwickshire had been admitted to the County Championship in 1895 the County fixture list was not as full as it is today.   Three day County games started on Mondays and Thursdays and players could often hurry from an early Saturday finish of a County game to play for their clubs.   On one occasion, Alf Law

ASTON UNITY CRICKET CLUB. LEAGUE CHAMPIONS

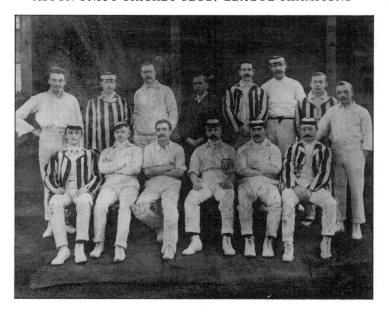

A. Devey, E.T. Edden, E. Markwick, James Evans, W.E. Crook,
E.J. Leake, F.G. Hurst, F.W. James,
C.M. Sykes, A.H. Crane, H. Holland, J. Rhodes, C.R. Durban,
W.E. Dimelow.
1906

scored 58 on Saturday morning to help defeat Yorkshire and then took his bat to Aston Unity to score 40 against West Bromwich Dartmouth, whose County player, Jack Shilton, was entered in the score-book as "Absent".

Season 1890 saw the first games where, in accordance with the Laws of Cricket, the captains elected to play a second innings when the result had been achieved early in the first innings.

	West Bromwich Dartmouth	101
	Walsall 24 and 36 − 8	
and	Moseley 98 and 58 − 1	
	Wednesbury 89	

The League table in the 1893 season had an odd look with some clubs finishing with minus points.   This was because the League, for this season only, used the then County system of ignoring draws and deducting losses from wins e.g. bottom club Wednesbury read:—

P16	W2	L9	D5	Pts − 7 instead of
P16	W2	L9	D5	Pts 9

By 1894 the games were arousing more spectator interest and press coverage had increased from a mere score, mixed in with other local cricket, to a separate column report.

In the 1898 season, five weeks were completely washed out. This badly affected gates, so West Bromwich Dartmouth and Smethwick followed Mitchells   and Stourbridge's lead of arranging fetes to raise money to offset losses in gate money.

Aston Unity

Aston Unity followed up their success in the inaugural season by winning the title in 1894, 1900, 1906 and 1913 and sharing it in 1896, 1905 and 1910.   The club had a triple success in 1894 when they also won the Second Division and the Charity Cup.   Aston Unity's successful span was graced almost throughout by club stalwarts Charles Durban, Jack Leake, John Devey and James Rhodes with Sam Durban making important contributions in the early years. E.T. Edden, C.H. Hartwell, George Rea, Harry Holland (wicketkeeper), A. Devey, S.A. Marlow, Billy George joined in as the period progressed.   The major professional assistance came from 'Harry' Pallett, C. Vale and Billy Bird.   John Devey frequently showed his county form with the bat, G.W. Rea, E.J. Edden and E.J. Leake took most of the bowling honours.   Billy George, the famous Aston Villa and England goalkeeper proved a great attraction and delighted his fans with attractive and forceful cricket.   John Devey also played soccer for Aston Villa F.C. and for England.   He scored the quickest goal in a Football Association Cup Final when, in 1895, he scored after only 30 seconds play against West Bromwich Albion.

Moseley

The attraction of the Moseley side undoubtedly was derived in the early 1900's from the appearance of the Stephens brothers, Frank and George, preceded a few years earlier by James Byrne. Moseley won the championship on five occasions and shared it twice. These three played exhilarating cricket, making Moseley an attraction at all away grounds, though unfortunately for the Moseley finances, not on their own ground.   James Byrne was an aggressive

No 2

Of course it is understood that [you are] to be released for County Matches when required & that you are to have the use of the grounds for the purpose of arranging a benefit match which you will act yourself ~~~~ on a date hereafter to be arranged between us.———

Mr W. G. Quaife.
77 Bristol Rd

Sir,
At a Committee Meeting of the above Club held on Friday 2? inst it was agreed to engage you for next season (1894) on the following terms viz: you to bowl every evening from 5. p.m. & play in matches for which we agree to pay you Two pounds five shillings (£2/9?) per week the engagement to last for 20 weeks.

A letter from you accepting these terms will form a binding agreement.

Yours truly,
C. E. _____
_____

W.G. Quaife letter of appointment as Moseley Pro.

batsman and bowled at 'tremendous pace'. On 2nd May 1903 it is recorded that he was accorded a flattering reception in the Moseley versus Handsworth Wood match to mark his appointment as Warwickshire's captain. He was also a leading Rugby Football International. The Stephens's were brilliant fielders, batsmen who hit the ball hard and more than useful bowlers. Rupert Smith and A.W. Smith can be picked out as outstanding from the many Smiths who turned out for Moseley. Frank Breedon, Howard Vaughton and G.H. Tyler, the League Auditor, were other names which regularly featured in Moseley performances. In 1892 Frank Breedon became the first bowler in the League to take ten wickets in an innings, but some of the wickets were taken after the opponents, Smethwick, had passed Moseley's score of 42.

The professional and groundsman for twenty two years was Bill Riley, a tubby, slow bowler who always wore a coloured sash below the normal belt line. He was assisted for short periods by William Quaife and Edwin Diver but generally Moseley, with their strong Warwickshire amateurs did not use up their full quota of professionals.

Walsall

In 1893 Walsall were winners of the First Division, Albert Bird, their slow bowler, taking 68 wickets and in one match versus Wednesbury he took 4 wickets in 4 balls. The score sheet for Walsall's match v West Bromwich Dartmouth records that Dartmouth's last man 'refused to bat' but the account does not say why. Walsall shared the Championship with Aston Unity in 1896 and won it outright in 1912.

The Walsall amateur strength lay in the steady batting of League President, Fred Cozens, W.H. Barnsby and S.E. Thomas with Bob Colston picking up the wickets not taken by the professionals. Their longest serving professional was A.H. Hawke who was reinstated as an amateur in 1896. He was followed by A. Bird and from 1903 W. Brammer who was to give legendary service. J.C. Eaton, David Barnsby, W. Wistance, C.H. Gilbert, Norman Hewson and Leonard Taylor joined to make substantial contributions in the pre-war years. Leonard Taylor came into the side straight from school and quickly made his mark as an accomplished batsman but he was one of the many League players who fell in the Great War. Another entry to the scene was Billy Preston, a useful bat who became a driving force as President of the Club in post war years. When Walsall won the title in 1912 he provided large peaked caps for the players resembling the head-gear of jockeys. This evoked a good deal of banter from spectators and a Black Country cry of 'Weer'es yower osses.'

Mitchells and Butlers

Mitchells and Butlers shared the title in 1909 and won it in 1911 and 1914.

Seven names which will be indelibly linked with Mitchells in these years will be Albert Lones, brothers Tom, Jack and George Stevenson, W.C. Smith, H.J. Powell and professionals Jack Fereday and Billy Wilkinson. Albert Lones played in the first season and eventually became Club President. Tom Stevenson took all ten wickets v Dudley on August 23rd 1902 when Dudley were dismissed for 115 in reply to Mitchells 144. Jack Stevenson and Billy Wilkin-

son were to continue their service with distinction in the post War period. Jack Fereday who scored 831 runs in 1906 was an exceptional allrounder. He moved to Handsworth Wood in 1911 but returned post War to play for and ultimately became coach to Mitchells and Butlers, demonstrating his shots with his walking stick.

In 1906 Jack scored three successive centuries in home matches, 101 v Smethwick, 100 not out v Moseley and 103 not out v Stourbridge.

W.C. Smith was also a good allrounder whilst H.J. Powell added to a strong batting line up. E.F. Bray, F.S. Litherland, F.W. Podmore and Alfred Parsons served for a number of years as did Frank Lawday. Frank Lawday eventually took up umpiring and became a leading member of that fraternity.

Mitchells were able to share the championship with Moseley in 1909 in unusual circumstances. On the last day of the season they played Aston Unity who scored 80. With Mitchells on 69 — 5 Aston Unity appealed against the light! The umpires turned down the appeal and Aston Unity walked off the field. The League awarded the match to Mitchells who finished equal points with Moseley, whose game had, unfortunately for them, been rained off.

Kidderminster

Kidderminster, known as the 'Carpetmen', joined the League in 1895 and enjoyed their first success in 1899 and then again in 1901 when their attack was strengthened by George Wilson the Worcestershire fast bowler. On two occasions he was unexpectedly able to travel to play due to early finishes of the County games and on each occasion he took six wickets in a Kidderminster victory. Kidderminster's nearest neighbours, Stourbridge, the 'Glass Boys', had a less successful season in 1899 suffering twice at the hands of the Champions. They were dismissed for 25 and then in the return game for 13, the lowest score in the First Division of the League at that time. In mitigation of this indignity it should be mentioned that they sportingly carried on in the rain.

Scores:—

Kidderminster	148 — 5 S. Gethin 36 G. Wilson 36 n.o. .
Stourbridge	13 J. Hingley 7 four of which came from overthrows to the boundary. Extras 3. 8 'ducks'. Bannister 6 — 7 G. Wilson 3 — 3. All out in 35 minutes.

Kidderminster brought some fine cricketers into the arena including two cricketing families, the Tomkinsons and the Gethins each of which fielded three players. The Tomkinsons, a well known name in the carpet trade fielded Herbert, Martin and Geoffrey who were prolifically scoring batsmen. Herbert and Martin played regularly but Geoffrey, who worked in Brazil, only played when on holiday but was to return after the Great War to become a leading member of the side. Stanley Gethin was another free scoring batsman whose innings were eagerly anticipated, and usually enjoyed, by the spectators. He was also a more than useful support bowler who could be relied upon to back up the professionals and his brother W.G. Another brother, Herbert Gethin, did not appear very regularly but gave the Club good service. The opening bat position posed no problems with Harry Wilkes at No.1 who had been notching up good scores since he joined the Club in 1888. On 24th August 1907 there was a good crowd, not only to see the eventual champions Moseley, but also to pay tribute to Harry, who had captained the Club for twenty years. Harry was presented with an Illuminated Address and Silver Epergne to mark the occasion.

Leslie Butcher, R.S. Brinton, Harry Austin, A.T. Cowell and H. Humphries are other names to appear regularly in the scorebook together with professionals George and H. Wilson, Bannister, Alec Skelding, Simms and Jesse Pennington the West Bromwich Albion and England footballer. When Alec Skelding applied for the post of professional in 1910 some of the Kidderminster committee did not think he could be any good because he asked for a small fee! In his four seasons he took 240 wickets so he did not do badly! After a successful first class career with Leicestershire he became a first class umpire.

Handsworth Wood

Grosvenor Hill the League Secretary and Treasurer until 1909 effectively spearheaded the Handsworth Wood attack until the same year. With J. Barton, the groundsman and professional, he formed one of the longest serving opening attacks in the history of the League extending over 18 seasons, and most seasons taking a hundred wickets between them. H.G. Hill established an individual record in 1902 with 83 victims in a season.

Grosvenor Hill and J. Barton had the support from 1895 of J.H. Cooper who could be relied on as a first change bowler to bowl tight and get his own bag of wickets. These three were the foundation of the Handsworth successes with the batting in the capable hands of Ernest Hill, R.S. Everett, E.H.Wigley, A.S. Cooper and for a few seasons Tom Fishwick, Walter Quaife, T.S. Haswell, J.P. Kingston, P.A. Pettifer and A.E. Mainwaring. Ernest Hill had the distinction in 1894 of scoring the first century for Warwickshire in the First Class game. Jack Fereday joined as professional in 1911. Two other famous names who played for Handsworth were Hon. F.S.G. Calthorpe, later to become an England and Warwickshire captain and Arthur Lilley the England and Warwickshire wicket-keeper. Arthur was offered a benefit by Handsworth but declined as he felt he had not made sufficient appearance for the Club because of his Test and County commitments.

On 9th June 1894 the Hill—Barton combination shocked eventual champions Aston Unity. Aston opened steadily with H. Widdowson and James Rhodes putting on 30 for the first wicket, then Grosvenor Hill took 8 wickets and Barton two to dismiss Unity for the addition of only one more run, scored by Frank Burgoyne, and Handsworth won by 72 runs.

The 1st September, 1894, saw an historic match when Stourbridge were defeated by Handsworth Wood by an innings and 15 runs after the Wood had only managed to score 84. Stourbridge were all out for 27 and 42. Grosvenor Hill had a performance which is sure to be unequalled taking 6 — 10 and 7 — 23.

West Bromwich Dartmouth

Supporters who today are accustomed to West Bromwich Dartmouth occupying leading positions in the League may be surprised to find that the Club was firmly entrenched at or near the bottom of the League prior to the Great War, apart from a title success in 1890 and a third place in 1891.

At the close of the 1890 season, with West Bromwich Dartmouth bracketed with Moseley at the top, Dartmouth protested that they were outright champions since in a game with Wednesbury the Wednesbury skipper had refused to let a Dartmouth substitute bat when nine Dartmouth wickets had fallen. Mr. J.G. Keys, Dartmouth's secretary, claimed that the M.C.C. had advised him that the substitute should have been allowed to bat and therefore the game should be recorded as a draw. The League made their own investigation and ruled that the result should stand and the title shared.

It is interesting to note that in season 1892, when Dartmouth and Wednesbury again met, Wednesbury were all out for 14 and the newspaper report shows a substitute batting last man for Wednesbury. This may be why Wednesbury had points deducted in the League table that season.

The brothers Walter and Frank Perks and W.J. Phair were the club men around whom the sides were built. All three were with the Club when the League was formed and members of the successful side in 1890 together with professionals Jack Shilton and W. Treadwell, E. Wright and H.J. Phillips. Other players featuring later were G.W. Field, C.S. Bache, the Langwell brothers, W and Edward, H.E. Mitchell, A. Holloway, F. Avery, Rabjohns and the old professional campaigner Harry Pallett who over seven seasons regularly scored around 300 runs and took 60 wickets in each season. A. Holloway provided additional all round support and the Perks and H.E. Mitchell the main batting whilst professionals J.E. Nichols and Corfield succeeded Harry Pallett. There was a golden week in 1909 when Maurice Foster turned out the scores reading, West Bromwich Dartmouth 272 — 5 M.K. Foster 132 C.S. Bache 44 H.E. Mitchell 24 F.J. Clare 3—48.

Stourbridge 67 W.K. Harrison 20 n.o. F.J. Clare 16 P. Davis 11 J.E. Nichols 6—27 (He was 4—0 at one time)

Maurice Foster, age 20, had joined Worcestershire but was to return to join Walsall and bring fresh impetus to the game on completion of his first class career.

Dudley

Dudley achieved two titles, one in 1898 and jointly with Kidderminster and Aston Unity in 1910, when they beat the Unity in the last match to join them at the top. Billy Eve, Arthur Fereday and C.P. Blewitt, all useful bats and change bowlers, played in both championship winning sides. The first success was chiefly the work of the two professionals Frank Davidson and Forrester, showing the effectiveness of combining two really fast and accurate bowlers in an opening attack, dismissing the opponents for less than 100 in all but five games. Their best performance was against Mitchells. Dudley batting first had made only 75, Frank Davidson 13 F. Bodison 19 A. Millington 19, but Mitchells were soon despatched for 22, Forrester 5—8 F. Davidson 5—6. These two also made useful runs during the years with further support from T.H. Simmonds, Frank Bodison, A. Millington and M. Bullock.

The Dudley success in 1910 and runners up position the following year was achieved with C.H. Grimshaw as professional with H.F. Baker, Wally Hatfield, B.G. Stevens, C.E. Crawford and J. Bateman joining the Eve, Fereday, Blewitt trio. Arthur Fereday, brother of Jack Fereday, was a youngster when the first title was won, had by 1910, developed into a dependable bat. H.F. Baker and Wally Hatfield took most of the wickets and made useful runs, Wally's in a most pugnacious manner which he contrived to employ when playing after the war with the Mitchells and Butlers side. On 27 July 1912, playing against Handsworth Wood on the large Dudley ground, he hit nineteen off 3 balls, 2—6's and an all run 7 with no overthrows included. There was similar running between the wickets on 13 June 1914 when playing Stourbridge, Dudley scored 308 H.A. Parkes 102 n.o. B.G. Stevens 101 n.o. H.A. Parkes's score included an all run 5 and an all run 8. Jim Naden had earlier taken 7—14 as Stourbridge were dismissed for 56.

In 1906 Dudley had signed another fast bowling professional Thomas Stringer. He took 85 wickets in his first season and established a new record in 1908 when he totted up 90 victims. On 30th June 1906 he took all ten Smethwick wickets for 48 runs off only 13.4 overs. In this game there was an unusual dismissal. H.F. Baker drove a ball back hard and hit J. Bateman, the ball flying to a fielder who completed the catch. Baker was therefore out caught and with Bateman injured and unable to continue, two new batsmen had to take their place. Despite this Dudley won 135 to 107. During the 1900's Dudley introduced to the League Kenneth Hutchings and his brother William, two stylish amateur batsmen from Kent. Kenneth became an England Test player.

Dudley spectators were to become renowned for their partisanship. In 1894 when Dudley played at Walsall, the 1893 champions, two thousand spectators were present. This game entered into two innings. Walsall scored 50 and 70 — 7 declared and Dudley 52 and 28 — 3, Dudley thus winning on the first innings. The spectators are reported to have gone wild with excitement and Jack Shilton (Dudley) and Albert Bird (Walsall), who had each taken seven wickets in the first innings for their sides, were carried shoulder high from the field.

In the return encounter at Dudley, Walsall obtained their revenge and again two thousand spectators were present. This time fighting broke out in the crowd and Walsall had to be escorted by the police from the dressing room to the railway station. Owing to further incidents, Dudley were ordered in 1897 to post notices warning spectators about using bad language or molesting umpires or players.

Smethwick

Smethwick maintained a middle of the table position but provided strong opposition and plenty of interesting cricket for their supporters. J.W. Fletcher and T. Roberts played throughout the period mainly supported in early years by R.L. James and T. Hedges with A.W.M. Boneham, S. Field and A. Prince taking over in the late 1890's to be joined later by F. Burgoyne, J. Pigott and 3 Dormans (W, G and D). Cowley acted as professional for six years to be followed by Bucknell. Leslie Neale, a future stalwart, gained a regular first team place in 1913. From 1896—9 Harry Pallett also had a turn with Smethwick.

In 1891 an eighteen year old local lad, Sydney Barnes, played in Smethwick's non League Second Eleven side. He made his debut in the First Division of the League on 29th August of that season when he scored 5 and took one wicket playing against Mitchells. He

25

gained a regular Smethwick first team place in the middle of the 1892 season scoring 70 runs in 8 innings. His highest score was 21 not out against Aston Unity, batting against bowler Harry Pallett who was then a leading bowler for Warwickshire. The only reference to Sydney's bowling was when the big hitter J. Manton of Handsworth Wood scored 18 off one 5 ball over! Sydney played mainly as a batsman in seasons 1893 and 1894 but gave an indication of his future potential as a bowler when he took 7 wickets in matches against Handsworth Wood and Wednesbury. In the former game he had taken 6 wickets for 7 runs when the last man hit him for three fours before Sydney had his revenge to finish with 7 — 19. In the season he bowled 121 overs and took 26 wickets for 313 runs. In 1894 Sydney scored 309 runs, nearly a fifth of the total of the side, with a highest score of 42 compiled against Warwickshire Club and Ground. Sydney found his opportunity to bowl limited by the successful bowling of the two professionals, T. Rollings and Schofield, but as a change bowler he did get a chance to pick up 15 wickets in the season.

Sydney joined Rishton (Lancashire League) as professional in 1895 and also played twice for Warwickshire C.C.C.

In 1911 Smethwick supporters had three weeks of entertaining batting when three successive 300's were scored on the ground.

15th July Aston Unity 65 J. Devey 33 J.W. Roberts 8 —22 Smethwick 352 — 6 F. Burgoyne 135 Bucknell 87 When Smethwick were 142 — 2 the Smethwick captain suggested tea be taken!

22nd July Smethwick 301 H. Walker 61 J. Fletcher 68 n.o. Bucknell 54

Moseley 224 G.H. Tyler 63 C. Denning 57 A.W.M. Boneham 5—44

29th July Walsall 301 — 4 W. Brammer 87 N.P. Hewson 68 L.F. Taylor 72 n.o.

Smethwick 252 — 8 H. Walker 91.

Stourbridge

Stourbridge only enjoyed two successful seasons in terms of League position when in 1903 and 1904 they finished second and third respectively. All-rounder J.O. Hingley was the only player regularly to feature in the side throughout the period, the main professional assistance coming from Robert Burrows, William Quaife, John Nichols, in two spells, Charles Grimshaw, William Hickton and Cyril Bland. The Club were never in a position to offer much financial inducement and unsuccessfully lobbied for the League to admit no professionals. Nichols was the professional in 1903 & 4 his good all round performance being backed up by J.O. Hingley, D. Ganner and A.E. Skidmore with good batting from W.H. Hartley (1903), Tom Clare, A.W. Robinson, W.S. Mobberley, H. Southall and also coming on to the scene Percy Davis followed by his brother Major Davis. At one time three Clares played — Tom, F.J. and P.R. Tom Allchurch made his first appearance in 1910 but like many other League newcomers at this time the full development of his potential was curtailed by the Great War.

On 18 August 1900 when playing at Walsall a Walsall favourite Rev. W.L. Thomas was on 49 when time was called. In response to the crowd, Stourbridge agreed to bowl another over to give him his 50. A full toss was sent up which he missed and he was bowled!

On 6 July 1912 Kidderminster were 56—0 when C.H.G. Bland took 6 wickets for 2 to dismiss them for 75. Stourbridge batsmen did not take the opportunity to register a win and were all out for 64 W.G. Gethin 5—29 A. Skelding 4—16. One of Stourbridge's most convincing wins occurred against Walsall on 3rd July 1897 and featured William Quaife.

Stourbridge 255—2 dec. W.G. Quaife 127 F.G. Green 65 n.o. Walsall 80. E.G. Arnold 6 wickets.

Three weeks later Quaife was in the runs again

Stourbridge 261—6 W.G. Quaife 151 n.o. J.O. Hingley 34 Mitchells 155—5 G. Stevenson 75 J.B. Fereday 27.

Warwickshire Club and Ground

The Warwickshire Club and Ground side which played for one season in 1894 had an indifferent season because of constant changes caused by County commitments. Harry Pallett, Sidney Santall, J. Wharton and L. Bates figured in the bowling Edwin Diver, F.W.D. Pinney, Ludford Docker, Rev. Edward Pereira, William Ansell and H.W. Bainbridge in the batting. The latter scored 183 not out against League leaders Dudley on June 26th and helped by 64 from Edwin Diver and 43 from F.W.D. Pinney the Warwickshire Club became the first side to score over 300 in the League declaring at 301—3. Dudley were then dismissed for 99 of which Jack Shilton, another Warwickshire player, scored 30. To illustrate the unpredictability of their performances the County side were dismissed on 7 occasions during the season for less than 100.

Salters, Small Heath and Wednesbury

Outstanding players for Salters in their one season were Jack Shilton, J. Horton and W. Richards.

Professionals James Whitehead, Alf Law and Cort were principal performers for Small Heath and Hawkins, J. Wharton, Brownsword and Flowers for Wednesbury but neither of these clubs were to challenge the leaders during their brief career in the League.

Shadows of War

Interest in the game towards the end of the 1914 season was overshadowed by the threatening cloud of war which culminated in the declaration of war on Germany on August 5th. At a special meeting of the League on the 14th August it was agreed to carry on and complete the season's fixtures. Consideration of the policy to be adopted for the 1915 season was deferred until a meeting on 30th March when, owing to the large number of players who had joined the forces it was reluctantly decided that League Cricket should be abandoned. No one then envisaged the catastrophic loss of life that was to occur in that generation of cricketers some of which is recorded in the Rolls of Honour in the Clubs' pavilions.

Extra Cover 1889—1914

29.6.89	Handsworth Wood 25 H.J. Pallett 6—9, E.J. Leake 4—14 F. Stevenson 12
	Aston Unity 231—9 C.R. Durban 43, S. Durban 41 n.o.
12.5.90	Harry Pallett took 7—38 v Australians playing for Warwickshire
26.7.90	Aston Unity 126 T. Stevenson 54 n.o. H.B.G. Hill 9 w. Handsworth Wood 22 E.J. Leake 7—8

BENETFINK & CO.,
BEST HOUSE FOR
Cricket, Cycling, & Tennis Outfits.

CRICKET SHIRTS.
WHITE FLANNEL, well
shrunk ... ...3/3, 4/6, 5,11 *nett.*
"THE COUNTY," Fine White
Twill, *as worn by all the
leading professionals*... ...4/6 ,,
"THE CLUB," Oxford Mat,
White ... ... 2/6, 3/6 ,,

TROUSERS.
WHITE FLANNEL, well　　*Men's.*
　　　　shrunk, 4/11, 5/11
　　,,　　,,　　Super ... 7/9, 9/11
GREY STRIPED or
PLAIN FLANNEL 5/11, 7/6, 9/6
　　　　Postage, 4½d.
PATTERNS, POST FREE.

CRICKET BALLS.
DUKE'S 5/3
DARK'S 5/-
GRASSHOPPER 4/10
BENETFINK'S B.C.B. 4/6
　　,,　　B.C.B., *Boys'* ... 3/3
　　　　Post Free.

CRICKET BATS.
MEN'S ALL CANE 5/3, 6/-
　　,,　　,,　　Super 8/5
　　,,　　,,　　Selected... ... 9/8
　　,,　　"RESILIENT" 14/10
WARSOP'S "CONQUEROR" ... 16/10
　　Single Bat sent Post Free.

Immense Stock of { LILLYWHITE, COBBETT, BRYAN,
　　　　　　　　{ CLAPSHAW, DARK, GARDINER,
CRICKET BATS by { AYRES, SYKES, NICOLLS.

CATALOGUES POST FREE.

89, 90, 107, & 108, CHEAPSIDE, LONDON, E.C.

The Cost of Cricket Equipment 1896

7.7.94	Warwickshire Club & Ground 59 T. Rollings 9—46 Smethwick 74 H.J. Pallett 9—32 T. Rollings 40 A collection for Rollings raised £2.0.0. William Ansell, Warwickshire Secretary, played for Warwickshire and scored 17 n.o.
6.7.95	Walsall 295—5 A.H.L. Hawke 97 F.T. Cozens 101 Opening stand of 171 Moseley 204—1 H. Vaughton 96 J.F. Byrne 78 n.o. Opening stand of 172
6.6.96	Dudley 49 W.Eve 21 H.B.G. Hill 4—19 J. Barton 5—23 Handsworth Wood 333—5 W. Quaife 144 n.o. J.E. Hill 68 T.S. Fishwick 60 A trio of Warwickshire players getting in some batting practice
15.5.97	F.B. Young, Smethwick given out 'Handled the ball' in a game versus West Bromwich Dartmouth
24.7.97	Handsworth Wood 295—5 W. Quaife 106 J.E. Hill 70 Walsall 97 J. Barton 6—22
	Stourbridge 261—6 W.G. Quaife 151 n.o. W.E. Round 5 wickets Mitchells 155—5 G. Stevenson 75 A Good day for the Quaifes
16.7.98	Albert Blackham, Wicket-keeper of Mitchells struck an opponent after an unsuccessful appeal. The League suspended Blackham for two weeks — the only time the need for such disciplinary action has occurred. Dudley 111 E.J. Thompson 44 Mitchells 97 E.Kirk Mitchells best bat 'refused to bat' after the dispute, otherwise Mitchells may have won.
17.6.99	A distinguished Japanese visitor attended the Kidderminster versus Smethwick game but his views on the game were not recorded.
7.7.1900	Aston Unity 256—2 E.T. Edden 125 n.o. J.H.G. Devey 72 Stourbridge 63 W. Bird 8—29 the last 5 wickets for no runs in 9 deliveries
13.5.05	Smethwick 25 'Extras' 7 G. Wilson 7—9 W.G. Gethin 3—9 Kidderminster 196 F.M. Tomkinson 40 S. Field 5—46
28.4.06	Handsworth Wood 91 C.H. Grimshaw 6—38 G.W. Rea 4—41 Stourbridge 18 C.H. Grimshaw 9 H.B.G. Hill 5—11 Barton 4—6
14.7.06	D. Witcombe of Handsworth Wood was credited with a boundary when a Dudley fielder, having dropped a catch kicked the ball over the boundary in disgust.
1.5.09	Walsall 63 versus Mitchells & Butlers when snow stopped play. In the morning there had been 1" of snow on the ground.
7.5.10	The President and Honorary Secretary cancelled all games due to death of King Edward VII.

29.7.11	At Stourbridge the home side were 197—8 in reply to Kidderminster's 238 when a storm of sand and dust drove the players from the field and the game had to be abandoned.
18.5.12	After Dudley had been dismissed for 115 Moseley scored 354—3 F.G. Stephens 116 P.Jeeves 106 n.o.

29.7.11 At Stourbridge the home side were 197—8 in reply to Kidderminster's 238 when a storm of sand and dust drove the players from the field and the game had to be abandoned.

18.5.12 After Dudley had been dismissed for 115 Moseley scored 354—3 F.G. Stephens 116 P.Jeeves 106 n.o.

G.H. Tyler, Moseley captain, declared with his score on 86 n.o.

There was still 15 mins playing time left and he may have been able to create a record of 3 centuries being scored in one innings.

24.5.13 When Walsall played at home against Dudley the crowd striving to get into the ground, rushed the gates and many gained free entry into the unreserved side.

Highest Club Scores in Period

Aston Unity	375—3	v	West Brom. Dartmouth	(H)	1907
Dudley	334—8	v	Walsall	(A)	1905
Handsworth Wood	333—5	v	Dudley	(H)	1896
Kidderminster	300—9	v	West Brom. Dartmouth	(A)	1913
Mitchells & Butlers	382—9	v	Stourbridge	(H)	1912
Moseley	405—8	v	West Brom. Dartmouth	(H)	1908
Salters	229—5	v	Kings Heath (Moseley)	(A)	1889
Small Heath	221	v	Smethwick	(A)	1893
Smethwick	352—6	v	Aston Unity	(H)	1911
Stourbridge	289	v	Dudley	(H)	1908
Walsall	377	v	Smethwick	(H)	1896
Warwicks.Club & Ground	301—3	v	Dudley	(H)	1894
Wednesbury	158—5	v	West Brom. Dartmouth	(H)	1892
West Brom. Dartmouth	301—6	v	Handsworth Wood	(A)	1909

Lowest Club Scores in Period

Aston Unity	31	v	Handsworth Wood	(A)	1894
Dudley	32	v	Handsworth Wood	(A)	1902
	32	v	Mitchells	(H)	1896
Handsworth Wood	22	v	Aston Unity	(A)	1890
Kidderminster	23	v	Dudley	(A)	1898
Mitchells & Butlers	22	v	Dudley	(A)	1898
Moseley	20	v	Walsall	(H)	1912
Salters	57	v	Handsworth Wood	(A)	1889
Small Heath	20	v	Stourbridge	(A)	1894
Smethwick	25	v	Kidderminster	(A)	1905
Stourbridge	13	v	Kidderminster	(A)	1899
Walsall	24	v	West Brom. Dartmouth	(A)	1890
Warwicks.Club & Ground	37	v	Aston Unity	(A)	1894
Wednesbury	14	v	West Brom. Dartmouth	(A)	1892
West Brom. Dartmouth	20	v	Moseley	(A)	1897

League Positions 1889–1914

First Division

	1800's												1900's													
	89	90	91	92	93	94	95	96	97	98	99	00	1	2	3	4	5	6	7	8	9	10	11	12	13	14
Aston Unity	1	3	2	2	3	1	2	1*	2	5	6	1	5	5*	3*	5	1*	1	2	4	3	1*	8	3	1	9
Dudley	.	.	.	.	4	2	7*	10	7	1	4*	9	6*	9*	7*	2	6	2	5*	6	9	1*	2	7	4	5*
Handsworth Wood	3	4	3*	1	2	4	3	3*	1	2	3	4	4	1	1	3*	1*	4*	10	7*	7	9	4	8	5	8
Kidderminster	.	.	.	.	.	.	6	5	4*	3	1	5	1	3*	9	6	3*	6	5*	5	4	1*	7	5	6	4
(2) Mitchells & Butlers	2	7	8	6	.	.	.	9	10	6*	7*	3	6*	2	7*	7	8	3	3	7*	1*	5	1	2	2	1
(1) Moseley	6	1*	1	3	5	5	1	3*	4*	6*	4*	2	2	9*	6	1	3*	7*	1	1	1*	4	6	4	8	2
Salters	4	.	.	.	.	.	.	.	.	.	.	.	.	.	.	.	.	.	.	.	.	.	.	.	.	.
Small Heath	.	.	.	9	8	10	.	.	.	.	.	.	.	.	.	.	.	.	.	.	.	.	.	.	.	.
Smethwick	.	5	5	4*	6	6*	7*	7*	3	9	2	7*	3	3*	3*	9	5	7*	4	2	5	8	5	6	7	5*
Stourbridge	.	.	.	.	.	8	4*	6	6	8	10	10	10	7	2	3*	9	9	7	7*	10	6	10	10	10	7
Walsall	7	6	6	4*	1	3	4*	1*	8*	4	7*	6	6*	5*	10	10	7	4*	8*	3	6	7	3	1	3	3
Warwickshire Club & Grd.	.	.	.	.	.	6*	.	.	.	.	.	.	.	.	.	.	.	.	.	.	.	.	.	.	.	.
Wednesbury	.	5	7	8	9	.	.	.	.	.	.	.	.	.	.	.	.	.	.	.	.	.	.	.	.	.
West Bromwich Dartmouth	5	1*	3*	7	7	9	9	7*	8*	10	9	7*	9	8	5	8	10	10	8*	10	8	10	9	9	9	10
No of Teams	7	7	8	9	9	10	9	10																		

* Position held jointly

(1) Played as Kings Heath in 1889

(2) Played as Mitchells 1889 to 1897

31

Individual Performances

Highest Scores

Aston Unity (J.H.G. Devey)	147*	v	Stourbridge	(H)	1907
Dudley (W.E.C. Hutchings)	138	v	Smethwick	(H)	1905
Handsworth Wood (J. Manton)	170	v	Kidderminster	(H)	1908
Kidderminster (S.J. Gethin)	138*	v	West Brom.Dartmouth	(H)	1910
Mitchells & Butlers (W.H. Wilkinson)	185	v	Stourbridge	(H)	1912
Moseley (F.G. Stephens)	200*	v	Stourbridge	(H)	1913
Salters (W. Richards)	115*	v	Kings Heath (Moseley)	(A)	1889
Small Heath (J. Gibbons)	104*	v	West Brom.Dartmouth	(H)	1894
Smethwick (F. Burgoyne)	135	v	Aston Unity	(H)	1911
Stourbridge (W.G. Quaife)	151*	v	Mitchells	(H)	1897
Walsall (L.F. Taylor)	175	v	Smethwick	(A)	1914
Warwicks. Club & Ground (H.W. Bainbridge)	183*	v	Dudley	(H)	1894
Wednesbury (Hawkins)	51*	v	West Brom.Dartmouth	(H)	1892
West Brom. Dartmouth (M.K. Foster)	132	v	Stourbridge	(A)	1909

Best Bowling

Aston Unity (H.J. Pallett)	9–19	v	Moseley	(A)	1891
Dudley (T. Stringer)	10–48	v	Smethwick	(H)	1906
Handsworth Wood (H.B.G. Hill)	10–11	v	Mitchells & Butlers	(A)	1905
Kidderminster (G.A. Wilson)	9–31	v	Stourbridge	(A)	1897
Mitchells & Butlers (T. Stevenson)	10–61	v	Dudley	(H)	1902
Moseley (F. Breedon)	10– ?	v	Smethwick	(H)	1892
Salters (J. Horton)	9–19	v	Walsall	(A)	1889
Small Heath (J. Whitehead)	8–24	v	Moseley	(A)	1893
Smethwick (Bucknell)	9–44	v	West Brom.Dartmouth	(H)	1912
Stourbridge (R.D. Burrows)	9–?	v	Aston Unity	(H)	1894
Walsall (A. Bird)	9–20	v	West Brom.Dartmouth	(A)	1894
Warwicks. Club & Ground (H.J. Pallett)	9–32	v	Smethwick	(A)	1894
Wednesbury (Flowers)	8–?	v	West Brom.Dartmouth	(H)	1891
West Brom. Dartmouth (Treadwell)	9–?	v	Smethwick	(H)	1894

Second Division 1893–1914

Second Division Winners

1893	Aston Unity	1904	Aston Unity
1894	Aston Unity	1905	W.B. Dartmouth
1895	Walsall	1906	Aston Unity
1896	Aston Unity	1907	Mitchells & Butlers
1897	Aston Unity	1908	Kidderminster
1898	Dudley/Walsall	1909	Smethwick
1899	Aston Unity/Handsworth Wood	1910	Mitchells & Butlers
1900	Mitchells & Butlers	1911	Smethwick
1901	Mitchells & Butlers	1912	Stourbridge
1902	Handsworth Wood	1913	Mitchells & Butlers
1903	Handsworth Wood	1914	Smethwick

Highlights

5.8.93
Small Heath 82
Moseley 9 Bowser 5–0 Bryan 3–7
This is the lowest total ever recorded in the League

14.7.94
Small Heath 59 and 55
West Bromwich Dartmouth 47 and 74–8
Small Heath having won the first innings then lost on the two innings.

1.9.94
West Bromwich Dartmouth 27 J. Evans 9–10
including 'hat-trick' with his first 3 balls
Walsall 112

22.8.96
Dudley 76 A. Vernon 7–1
Moseley 43

8.5.97
Stourbridge 91
Moseley 60 P. Bidmead 9–10

17.7.97
Kidderminster 293–8 dec. W.G. Gethin 76 n.o.
Walsall 294–6 R.P. Davis 143

12.5.1900
Walsall 182–4 F.Y. Wood 59
Moseley 43 C.H. Gilbert 9–9

2.6.06
Stourbridge 120
Aston Unity 53 J. Bidmead and his brother W. Bidmead 5 wickets each.

21.7.06
Mitchells & Butlers 363–4 Ted Hadley 221 Partnership with Frank Lawday 81 of 279 for First wicket after Walsall had scored 183

20.7.07
Dudley 130
Walsall 284–7 C.H. Gilbert 122 'Extras' 57

20.7.12
3 Cozens family played for Walsall

16.5.14
Walsall 176 P. Cozens 54 H.W. Beebee 57
Smethwick 106 L.J. Taylor took 7 wickets for 10 runs at one stage 7–0.

Stourbridge

34

1919–1929 – THE TWENTIES

Administration

In 1920 John Lones succeeded C. Herbert Smith as the Hon. Secretary and Treasurer and at the same time W.T. Clarke started acting as Assistant Hon. Secretary, in which capacity he was to do most of the background administration.

The following year Mr. F.T. Cozens was re-elected President for the 33rd consecutive season. The occasion was marked by the presentation of an Illuminated Address and a Silver Rose Bowl to mark his enthusiastic service to the League as a player and administrator.

The encroachment of the Football season into May began to be a source of concern to the League. The League supported by Aston Villa and West Bromwich Albion F.C. made numerous representations against the encroachment to the M.C.C. and the National and Local Football Associations but did not meet with any success.

1928 saw the introduction of the Complimentary Pass. This admitted the holder into League grounds and was stamped into the back cover of the Handbook and each was signed by the Hon. Secretary. Only enough to cover players and a limited number of officials were issued to each club. In 1935 and 1936 it was ruled that the passes covered one person only and players wives and sweethearts were to pay ground admission. The inclusion of the pass in the Handbook was not finally discontinued until 1986 but for some years it had been generally academic since, by then so few clubs charged for admission.

Engagement of Professionals

The period saw no relaxation of Rules relating to professionals. In fact, in 1923, the regulations were made more onerous by Clubs agreeing that professionals should be on full-time service on the ground or on coaching unless special permission was obtained from the League. This was tightened even further at the 1928 Annual Meeting when it was ruled that the professionals should, subject only to County calls, be available to coach on at least two nights of the week. This immediately meant that Abe Waddington, West Bromwich Dartmouth, who travelled from Bradford each week, and Aaron Lockett, Old Hill, who was employed as a pit fireman in North Staffordshire, had to resign their positions with their clubs.

During the period annual proposals that no professionals be employed were defeated, the voting in 1925 being evenly divided.

Playing Time

From the 1920 season the playing time was extended from 7.30 to 8.00 with provision for 10 minutes tea and in 1924 the provision included that, in event of start of matches being delayed through rain until 3.30, stumps should be drawn at 8.30.

The provision for 10 minutes tea interval was not universally popular, one writer exclaiming that players went to play, not eat cream buns! Similarly the alteration to allow play to 8.30 in the event of a late start drew remarks at the start of the season that clubs were becoming 'night clubs' instead of 'cricket clubs'. Before 1914 there had been a call for extending the playing time in the event of a delayed start but until the introduction of summer time during the 1914—18 war the light did not hold after 8.00 p.m.

Registered Players

In 1927 the Rules were tightened to ensure that players only played for one club during a season.

Match Balls

During the Twenties proposals were unsuccessfully tabled for only one ball each match with no provision for a new ball after 200 runs.

The M.C.C. new rule reducing the size of the ball was adopted by the League for the 1927 season. The verdict was that the change gave the bowlers a better grip.

The Playing Scene

The dominant clubs from 1919 to 1929 were Mitchells & Butlers and Old Hill. Mitchells finished first on three occasions and were runners up for five consecutive seasons. Old Hill, who joined in 1920 in place of Handsworth Wood, won the League in what was only their second season, were second on four occasions and only twice dropped out of the first five. Moseley were champions twice and otherwise maintained a middle position in the table. Kidderminster also won twice. Stourbridge, Aston Unity and Walsall notched up one title each but these successes were isolated peaks for these clubs.

The first season after the 1914—1918 War proved a difficult one as clubs had to re-establish themselves. Grounds had to be brought back into shape, and wickets relaid; club members had to be rallied and players find their touch after the four year break. Handsworth Wood had lost their ground and had to play away and on borrowed grounds.

Dudley were the first side to meet the difficulties of team re-building. In their opening game of the 1919 season they fielded ten men only and were dismissed at Walsall for 12. This score still stands as the lowest recorded in the First Division. The previous lowest score was 13 by Stourbridge in 1899.

On the 9th August 1919 Moseley and Walsall, meeting at the Reddings, staged what has proved to be the highest scoring match in the League. Moseley scored 329—5 off 59 overs only to lose as Walsall amassed 330—8 off only 57.2 overs. The score card for the game is now proudly and prominently displayed in the Walsall pavilion and shows that the two captains scored centuries. The scorecard is reproduced over:—

As spectators flocked back to the cricket, record crowds were reported at all grounds. A record crowd at Aston Unity on July

Moseley v Walsall. Played at the Reddings on Saturday, 16th. August, 1919

Scores

MOSELEY		WALSALL	
G.H.Tyler run out	64	N.P. Hewson c Payne b Breeden	9
W.H. Harris b Hawley	45	L. Taylor b H. Tyler	46
C.A.F. Hastilow b Brammer	2	A.T. Lyons c and b Breeden	12
G. Payne b L. Taylor	21	P.B. Pearman-Smith c Payne b Breeden	106
F.G. Stephens not out	119		
G.E. Tyler c and b B. Taylor	19	B. Taylor b F. Stephens	41
H.A. Tyler not out	16	J. Ashwell c Harris b Breeden	35
P. Slattery		S. Eglington b F. Stephens	10
C.D. Stephens		P. Cozens b F. Stephens	26
J. Brake did not bat		G. Seldon not out	17
F.V. Breeden		Brammer not out	10
		G. Hawley did not bat	
Extras	43	Extras	18
Total (innings declared closed)	329	Total	330

Bowling Analysis

Moseley	O	M	R	W	Walsall	O	M	R	W
Hawley	11	0	76	1	Breeden	15.2	1	89	4
Brammer	23	7	72	1	Hastilow	12	0	60	0
L.Taylor	16	0	77	1	H.A. Tyler	6	0	40	1
B. Taylor	7	0	37	1	Brake	5	0	26	0
P.Pearman-Smith					F. Stephens	12	0	65	3
	2	0	24	0	C. Stephens	6	0	32	0

26th 1919 had more excitement than they wanted when a swarm of bees forced players and spectators to seek shelter!

Stourbridge

In 1919 Stourbridge obtained their first championship of the First Division when they held off a strong challenge from Walsall and Mitchells and Butlers.

Stourbridge's success was based almost entirely on the bowling of school teachers Jimmy Higginson and Tom Allchurch, and the batting and outstanding fielding of Tom Clare, aided by useful contributions from Percy Davis, Harvey Bryant and H. Walker. Tom Clare and Percy Davis were to continue to apply their skill and enthusiasm throughout the period. In 1929 when Percy was in his 27th year with the Club and in his 60th year he scored 109 not out when the whole Walsall side had only made 108. Harry Perry made a youthful appearance in the early twenties, his prowess growing in stature as each season progressed. These three players together with batsmen 'Dicky' Williams, left arm bowler Colin Mobberley, all rounder Dan Harris, Joe Brookes and wicket-keeper Frank Tate were to be the Club's mainstay as five professionals arrived and left in the 11 years.

Moseley

Moseley won the title in 1920 and 1923 and on each occasion the margin was one point more than Mitchells and Butlers, the issues being decided on the last day of each season. 1923 was a close call. Moseley had their penultimate game rained off whilst Mitchells and Butlers were trouncing Aston Unity who were dismissed for 23 in reply to Mitchells and Butlers 184—9. This left Moseley one point in front with one game to play. Rain again took a hand and, although Moseley could only play a few overs, Mitchells and Butlers could not overcome Smethwick in a rain reduced match.

On June 14 1919, Tom Ullathorne, playing for Moseley v West Bromwich Dartmouth, was reported to have been missed in the long field by G. Baddeley and then hit the next ball for six the ball hitting the chimney of Baddeley's house. Tom Ullathorne died tragically in 1926 when the house in which he was lodging burnt down.

Jim Morter was the outstanding bowler for Moseley in the period backed up by the dashing batting of George Stephens and his brother Frank Stephens, with steady contributions from Robert Baynton, W. Baines, 'Rusty' Scorer, Alec Hastilow and the long serving wicket keeper, Eric Cross.

George Stephens had captained Warwickshire in 1919 whilst still playing for Moseley. On 15 May 1920 he scored 170 out of a Moseley total of 204 scored in 57 minutes against Old Hill. His 100 had taken 45 minutes and the other 70 only 12 minutes but this fast scoring did not eclipse that of Wally Hatfield the Mitchells and Butlers big hitter who scored 100 in 27 minutes off the Walsall attack. Alec Hastilow, no mean performer with bat and ball, was to become Chairman of Warwickshire from 1948—1962. Robert Baynton and his brother Gerald, a Moseley 2nd XI player, were killed in a car crash in October 1924 and were a great loss to Moseley and the League. 'Rusty' Scorer had joined Moseley on the demise of Handsworth Wood and his name will always be synonymous with that of the League and Moseley. As a player he was an established attraction at all grounds loving his duels with opposing supporters as much as the ones with their players. His forceful, if abrasive, personality was to achieve much for Moseley and the League.

Old Hill

1920 saw the first League game staged at Old Hill but rain stopped play when Kidderminster were 51—4 in reply to Old Hill's 157. It was reported that "there was a good crowd and League cricket should be popular in that area". This has proved to be the case and even today it is worth the club's while to charge for the privilege of watching League cricket from the grassy banks of their most attractive ground.

Old Hill's admission to the League introduced two names which are to be coupled with outstanding League performances for many years, namely Homer and Hollies. Bert Homer was to prove a leading run scorer and Billy Hollies, an underarm lob bowler, was to play with and introduce his son Eric who was to become one of Warwickshire's and England's great leg spinners. Eric is renowned for dismissing Don Bradman for a 'duck' on the Don's last Test appearance for Australia in England! Bert Homer, Billy and Eric Hollies were to break several League records.

An accomplished bat, Bert Homer, in 1928, scored 854 runs in the season to exceed the record 831 scored by Jack Fereday in 1906. He was to plague bowlers over a period of twenty five years with his immaculate stroke play. He captained Staffordshire and later, when his playing days were over, willingly gave his time to the affairs of the Old Hill Club and the Warwickshire County Club, serving on the selection Committee and later as Vice Chairman. He was President of the League in 1950 and 1959. Bert's views on cricket were highly respected by all players and administrators.

Billy Hollies also created a record, in 1928, when he took 94 wickets in the Second Division, then on the last day of the season, in the Champions v The Rest match, he reached a century of wickets when he took 6—105. Billy bowled his 'lobs' with deceiving accuracy and is reputed to have practised by pitching the ball so that it would turn past a beer barrel to hit the wickets.

Under the astute leadership of old campaigner Billy Edwards, then in his 30th season as captain of the club, Old Hill won the title in 1921. Bert Homer and his namesake F.T. Homer, no relation, provided the stability in batting to supplement the penetrating bowling of Joe Mantle and professional George Platt. Old Hill led the table by a substantial margin winning 14 of their 18 games. Billy Lee, Percy Yates, Ben Forrest, H.H. Millichip, Frank Wood-house and Jim Eley provided the additional amateur back up to ensure a strong side was maintained, with Aaron Lockett replacing George Platt as professional in 1926.

In May 1926 Aaron Lockett took all ten wickets for 14 as Stourbridge collapsed to 21 all out. Colin Mobberley scored 12, but eight batsmen got "ducks" and eight were bowled. Dicky Williams carried his bat to finish 0 not out. Lockett's wickets included four in four balls and he achieved the wonderful feat of taking the first seven wickets for no runs.

Walsall

Walsall pushed Mitchells & Butlers into second place in 1922. Walsall's professional, Bert Sedgwick was at the forefront of their success creating a club record for wickets taken by dismissing 85 batsmen in the course of which he took 5 or more wickets in an innings in eleven games. Fellow fast bowler, Joe Churm chipped in with wickets at the other end as he was to do for the next three seasons until he died in 1926 after contracting pneumonia after catching a chill whilst playing in the first match of that season. Bert Taylor, Norman Hewson and Hal Thacker provided most of the runs together with Jimmy Ashwell. These four together with professionals Bert Sedgwick and later Billy Wilkinson gave unstinting service but the club had little reserve strength and towards the end of the period languished at the bottom end of the table. Hal Thacker later rose to eminence becoming a Judge in the High Court.

Kidderminster

Kidderminster's successes came in 1924 and 1929. By coinci-dence they had identical playing records in the League Table in those years. Martin and Geoffrey Tomkinson, Charles Anton, Gilbert Ashton and W.E. Richardson were members of both success-ful sides but L.H. Greenwood and W.G. Gethin were missing from the 1929 side to be replaced by Alec Wyers, Harvey Perry, Gerald Humphries and Lawson Winwood. Jack Bowles, the professional, took 83 wickets in 1924, and 87 in the following year. Jack Bowles then left the club to try his hand with Worcestershire before returning to the League at Old Hill in 1929. George Brook the professional in 1929, took 80 wickets.

In 1925, Kidderminster and Moseley figured in a game with a dramatic finish. Moseley scored 91, Jack Bowles 9—47. Facing this mediocre total, Kidderminster were cruising to victory at 91—4 when five wickets fell without addition to the score. The last man, Harry Morgan, who was in the team for his fielding, went to the wicket with the crowd and the players, and no doubt himself, in a state of great excitement but he proved equal to the situation and the winning run was at last achieved.

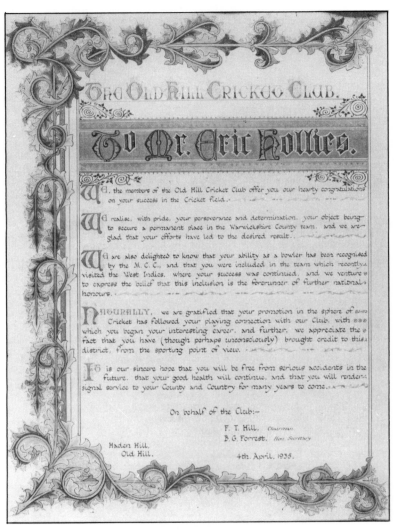

Illuminated Address presented to W.E. Hollies by Old Hill C.C.

Mitchells and Butlers

Mitchells and Butlers had to wait until the second half of this period for their successes but they celebrated in style, winning in 1925, 1926 and 1928. Billy Wilkinson, their professional for sixteen years, had a big hand in the 1925 and 1926 successes but had moved to Walsall by 1928, to be replaced by George Paine.

These professionals were, however, backing up a formidable team of amateurs. Harry Kirton, Jack Stevenson, Wally Hatfield, Jimmy Williams, Reg Stimpson, Fred Broadbent, Charlie Harbage, Harry 'Bowie' Payne and Arthur Melley. Arthur Melley joined at the start of the 1925 season and his success with the ball was just what was needed to turn draws on the good Cape Hill wicket into victory. In a rousing match at Walsall in 1929, Arthur took 6—51 as Walsall chased a total of 211. With Walsall at 201—7 he took two wickets in two balls then George Paine took an outstanding catch and the report says 'hundreds of caps went into the air.'

Harry Kirton first made his entry into the First Division in 1923. He just missed his first century when he was dismissed for 98 in another memorable match at Cape Hill. Dudley set Mitchells & Butlers 256 in 125 minutes, a total they achieved as Dudley bowled 50 overs in the time. It is interesting to note that 50 overs were bowled in 125 minutes yet nowadays some clubs are losing points because they do not bowl the same number of overs in 3 hours.

Some idea of the powerful batting line up of Mitchells and Butlers can be gauged from three successive games where they scored 214—2 in 41 overs to beat Walsall; 285—7 in 57 overs, to beat Smethwick's 283; and 280—3 in 49 overs to beat Dudley. They did fail on 7th August 1926 when West Bromwich Dartmouth dismissed them for 130, to inflict upon them their first defeat since July 1924, and only their second in three seasons.

When Smethwick and Mitchells and Butlers met in 1920 the Presidents of the two clubs arranged that the President of the losing side should pay for the entertainment of the players. The first game finished as a draw but the return was won by Mitchells. W.O. Butler, son of the Mitchells President scored 50 and presumably the Smethwick President, Major S.N. Thompson, footed the bill for the entertainment.

Smethwick

Smethwick only managed to get into the top half of the table during the last three years of the period but they did achieve one record. On 7th June 1922 they scored 410—5 off only 53.4 overs batting first against Kidderminster who, weary of leather chasing, were all out for 82. Shipman, the Smethwick professional, scored 102 not out and then clean bowled eight. The busiest people on the ground were the 8d side spectators kept occupied throwing back the ball. This tremendous score has only once been surpassed when, on 29th August 1931, Old Hill scored 413—6. This score was, however, in reply to a Unity score of 82 and serves as an illustration that records and averages are not truly comparable if they were achieved before 1945, when the League ruled that the score books should be closed when a result was achieved.

Smethwick came close to winning the title in 1927. They led the Table for most of the season but faltered towards the close when

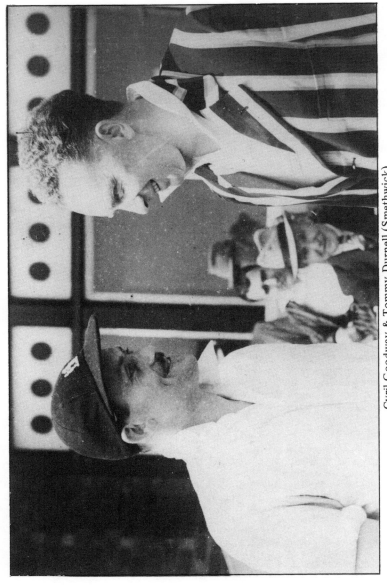

Cyril Goodway & Tommy Durnell (Smethwick)

42

Aston Unity took a one point lead. Smethwick's last game was at home against West Bromwich Dartmouth. Tommy Durnell took 8—25 to polish off the visitors and Smethwick knocked off the runs before tea. The game was then declared finished so that the Smethwick players could rush over to Trinity Road to check on Aston Unity's progress against Mitchells and Butlers. For once, the M & B run machine had failed, Harry Howell had taken seven of their wickets and, to Smethwick's disappointment, they were to see Aston Unity score the runs required and receive the trophy.

Early in the period the Smethwick side did not have sufficient strength in depth to support batsmen Leslie Neale and Billy Ellerker and the professional Shipman. Later in the period, these were joined by fast bowler Tommy Durnell, R.N. Webster, E.J. Rooker, free scoring Norman Mathews and wicket-keeper Cyril Goodway. Cyril was to become wicket-keeper and later Chairman of Warwickshire and play a leading part in League administration. Cyril joined Smethwick at the age of 15 and made his Second XI debut two years later, on 4 July 1927, scoring 53 against Moseley 2nd XI. His First Eleven debut was on 27 August 1928, when he scored 15 not out against Mitchells and Butlers, hitting his first two balls for 6 and taking 45 minutes to score the other three.

Cyril was to become renowned for his carefree yet dedicated approach to the game and to always be on hand when any practical jokes were afoot. In the middle of his bat he drew a circle the size of a cricket ball with an inscription to bowlers 'Aim Here'. In his League career he was to score one century which included 3 — 6's and no fours!

In 1927 Tommy Durnell was to achieve a unique feat by finishing top of the League, Warwickshire and English averages. Leslie Neale and Billy Ellerker featured in one of Smethwick's finest wins on 22 June 1929, when they defeated Mitchells and Butlers by 9 wickets scoring 254—1 in reply to M & B's 191. Leslie Neale 102 not out, Billy Ellerker 136 n.o.

On 27 August 1927, Tommy Durnell was bowling in his best form against West Bromwich Dartmouth when Georgie Dodd came to the wicket. After dodging the first delivery the next struck him on the side. Instantly, a cloud of smoke issued from the batsman's pocket from which a burning box of matches was extracted. The next ball hit him on the body and he had to be assisted to the pavilion.

Aston Unity

Aston Unity's one success, in 1927, came in the absorbing finish to the season when they led Smethwick and Old Hill by one point and Moseley by three, so that a slip could have given any of the four the title or a share. Aston's success can be attributed to the arrival of Harry Howell as professional. Harry had done a lion's share of the bowling for Warwickshire crowning this with ten wickets in an innings against Yorkshire in 1924. His presence was the tonic that was needed to stimulate a rebuilt side previously stuck in the bottom half of the table. Teddy Edden, J. Rhodes and Wally Ogle, who were the only players from the successful pre-War side, had retired or left the Club by the middle of the 1920's but George Peare, Jim Beevers, Ric Hunt, Norman Pulley and Eric Heywood were to be the base on which the side was to be rebuilt.

The significant result of the season occurred on 23 July, when

Smethwick were leading the table. Aston Unity were all out for 66 but then Harry Howell took 7—29 and, with 'Ric' Hunt taking 1—4 off 8 overs and sealing up the other end, Smethwick could only muster 61. Aston were later again dismissed for 66, this time by Kidderminster who only managed 27; Harry Howell 6—13. That Aston's bowling won the league can hardly be an exaggeration since only two 50's were scored one by George Peare and the other by — Harry Howell, and that in a 'batting on' situation.

West Bromwich Dartmouth

West Bromwich Dartmouth and Dudley failed to achieve any championship honours but Dartmouth were building up the nucleus of a side which was to be a strong force in the 1930's. Eric Perry, like his namesakes Harvey Perry, Kidderminster and Harry Perry, Stourbridge, was to mature and develop his skills to form a trio of Perrys, not related, who would be a scourge to opponents, and heroes in the eyes of their supporters.

In 1923, Eric Perry joined a Dartmouth side featuring Stacey Jackson, B.H. Langwell, Douglas Perks, Gordon Field, Norman Partridge and Ephraim Smith who kept wicket brilliantly. These, with Arthur Fitton, who returned to the club at the end of the period after a short spell with Kidderminster and with professional Yorkshireman Abe Waddington, and Cecil Tate, were to bring the club close to honours at the end of the period. On 9 June 1928, playing against Aston Unity, Abe Waddington had one spell when in 7 balls he took four wickets, hit the stumps twice off no balls eventually finishing with 9—43.

Dudley

Dudley rose from the bottom half of the table in 1920, 1922 and 1926 when Fred Root and Doc Gibbons were the respective professionals. Fred Root served for three seasons, 1920—1922, whilst qualifying for Worcestershire before embarking on an outstanding career in the National and County game. In 1920 he had taken 9—29 against Moseley when the last man was dismissed by Joe Mantle. Earlier in the season he had the same figures against Mitchells and Butlers. With the bat he scored 162, out of a team total of 332—5 against Stourbridge in 1921, and followed this up by bowling thirty overs to take 6—70. Fred Root's fast bowling partner, Jim Naden, started his career with the Club before the war. He attracted the attention of Worcestershire in 1922 but was unlucky to have his debut cancelled when Fred Root declared himself fit at the last minute and played in his place. When Jim eventually made his debut, he met a fearsome Kent batting side on a good wicket and managed two wickets in the Kent score of 509—5 but only played one other game for the County.

The Club stalwarts in the period were the brothers Barney and Frank Adshead, Jack Wilkinson, who picked up wickets regularly with his slow donkey-drops, Percy Jeavons and the brilliant all-rounder Leslie Gale who could be depended upon to acquit himself well in every game. In the second half of the period another pair of brothers Horace and Jack Pearson together with Jim Wrightson made steady contributions.

A Note of Optimism

The era which had started by picking up the threads severed by the Great War ended on a high note of optimism. Record crowds were flocking to the grounds, many ground improvements had been or were being undertaken, wickets were better prepared. The stage was set for the great performances to come from the three Perrys, Harry Kirton, Eric Hollies, George Peare, Ric Hunt, Jack Hossell (Jnr.), Norman Plowright, Billy Jones, Gerald Humphries, Alec Wyers, Leslie Gale, Cyril Goodway and Tommy Durnell along with many others.

Extra Cover 1919—1929

29.5.20   When Aston Unity played Stourbridge rain stopped play after 35 minutes. When play was resumed a new pitch was cut and the game continued.

27.8.21   Championship cup presented to W.L. Edwards, Old Hill Captain for 30 years — also a presentation to mark his Silver Wedding.

27.5.22   Walsall 255—8 B. Taylor 99 G.W. Platt 4—63
Old Hill 43 W. Sedgwick 8—20
3,500 spectators, Sedgwick carried shoulder high
Previous week a 'poor gate' at Walsall of 1,000!

23.6.23   Kidderminster 115 all out and all bowled: G.W. Platt 7—43:
Old Hill 140

21.7.23   Aston Unity 20 in 10.4 overs. W.Beaver 5—7 Shipman 4—11 G.A. Holloway retired hurt.
Smethwick 159—8

11.8.23   Both Kidderminster sides declare at 300 versus Mitchells and Butlers

26.7.24   Mitchells and Butlers 196 H.O. Kirton 84 W. Wilkinson 68 W. Lee 7—54
Old Hill 197—4 H.W. Homer 102 not out: scored first century in First Division of League for Old Hill.
Mitchell's first loss since 23.6.1922

6.6.25   Walsall 19 W. Lee 7—13
Old Hill 88 J. Churm 5—44

15.8.25   Mitchells and Butlers 251—9 W.E. Hatfield 93 including 6 - 6's and 10 - 4's
West Bromwich Dartmouth 73 W. Wilkinson 6—28
One of Hatfield's drives out of the Dartmouth ground just missed two passing tram cars.

14.5.27   Stourbridge 286—8, were 4 wickets down for one run F. Tate 59 not out, H.Hunt 78 n.o. put on 127 for ninth wicket in 50 minutes — earlier Joe Tate, Fred's brother scored 71
Mitchells and Butlers 115—3

25.6.27   Walsall 117 J. Chattin 43 E. Perry 6—51. At one time Walsall were 0—2, recovered to 108—5 and then collapsed.
West Bromwich Dartmouth 177—6 L.J. Taylor 107 n.o. E. Perry 42. Dartmouth lost half their side for 9 runs but Perry and Taylor hit them to victory. At one point in the partnership Perry and Taylor were at the same end

45

and a fielder made the extraordinary blunder of walking to the same end to take off the bails! Taylor formerly played for Walsall.

23.6.28   Mitchells and Butlers 92 H.O. Kirton 39 N.E. Partridge 5−23 A. Waddington 4−51
West Bromwich Dartmouth 65 G.A.E. Paine 7−33 A. Melley 3−30.
A good day for four splendid bowlers.

1.9.28   Martin Tomkinson, Kidderminster, hit Aaron Lockett, Old Hill for 6 at Kidderminster. The ball fell in a passing train and was not recovered.

13.7.29   Aston Unity 255−8 N. Pulley 50 A.E. Morgan 75
Mitchells and Butlers 248−3 J. Williams 120 H.O. Kirton 80 n.o.
Mitchells wanted eight off the last four balls. The large crowd got so excited and vociferous that the players stopped the game and appealed for something like quietness! (what would those players have thought of the noise of some crowds at First Class one day games and Test Matches nowadays).

League Positions 1919—1929

First Division	1919	1920	1921	1922	1923	1924	1925	1926	1927	1928	1929
Aston Unity	4	3	3	10	7*	10	9	10	1	8	3
Dudley	6	4	7	5	10	8	7	4	6	10	7
Handsworth Wood	9	-	-	-	-	-	-	-	-	-	-
Kidderminster	8	5*	9	9	6	1	2	6	10	5*	1
Mitchells & Butlers	2	2	2	2	2	4	1	1	7	1	6
Moseley	5	1	5	6	1	5	3	2*	4	5*	10
Old Hill	-	9	1	4	4	2	8	2*	2*	2	5
Smethwick	7	10	6	8	9	7	5	7	2*	4	2
Stourbridge	1	8	4	7	7*	9	6	8	5	9	8
Walsall	3	7	8	1	3	3	10	9	9	7	9
West Bromwich Dartmouth	10	5*	10	3	5	6	4	5	8	3	4

* Position held jointly

Highest Club Scores in Period

Aston Unity	286–8	v	Smethwick	(A)	1919
Dudley	332–5	v	Stourbridge	(A)	1921
Handsworth Wood	223–4	v	West Brom. Dartmouth	(H)	1919
Kidderminster	302–6	v	Moseley	(H)	1929
Mitchells & Butlers	307–9	v	Dudley	(H)	1921
Moseley	329–5	v	Walsall	(H)	1919
Old Hill	298–6	v	Smethwick	(H)	1927
Smethwick	410–5	v	Kidderminster	(H)	1922
Stourbridge	286–8	v	Mitchells & Butlers	(A)	1927
Walsall	330–8	v	Moseley	(A)	1919
West Brom. Dartmouth	305–8	v	Smethwick	(H)	1923

Lowest Club Scores in Period

Aston Unity	20	v	Smethwick	(A)	1923
Dudley	12	v	Walsall	(A)	1919
Handsworth Wood	27	v	Moseley	(A)	1919
Kidderminster	24	v	Smethwick	(A)	1919
Mitchells & Butlers	58	v	Stourbridge	(A)	1919
Moseley	40	v	Walsall	(H)	1922
Old Hill	43	v	Walsall	(A)	1922
Smethwick	33	v	Kidderminster	(A)	1920
Stourbridge	21	v	Old Hill	(A)	1926
Walsall	19	v	Old Hill	(H)	1925
West Brom. Dartmouth	27	v	Aston Unity	(A)	1920

Individual Performances

Highest Scores

Aston Unity (S. Ogden)	174	v	Stourbridge	(A)	1923
Dudley (C.F. Root)	162	v	Stourbridge	(A)	1921
Handsworth Wood (A.J. Wharton)	107 n.o.	v	West Brom. Dartmouth	(H)	1919
Kidderminster (G.Ashton)	123	v	Stourbridge	(H)	1922
Mitchells & Butlers (W.H. Wilkinson)	169n.o.	v	Aston Unity	(H)	1919
Moseley (G.W. Stephens)	170n.o.	v	Old Hill	(H)	1920
Old Hill (F. Woodhouse)	123	v	Aston Unity	(H)	1928
Smethwick (A.J.L. Neale)	154	v	Walsall	(H)	1926
Stourbridge (T. Clare)	111	v	Mitchells & Butlers	(H)	1920
Walsall (J. Ashwell)	168n.o.	v	Mitchells & Butlers	(A)	1929
West Brom. Dartmouth (Spring)	153n.o.	v	Smethwick	(H)	1923

Best Bowling

Aston Unity (E.T. Edden)	9–103	v	Mitchells & Butlers	(A)	1922
Dudley (C.F. Root)	9–29	v	Mitchells & Butlers	(H)	1920
Dudley (C.F. Root)	9–29	v	Moseley	(A)	1920
Handsworth Wood (A.J. Wharton)	8–35	v	Kidderminster	(A)	1919
Kidderminster (W.G. Gethin)	9–30	v	Aston Unity	(A)	1921
Mitchells & Butlers (W.H. Wilkinson)	9–61	v	Smethwick	(A)	1923
Moseley (C.A.F. Hastilow)	9–40	v	Dudley	(A)	1929
Old Hill (A. Lockett)	10–14	v	Stourbridge	(H)	1926
Smethwick (W.H.Ellerker)	8–17	v	Dudley	(A)	1925
Stourbridge (T. Allchurch)	8–17	v	Kidderminster	(H)	1919
Walsall (Sedgwick)	8–20	v	Old Hill	(H)	1922
West Brom. Dartmouth (A. Waddington)	9–43	v	Aston Unity	(H)	1928

Second Division 1919—1929

Second Division Winners

1919	No Competition	1925	(Mitchells and Butlers
1920	(Aston Unity		(Old Hill
	(Moseley	1926	Moseley
1921	Aston Unity		
1922	)	1927	)
	) Old Hill		) Mitchells and Butlers
1923	)	1928	)
1924	Mitchells and Butlers	1929	West Brom.Dartmouth

Highlights

20.8.21   Old Hill 304—2 C. Palmer 129 W. Eley 126 n.o. added 275 for second wicket.   Palmer's 129 was first century in League at Old Hill.
Mitchells and Butlers 64 S. Adams 8—21 including 'hat-trick'

29.4.22   Old Hill 115
Smethwick 88 S. Adams a 'lob' bowler took 5 wickets and W. Hollies one with his 'lobs'

17.5.24   Mitchells & Butlers 367—4 W. Ogle 225 to break League individual batting record previously held by E. Hadley who in 1907 made 221 also for Mitchells and Butlers and against same opponents Walsall
Walsall 190

9.7.27   The game Moseley 2nd's won then lost.   Moseley dismissed Walsall for 43 and then scored 48.   The captains agreed to play a second innings.   Walsall then scored 62—5 declared and Moseley were all out for 12 to give Walsall victory.   This also denied Moseley of their first win of the season.

28.7.27   After Smethwick had been dismissed for 78 Old Hill batted on to score 398—6.   All ten Smethwick fielders bowled.   This is another illustration of the fallacy of 'Batting on'.

1928   Fred Broadbent, of Mitchells and Butlers, scored 924 runs in the Second Division and, with 68 in the Champions v The Rest match finished only 8 short of 1,000 runs in the season (15 innings).

15.6.29   Moseley 167.   The Old Hill Hollies, 'Father and Son' took all ten wickets.   W. Hollies 7—59 and his son Eric 3—63.   W. Hollies, Lob bowler, known as the 'twiddle-de-de-King'
Old Hill 231—7 E. Hollies 33 W. Hollies 39 J. Newton 55.

15.6.29   Mitchells and Butlers 290—1 F. Broadbent 110 not out C. Harbage 157.   A record stand.
Stourbridge 147

20.7.29   Kidderminster 253   F.R. Pearsall 92 W.E. Beresford 47 added 148 for the last wicket.
Walsall 126

Dudley

1930–1939 – THE GOLDEN YEARS

Administration

The decade started with the President, Mr. F.T. Cozens, relinquishing his post thus breaking 42 years unbroken service and bringing to an end the last serving officer's link with the founder members. His retirement was occasioned by his decision to move to the South Coast. During his term he had guided the League to the forefront of League cricket in the country and his geniality and tact in control of League meetings had contributed greatly to the unanimity of spirit amongst the members of the clubs. To mark his retirement he was, in 1931, presented with an Illuminated Address, a gold watch and the First Division Championship Cup. Part of the contributions to his Testimonial collection were spent on a replacement cup which is still in use today and bears his name.

Another of the Founder members of the League, Mr. W.J. Phair of West Bromwich Dartmouth, was honoured by his Club in 1932, having completed 50 years service with the Club. He had the record of being the only person to have attended every League meeting and League Dinner since the League had been founded.

Following Mr. Cozen's retirement, it was agreed that a new President should be elected annually to enable the honour to be shared by individuals who had given meritorious service to the League. Proposals that Vice Presidencies should be shared equally by all clubs were also tabled but it was agreed that the practice should be retained of making these appointments in recognition of meritorious service only. It was also ruled that the principle of "one club, one vote" should continue to apply and the President and Vice Presidents would have no vote.

Discussions on the effects of new Government Legislations relating to Land Tax and Entertainment Tax were at this time taking up time at the League meetings. Club Treasurers were now faced with the need to pay the Customs and Excise Tax element of admission fees and a number of Clubs found it necessary to change their rules relating to members and Vice Presidents whose contributions were subject to tax if they did not have full use of sports facilities of the Club.

In 1937, Mr. W. Preston, Walsall, presented a flag to the League to be flown at the grounds where the Champions were playing.

Engagement of Professionals

The first sign of the League clubs relenting on their strong line regulations regarding professionals occurred in 1935, when sympathetic consideration was given to the reinstatement of young players who had tried their luck with the Counties and were then not retained. Such consideration was only to apply if they had not played County cricket regularly and returned to the clubs for whom they had played before turning professional.

This relaxation of the Rules did not assist the case of Eric Hollies or Ronnie Bird who were qualifying for Warwickshire and Worcestershire respectively since it was considered they would make the grade as professionals.

Wickets

The 9" wicket recommended by the M.C.C. was adopted for all League matches for season 1931. It did not become compulsory in all cricket until 1947.

Playing Time

In 1935 it was ruled that the last over should be completed. Following a number of complaints by clubs about the "Calling of Time" by umpires in 1938 the Honorary Secretary was instructed to write to every club asking them to provide a clock on all grounds, and umpires were instructed to synchronise their watches with the clocks before the start of play.

Players

It was ruled in 1930 that a player who had played in a first team match or had been selected to play in an abandoned First team match was not eligible to play for the Second Eleven on the same day.

Match Balls

Each year, from 1933 to 1937, motions were tabled to legislate for a new ball for each innings, and finally in 1937, this provision was adopted.

The Playing Scene 1930—1939

This decade can well justify the sub-title "Golden Years", with great team and individual performances, outstanding and famous players of past, present and future performing in front of excited and record crowds.

West Bromwich Dartmouth and Walsall took most honours with seven championships between them, with Mitchells and Butlers also thereabouts, winning twice, one shared with Aston Unity. Moseley managed one title by 1½ points when one run denied Walsall a victory when they tied a game with Mitchells and Butlers. Despite this domination of the championship awards by West Bromwich Dartmouth and Walsall, all the Clubs introduced amateur and professional players of exceptional ability to provide testing opposition, and lower positions in the Championship Table were by no means an indication of a shortfall in performance or entertainment value.

West Bromwich Dartmouth

With four titles in 1930, 1932, 1933 (shared with Walsall) and 1934, the West Bromwich Dartmouth success was built around Cecil Tate as professional. Significantly he left to play for Warwickshire in 1931 the one lean year. Amateur support came from Eric Perry, Ron Lawton, a fast bowler and hard hitting batsman, Billy Jones, Arthur Fitton, Doug Perks, Arthur Perry, Charlie Mitchell, George Dodd and wicket-keeper Ephraim Smith. All these players would justify a chapter to themselves but this applies to so many League players that this full cover must be left in the hands of Club Historians. There must, however, be exceptions and one such is Eric Perry, whose name constantly comes to the fore when League players are discussed today.

Eric first made an impact in the Dartmouth first eleven in 1925 at the age of 17, with 59 and 5—17 against Walsall. He was to develop into a great all-rounder and be a dominant member of the side until 1951. He became a great driving force in the side, showing no mercy his appealing being described as 'as venomous as his bowling'. He opened the Dartmouth batting in the 1930's successes and later moved to the middle of the order, always willing to hit his way out of trouble. He had a reputation as an aggressive and uncompromising captain who controlled practice at the nets with the same thoroughness as the fielders in a match. He bowled seamers at first and sharp off breaks later in his career and older cricketers and followers of the League are almost unanimous in declaring him to have been the finest all-rounder within living memory — a man who could have walked into any County side if he had wished. In his career in the League, although he took 5 or more wickets on at least 28 occasions and scored 48 50's and 16 centuries, no statistics can reflect his immeasurable impact on the game. Many stories abound of his performances but perhaps one in relation to his uncompromising captaincy will indicate his commitment to the Dartmouth's fortunes. In a game versus Stourbridge, with Dartmouth batting out for a draw, two Stourbridge players collided trying to make a catch and, and as they lay on the ground, Eric ran out of the pavilion, past the injured fielders, to tell the batsman not to lose his concentration.

Walsall

Whilst West Bromwich Dartmouth were dominating the early 1930's Walsall were languishing in bottom place in the League and interest in Walsall had consequently declined.

This state of affairs was not acceptable to Mr. W. Preston, the town's Member of Parliament and a former captain of the Club, so that on his election as President of the Club in 1931, he took steps to improve the playing standards. With little reserve strength available he embarked on rebuilding the side with imported players. His first two signings, namely Maurice Foster, 1932, and professional Norman Backhouse, 1933, were probably the most significant and brought a change in the Club's fortunes, enabling them to rise from bottom position in 1932 to joint champions in 1933. Maurice Foster, a wiry sun-tanned 44 year old former captain of Worcestershire, brought into the game not only his batting and wicket-keeping expertise but also an adventurous style of captaincy, setting achievable targets for his own players and the opposition, and playing for a draw only as a last resort. One illustration of his approach was a rain affected game versus Smethwick in May 1933. Walsall declared at 151—7 Hubert Lindop scoring a dashing 63, and although the umpires suggested the ground was unfit, Maurice Foster and Smethwick's captain Norman Mathews agreed to play on. Maurice saying "We will bowl for wickets! If Smethwick get the runs good luck to them!" Walsall did get six wickets, four for 'ducks', but Smethwick's new professional 'Tom' Dollery, qualifying for Warwickshire, joined his captain to score 99 in 45 minutes for Smethwick to win by four wickets. This match was described in the press as

"Champagne of the game."

The spirit in which Maurice Foster led his side can be gauged from frequent references to the Walsall side applauding their opponents on leaving the field even when Walsall had lost.

Norman Backhouse, a Yorkshireman and a left arm spinner, who may have played for his County had he not been in the same era as Hedley Verity, proved to be as good a professional as any who have served the Walsall Club. For four years, until his untimely death in a car accident, he was an outstanding performer with bat and ball, twice taking all ten wickets and in 1935 taking a record number of 95 wickets in a season. The first 10 wicket success was in 1934 when he took 10−37 to dismiss Stourbridge for 82 in reply to Walsall's 167. In this match, he also achieved a hat-trick for the second week running. His second achievement of ten wickets came the following year when he took 10−34 as West Bromwich Dartmouth were dismissed for 95 to enable Walsall to win by 5 wickets. There was added pleasure in this performance for it mollified in some measure Walsall's defeat at the hands of West Bromwich Dartmouth in a thrilling game the previous season which had decided the championship.

This decisive game was played in front of 4000 spectators crowded into the Dartmouth ground, including over 1000 who had made the journey from Walsall. The match was full of surprises and generated high excitement throughout. Dartmouth batted first and were shocked to lose Eric Perry off the second ball. Worse was to follow as John Wardrop and Norman Backhouse ripped through the batting to reduce Dartmouth to 35−9. The last pair, A.R. Perks 29 n.o. and Charles Mitchell 12, slowly dragged the score to 69 when Mitchell was dismissed. Wardrop proved relatively expensive at 6−50, Backhouse 4−9. Walsall's supporters were 'cock a hoop' but their celebrations were short-lived, Walsall losing 2 wickets for 4 runs including that of Maurice Foster. Wickets continued to tumble as the total was edged forward with Backhouse, who had opened, standing firm until he too fell for 21 with the score 56−7. By now the crowd were at fever pitch and when Cecil Tate took the last wicket at 64 the crowd rushed on to the ground to chair their heroes. There was more sensation to follow, for Maurice Foster exercised his right, probably with his tongue in his cheek, to claim a second innings, much to the chagrin of the Dartmouth supporters. When Dartmouth slumped to 22−4, it seemed the game was not yet over but when they recovered to 126−5 Walsall conceded defeat and the Dartmouth supporters resumed their celebrations. Douglas Perks, the popular Dartmouth captain briefly addressed them and pointed out that apart from Ron Lawton, who had lived in the town for seven or eight years and Cecil Tate, the professional, all the team had been born and bred in West Bromwich and had been promoted from the second eleven.

Walsall however were building up a strong side with John Wardrop, Jack Hight, Freddie Bryan, Norman Partridge and Tom Troman. They were to be successful for the next three seasons during which time they were dubbed as "Billy Preston's Circus". A Championship dinner menu included the couplet:

"So long as we're champions why should it irk us
That Clubs less successful should dub us a Circus!"

When they played their last home game of the 1937 season,

incidentally against the Dartmouth who won 94—68, Walsall had already won the Championship and spectators, of which there were some 2000, were treated to a free bottle of beer each. This game included a landmark for 'Tich' Freeman, the new Walsall professional when he took 8 wickets to bring his total for the season to 98, thereby beating Backhouse's record of 1935. The previous week 'Tich' Freeman had joined the 10 wicket takers with 10—44, including a hat-trick, against Dudley.

Dudley

Dudley could not claim a ten wicket-taker but created a record with the bat on the 18 June 1932 when Leslie Gale 150 n.o. and Charles Bull, the professional, 107 n.o., made an opening stand of 264 in 66 overs. These two had a prolific season scoring a total of 1442 runs whilst the other thirteen batsmen who went to the wicket could only muster 773. Leslie Gale's total for the season of 836 was only 18 short of Bert Homer's record. When Bull left after one season, Dudley's batting frailty was exposed and although Jack Pearson, Norman Hartill, Jack Dalloway and Jim Wrightson gave support to Leslie there was not sufficient consistency to ensure steady batting in support of the bowling of Horace Lavender, Ernie Haycock and the professionals, of which Ted Sheffield was outstanding. They did, however, have two meritorious wins, the first on 10 June 1933 when they inflicted the first defeat suffered by Dartmouth since August 1931. Then on 12 May 1934, they dismissed the powerful Mitchells and Butlers batting for 34, Sheffield taking 9—6, all bowled, 5 of the 6 runs scored off one over. Dudley did not make easy work of winning this match and were 25—6 but a Norman Hartill gritty innings took them to victory.

The Dudley, Mitchells and Butlers match on 7th July 1934 was interrupted by a loudspeaker announcement that Miss Dorothy Round, the local girl, had won the Women's Singles at Wimbledon. The message was received with applause by both players and spectators.

Mitchells and Butlers

Mitchells and Butlers formidable batting had as its base the opener Harry Kirton, another of the great performers of this era, an immaculate and correct bat. He was another player who had no desire to enter the County scene although he had all the attributes of a County opening bat. He entered the League arena in 1923 and regularly compiled good scores until 1946 even though dogged by illness for part of the time. He topped the century on at least 32 occasions and fifty over 75 times. In 1935 he established a new League record of 878 runs in the season and on 10 June 1939 he scored 189 with Roger Wyatt 87 n.o. in a partnership of 288—1 off 49.5 overs versus West Bromwich Dartmouth. This exceeded the partnership of Leslie Gale and Charles Bull in 1932. The 288 partnership still stands as a record for the 1st Division. Some idea of the respect and veneration he was accorded can be gauged from a game near the end of his career when he slipped and fell when making a run, but the opposition, Moseley, laughingly helped him to his feet and into his crease without removing the bails. This was also a good example of the sportsmanship which has existed in the League. He had a spell as captain in the thirties but his captaincy matched the correct and careful approach of his batting with none of the aggression of Eric Perry or flair of Maurice Foster. Owing to

JUNE 3rd 1939 – 288 RUNS
MITCHELLS & BUTLERS v WEST BROMWICH DARTMOUTH
R.A.D. WYATT   H.O. KIRTON

his correct and careful approach, and in the absence of good support bowling for professional Freddie Gross and Arthur Melley, Mitchells became draw specialists, but although always close to the top, never pulled off enough wins to ensure outright success.

Mitchells, who opened their present ground in Portland Road in 1930, were, however, by no means a one man side. Jack Stevenson was a dependable bat and, when he scored 102 n.o. against Walsall on 10 June 1933, he had achieved a distinguished record of a century against every club in the 28 years he had played in the League. His father and 3 uncles had also previously played for the club. Charlie Harbage, Roger Wyatt, Ronnie Lake, Reg Stimpson and in later years Dick Jones, gave further good amateur support to professional Freddie Gross, a leg break and googly bowler who picked up a good number of victims each season, his best in 1934 when he took 86 wickets.

In the same season he played his last First Class game and his only one for Warwickshire taking one wicket, that of Len Hutton who was playing in his first game!

Mitchells shared the championship with Aston Unity in 1939, in unusual circumstances. With the outbreak of War, Stourbridge were unable to raise a side for the last match of the season versus Aston Unity. Mitchells beat Dudley to go three points in front of Aston Unity but then had to await the outcome of a League meeting before they knew whether they would be outright or joint winners. The League awarded three points for a win to the Unity, a precedent which was followed thirty seven years later when Worcestershire could not field a side, albeit for a different reason.

Aston Unity

The Aston Unity success in 1939 was achieved with the assistance of professional Albert Thomas who had been released two seasons previously by Kidderminster on the grounds that his type of bowling did not win championships! Albert, a former Northants player, was an extremely economical bowler and, coupled with Eric Heywood, and backing with bat and ball from Ric Hunt, Ted Whitehead, Jack Hossell (Jnr.) and the batting of Ray Sparkes, Stan Flavell, Dennis Hodgetts, Alf Woodroffe, Jim Beevers and the famous Aston Villa and England soccer international, Eric Houghton, Aston Unity were able to prove Kidderminster wrong. Other players who had served the Unity well during the thirties were Bill Wood, George Peare, Bernard Sanders, Wilf Harmer and Roy James.

Norman Ingram was also to make his appearance from time to time from 1932. He was an excellent Club man, always prepared to step from First to Second eleven cricket to serve the Club he has supported to this day as player, groundsman, secretary and club official. Norman took part in a record last wicket stand on 27 August 1932. He went in to face Moseley, with the Unity score at 47—9 but he and Ted Whitehead, who finished at 90 not out, added 102 before Norman was dismissed for 10. When the partnership was worth 42 he was given out stumped, but recalled when Eric Cross, the Moseley wicket-keeper, said he was not in possession of the ball when he broke the wicket.

Eric Heywood took 9—31 on 25 May 1931 in a match versus Dudley. He was robbed of the 10th wicket when, Jack Dalloway, last man in, was dropped off his bowling and then run out off the same ball.

Aston Unity had a long spell of leather-chasing on 29 August 1931. After being dismissed for 82 in 27.3 overs, they then fielded for 68.4 overs as Old Hill compiled a record 413—6 as they 'batted on' after winning. The Old Hill performance was nevertheless creditable, with Bert Homer scoring 170 n.o. He shared a third wicket stand of 234 with Jim Eley 82.

Old Hill

The Club lost the services of Eric Hollies in 1932, when he joined Warwickshire to start a First Class career spanning 25 years.

Old Hill signed up Dick Howorth as professional for seasons 1932 — 33 and, although he earned his fee with bat and ball including 10—38 in 14.2 overs, on 10th June 1933, against Smethwick, the side did not achieve any championship successes. Billy Lee took over as professional in 1936 and also performed well, but lack of support in the attack negated the professionals' and the batsmen's efforts. The Club even had to recall Billy Hollies from time to time and he proved his 'Lobs' could still be effective. Bert Homer, Jim Eley, Bert Millichip, Bert Edwards and J.I. Homer, and for one season only, Ronnie Bird, provided more than adequate batting strength. In a high scoring game on 28 May 1938, Smethwick hit 248—7 in 40.1 overs, Norman Mathews 140. Old Hill replied with 238—7 in 53.0 overs, Bert Edwards 66. In all twenty six 6's were struck.

The Club has always encouraged young players and one such, Charles Palmer, a nephew of Bert Homer, played at the age of 14 batting at number 11 for Old Hill Second Eleven. He was to rise from this lowly start to play for Worcestershire, Leicestershire and England. He also became Secretary to Leicestershire, President of the M.C.C. and eventually took the premier post in cricket as Chairman of the Cricket Council and the Test and County Cricket Board. Playing for Old Hill in the First Division, in 1938, he scored two successive centuries, one against Walsall the other against West Bromwich Dartmouth, in which match he also took 5—45. He started his First Class career with Worcestershire in the same season. He was awarded the C.B.E. in 1984 for his lifetime of service to cricket and the community.

Moseley

Moseley's visit to Old Hill on 17 May 1937 saw some further high scoring when Peter Cranmer hit 96 including 11 — 6's and 4 — 4's but he only had one season in the League for supporters to enjoy his belligerent play.

Moseley played without a professional until Ronnie Bird joined the Club in 1935 but they always had sufficient strength to provide tough opposition and stay in the top half of the table with players of the calibre of Jim Morter, 'Rusty' Scorer, Alec Hastilow, Andy Speed, Norman Plowright, Ken Wyatt, Dennis Harris, Cecil Addleman and wicket-keeper Eric Cross.

Moseley's single title came in 1938 when fire was added to the attack by a West Indian, R.C. Lightbourne, nicknamed 'Snow White', who brought a preview of the fast bowling that is today an accepted part of the West Indians' armoury.

Smethwick

A bowler of different vintage shattered Moseley on the 31

August 1935 when the great Sydney Barnes took 8—52. At 62 years of age he bowled 28 overs, bringing his total wickets for the season to 75. Sydney had returned to play for Smethwick having played for them from 1891 to 1894 before embarking on his exceptional career. He is credited with bowling every type of ball in the bowler's armoury in an innings and all delivered on a perfect length. His bowling partner in the match at Moseley Tommy Durnell only took one wicket but that wicket created an amateur record for the club of 69 wickets.

With Sydney and Tommy in partnership, it seems astonishing that Smethwick did not notch up a title but time and again batsmen failed when in a good position. They did however score two good wins against Walsall and West Bromwich Dartmouth. In the former game, Walsall were dismissed for 112, Sydney Barnes 6—30, Tommy Durnell 4—40, Smethwick winning by 5 wickets. Dartmouth fell for 57, Barnes 5—26, Durnell 5—26, Smethwick having already scored 163. Barnes 40, Cyril Goodway 17, Cecil Tate 6—38. On the other hand they dismissed Dartmouth in July 1936 for 59, Barnes 5—30, Durnell 3—9, only for Smethwick to collapse to 47, Barnes 13 not out, Tate 7—30, Ron Lawton 3—14.

Consistent performers and good club men were Leslie Neale, R.N. Webster, Norman Mathews, who also had two years at Moseley, W. Haines, R. Lee, Ron Pearson, to be joined in later years by Maurice Harvatt, Norman Downes, John Norris, and Eric Pole, an exceptional fielder and reliable middle order bat.

Stourbridge

In 1933, Stourbridge brought together another fine pair of bowlers when Sidney Shepherd was signed as professional to share the new ball attack with amateur Harry Perry. The previous season, Harry had destroyed Walsall for 40 when he took 7—6 off ten overs, his analysis at one stage being 6—1. Harry was always immaculately turned out and bowled in-swingers to a leg trap field. On May 15 1937 he and Sidney Shepherd reduced West Bromwich Dartmouth to 66—9 but Eric Perry was still there to score 102 not out, he and Charlie Mitchell adding 72 for the last wicket. Stourbridge then fell to a young leg break bowler, J.R. Robson, playing in his first senior game who took 8—33. Stourbridge had earlier had their own ninth wicket heroes when on 18 May 1935 Shepherd 19 n.o. and Denis Evers 48 added 56 to beat an Old Hill score of 106, Shepherd 6—56, Perry 4—43, Bert Homer 56 n.o. Evergreen Percy Davis scored 22 in this game and continued to play throughout the period flighting his tantalising deliveries and picking up useful wickets.

Jack Whitehouse, Jack Apse, John Bloomer and 'Bobby' Bowen supported Harry Perry in the batting joined towards the end of the era by Dennis Evers and Joe Tilt. John Bloomer continued as an outstanding wicket-keeper, standing up to the quick bowlers, and on 4 July 1936 catching 3 and stumping 3 Moseley batsmen. Two names which also make an entry are Norman Whiting and 15 year old Don Kenyon — a "promising bat."

Kidderminster

Stourbridge unsuccessfully combated another Perry, Harvey Perry of Kidderminster, in August 1937 when he shot them out for 46, his bag being 7—22 and bringing his total to 83, the highest taken by an amateur since Grosvenor Hill's 83 in 1902. The following season Harvey even surpassed this total with 86 wickets. In tandem with Albert Thomas, 1934-1937, and other professionals the Kidderminster attack was a good one by any standards. It is a good indication of the strength of the League that Kidderminster could not top third place, even with batsmen of the calibre of Geoffrey Tomkinson, Alec Wyers, Philip Thorp, Harry Dalloe, P.T. Chell and the three Humphries brothers, Gerald, Cedric and Norman. When Cedric scored a 100 n.o. at Stourbridge in August of 1939, each of the brothers had notched up a century in the era, Gerald against Dudley and Norman against Stourbridge, both in 1934. Their father, Henry Humphries, had played for the Club when they first entered the League. In 1930, Geoffrey Tomkinson, then Vice-Captain of the Club, was elected Mayor of Kidderminster — he said the Council knew where to find him on Saturday afternoons and umpires were assured that when he appealed, as wicket-keeper, they would not have to call him "Your Worship." In 1955 Geoffrey received a Knighthood.

Extra Cover 1930—1939

9.6.30   West Bromwich Dartmouth 140, were 28—7.   Ron Lawton hit a hurricane 69.
Kidderminster 74, were 74—6.

14.6.30   West Bromwich Dartmouth 71. Smethwick 47.
Smethwick claimed a two innings game although only one hour left. Dartmouth scored 27—2. F.D. Perry 1 in half an hour to register his protest.

23.5 31   Dudley v Stourbridge. Horace Lavender of Dudley twice recalled after being given out, once for caught and once for l.b.w.

13.8.32   Two matches finished early and rather than play on for second innings teams agreed to play 15 over exhibition games, but report says atmosphere was fun rather than entertaining cricket.

6.5.39   Aston Unity 94. Kidderminster 108 won by 2 wickets. "As if to mark Kidderminster's home success, the horse which pulled the roller galloped across the pitch."

13.5.39   West Bromwich Dartmouth 213.
Old Hill 226—1. H.C. Edwards 131 n.o. C.H. Palmer 54 n.o.

20.5.39   Dudley 97.
West Bromwich Dartmouth 115. Blakey 8—39 including hat trick with his first three balls.

22.7.39   L.J. Gilbert (Old Hill) given out "hitting the ball twice".

League Positions 1930–1939
First Division

	1930	1931	1932	1933	1934	1935	1936	1937	1938	1939
Aston Unity	7	8	8*	4	5*	9	8*	9	7	1*
Dudley	8	6	3	10	5*	4	8*	7*	10	9
Kidderminster	6	3*	5*	9	4	6*	5	3	3	3
Mitchells & Butlers	2	1	2	5	3	2	6	2	8	1*
Moseley	5	9	5*	6*	8*	6*	3	6	1	7
Old Hill	9	2	4	6*	8*	10	7	10	4*	4*
Smethwick	3*	3*	8*	3	10	3	4	5	4*	8
Stourbridge	3*	3*	7	8	7	8	10	7*	6	10
Walsall	10	10	10	1*	2	1	1	1	2	6
West Bromwich Dartmouth	1	7	1	1*	1	5	2	4	9	4*

* Position held jointly

1939 Jt. Champions (A.U. & M&B) v The Rest

B: F.C. Smith, H.C. Edwards, O.H., A. Wyers, K.C.C., W. Lee, O.H., E. Perry, W.B.D., C.C. Goodway, Sm., C.H. Palmer, O.H., P. Reed (Scorer)

C: W. Bridgman (Umpire), R.H. Cotton, C.B. Harbage, M&B., R.I. Scorer, Mos., A.E. Thomas, A.U., H.O. Kirton, M&B., J.Tilt, Stour.

F: J.D. Beevers, A.U., J.J. Hossell, A.U., F.H. Hunt, A.U., W.L. Edwards, (Pres.), J. Goodwin, M&B., R.A.D. Wyatt, M&B., F. Gross, M&B.

S: W.E. Jones, WBD., E.H. Perry, Kid., G.H. Humphries, Kid., R. Sparkes, A.U.

Highest Club Scores in Period

Aston Unity	309–5	v	Old Hill	(A)	1939
Dudley	285–3	v	Walsall	(H)	1939
Kidderminster	281–5	v	Old Hill	(H)	1930
Mitchells & Butlers	288–1	v	West Brom. Dartmouth	(H)	1939
Moseley	276–6	v	Old Hill	(A)	1939
Old Hill	413–6	v	Aston Unity	(H)	1931
Smethwick	269–9	v	Dudley	(H)	1938
Stourbridge	295–8	v	Mitchells & Butlers	(A)	1930
Walsall	280–8	v	Dudley	(H)	1930
West Brom. Dartmouth	323–5	v	Walsall	(H)	1931

Lowest Club Scores in Period

Aston Unity	44	v	Stourbridge	(A)	1937
Dudley	31	v	Smethwick	(A)	1930
Kidderminster	48	v	Smethwick	(A)	1934
Mitchells & Butlers	34	v	Dudley	(A)	1934
Moseley	34	v	Smethwick	(A)	1935
Old Hill	33	v	West Brom. Dartmouth	(A)	1934
Smethwick	25	v	Kidderminster	(A)	1936
Stourbridge	34	v	West Brom. Dartmouth	(A)	1935
Walsall	38	v	Aston Unity	(A)	1932
West Brom. Dartmouth	57	v	Smethwick	(A)	1935

Individual Performances

Highest Scores

Aston Unity (S.H. Flavell)	141	v	Old Hill	(A)	1938
Dudley (L.E. Gale)	150*	v	Aston Unity	(H)	1932
Kidderminster (H. Dalloe)	151*	v	Moseley	(H)	1933
Mitchells & Butlers (H.O. Kirton)	189	v	West Brom. Dartmouth	(H)	1939
Moseley (R.E. Bird)	157*	v	Old Hill	(A)	1939
Old Hill (H.W. Homer)	170*	v	Aston Unity	(H)	1931
Smethwick (N. Mathews)	140	v	Old Hill	(A)	1938
Stourbridge (R.D.M.Evers)	127	v	Moseley	(H)	1937
Walsall (M.K. Foster)	119*	v	Smethwick	(A)	1933
West Brom. Dartmouth (E. Perry)	176	v	Dudley	(H)	1930

* Not Out

Best Bowling

Aston Unity (E. Heywood)	9–61	v	Dudley	(A)	1931
Dudley (Sheffield)	9–6	v	Mitchells & Butlers	(H)	1934
Kidderminster (Hutchinson)	9–32	v	Moseley	(A)	1932
Mitchells & Butlers (F.A. Gross)	8–21	v	Stourbridge	(A)	1934
Moseley (A.W. Speed)	8–30	v	Dudley	(A)	1930
Old Hill (R. Howorth)	10–38	v	Smethwick	(A)	1933
Smethwick (T.W. Durnell)	9–20	v	Walsall	(A)	1938
Stourbridge (Shepherd)	8–44	v	West Brom.Dartmouth	(H)	1934
Walsall (E.N. Backhouse)	10–34	v	West Brom.Dartmouth	(A)	1935
West Brom.Dartmouth (C.F. Tate)	9–31	v	Smethwick	(A)	1936

Second Division 1930—1939

Second Division Winners

1930 Dudley	1936)
1931 Old Hill	1937) Mitchells & Butlers
1932)	1938)
1933) Mitchells & Butlers	1939 Kidderminster
1934)	
1935 Walsall	

Highlights

7.6.30   Walsall 349—4, Mitchells & Butlers 303—2 — not a bad afternoon's cricket!

25.5.31   Walsall 101, W. Hollies 6—24.
Old Hill 362. Ben Forrest 243 n.o. — the highest individual score in either Division. Playing at Old Hill Ben went to the wicket with the score at 39—2 and hit his runs in 105 mins., with 14 — 6's and 31 — 4's. Nine bowlers tried to curb him. The next highest score in the innings was 28!

16.7.32   Walsall 62, Harold Fereday 10—18.
Mitchells & Butlers 234—6. Harold was the son of Jack Fereday the Mitchells & Butlers Coach and former player.

5.5.34   Stourbridge 50. Kidderminster 245—2. Geoffrey Tomkinson 200 n.o.

5.5.34   Aston Unity 116, Old Hill 116.

21.7.34   Old Hill 66, West Bromwich Dartmouth 66. Old Hill two ties in one season.

20.6.36   Mitchells & Butlers 147. C. Grove 58. Moseley 17. C. Grove 6—9. Charlie Grove to become a good servant to Warwickshire.

4.7.36   West Bromwich Dartmouth 116. N.C. Downes 7—37 including 4 wickets in 4 balls.
Smethwick 112.

15.8.36   Mitchells & Butlers only lost 8 out of last 88 games.

26.6.37   Aston Unity 48 and 79—9 dec.
West Bromwich Dartmouth 75 and 55—0.
The Dartmouth won both the one innings and the two innings match.

4.6.38   Moseley 67 and 88. West Bromwich Dartmouth 36 and 42. Dartmouth lost both the one innings and the two innings match.

4.6.38   Stourbridge 48. B. Stanley 6—23 including 4 in 4 balls.
Old Hill 186—8.

Old Hill

1940—1945 THE WAR YEARS

Administration

At the League Annual General Meeting in November 1939 a recommendation was made that play should continue in 1940 but a decision was deferred to an adjourned meeting held the following February. At this meeting, Clubs decided to carry on with one Division only. This decision was probably influenced by the older members of clubs who remembered the ravages of neglect on clubs and grounds, due to the lack of play in the 1915—1918 years. The decision was also prompted by a desire to maintain the popular summer entertainment, for in those days the importance of the League in that field should not be overlooked, even if today there is less spectator interest. As a war-time measure, before play could take place, clubs were required to obtain permission from the local police.

News for umpires was not so good, for the Clubs reduced their fee to 3/6, including expenses, on grounds of economy, but for 1942 the fee was restored to 10/-.

Further wartime measures were permission to use reconditioned cricket balls and home clubs to provide batting pads. Applications by the League to the authorities for petrol coupons and cricket equipment were also made. At grounds where printing of scorecards was not possible, team lists were chalked on black-boards. Members of the armed forces in uniform were admitted to grounds for half price. Charges then were 1/6 reserved and 1/- unreserved, ladies and children half price.

County cricket was discontinued so a number of professionals turned to League cricket. The League, however maintained their policy of controlling their employment but, as a war-time measure, professionals were not required to coach and each Club was allowed to field one paid and one unpaid professional. Professionals joining were Charles Elliott, (Derbyshire), to Stourbridge, Dick Howorth, (Worcestershire) to Walsall, New Zealander Bill Merritt, (Northants), to Dudley, Reginald Perks, (Worcestershire) to West Bromwich Dartmouth, George Paine, (Warwickshire) to Smethwick, Tom Goddard, (Gloucestershire) to Kidderminster, Reg Santall, (Warwickshire) to Moseley and Eric Hollies (Warwickshire) to Old Hill. Bob Wyatt, (Warwickshire) also joined Moseley as an amateur.

By the end of the 1940 season the grip of war was beginning to make itself felt as air-raids brought the horrors of war to the civilian front. In one raid, Aston Unity lost their ground when a bomb fell in the middle of the square and another severely damaged their pavilion, as Norman Ingram and Billy Wood sheltered under the billiard table. Moseley found they could not afford to keep their ground going with a small number of members as players left to join the forces so Moseley and Aston Unity had to play all their games away for the next three seasons. Mitchells and Butlers' ground in Portland Road was requisitioned for use as a storage area so they moved back to the Cape Hill Oval. Walsall were also experiencing financial difficulties but when the Town Council offered to reduce their rent on the expiration of the lease in 1940 the club, faced with the alternative of having the ground ploughed up for agriculture, decided to struggle on. This was a wise decision, as events have proved.

With a general shortage of players, it was agreed to form a pool of players and that clubs, with the consent of the opposition, could have players on loan. Other bomb damage forced the League to move from their headquarters at The White Horse in the City to The Wernley on the Wolverhampton Road, the meetings being held in the late afternoon instead of evening.

Playing Scene 1940–1945

Not surprisingly, the professionals captured the headlines in 1940. On 18th May Eric Hollies, Old Hill took 10 wickets for 21, including a hat-trick v Mitchells and Butlers who were dismissed for 61 their No. 10, Crockett scoring 23. On 10th August Bill Merritt, Dudley, also collected 10 wickets and a hat-trick as Aston Unity were all out for 123. Merritt excelled with the bat and ball, on 8th September 1940, when he scored 197 against Smethwick bringing his total to 878 runs to equal Harry Kirton's record made in 1935. In the same game he took 6–82 and in the season 80 wickets. Dick Howorth took 60 wickets and scored 687 runs, just failing to become the highest scorer for Walsall. In the last match of the season Dick must have fancied his chance but Eric Hollies dismissed him for one and then went on to take 7–56, to bring his personal total to 99 wickets to create a record number of dismissals in the First Division. This record still stands. In addition, in the same game, he spun Walsall out for 129 in reply to Old Hill's 205 which gave his side the League title by one point over West Bromwich Dartmouth. Also in this match Maurice Foster, Walsall, scored 60 in what was to be his last League game, for he died before the year closed.

Eric Hollies record of 99 wickets in the First Division established a unique family record, his father Billy holding the Division 2 record with 94 plus 6 in The Champions v The Rest match in 1928.

Kidderminster featured in two high scoring sprees. The first on 6th July when they scored 315–1 Cedric Humphries 158 not out, Harry Moule 113 not out, Cedric Humphries score being the highest then recorded for Kidderminster in the Division. Mitchells and Butlers in reply could only muster 135–4. In Kidderminster's second highest score Cedric Humphries scored 104 not out, Alec Wyers 101 not out, in a total of 238–1 in reply to Dudley's 301–5, Bill Merritt 111. Cedric Humphries was to make more runs during his spells on leave until he fell in action in 1944.

West Bromwich Dartmouth were to win the League title in all Seasons 1941–45. It is significant that Eric Hollies played for them in 1942–1945, having been at Old Hill when they were champions in 1940 and in 1941 when they had finished second so he was a

Moseley's ground in wartime

member of five championship sides in six years. Eric Perry, Billy Jones, Charlie Mitchell, George Dodd and Tom Stanley were other regulars who made good contributions for the Dartmouth and no doubt this ability to field a fairly consistent eleven contributed to the club's success. Other clubs were unable to match this consistency and the two clubs without grounds, Aston Unity and Moseley shared bottom place from 1942—1945.

At Kidderminster, on 17th July 1943, Moseley were only able to field 8 men so three young locals made up their side. Kidderminster openers George Paine 131 and Ray McKinlay 100 took advantage to score 215 a club record opening stand in Kidderminster's total of 261—5. One of the Kidderminster youngsters, Geoffrey Darkes, caught and bowled both and finished with 3—43, whilst another youngster Albert Butt took 1—11. Led by the old fighter and only regular, Rusty Scorer, Moseley played for a draw but still scored 205—6 E.T. Cox 87 and Rusty Scorer 68. Geoff Darkes played seven games for Worcestershire after the war.

The Stourbridge side were kept together by professional Charles Elliott, Arthur Fitton, John Bloomer, K. Mitchell, Stan Grainger and teenage prodigy Don Kenyon. Don collected his first century (103) against Aston Unity on 3rd August 1940 and took his chance to sharpen his technique against the League professionals, so that in 1946 he signed up with Worcestershire to start his eminent career in Test and County Cricket. Charles Elliott was later to become a highly respected Test Umpire.

Cyril Goodway, Eric Pole, W.H. Haines kept the Smethwick side together Eric scoring a century in 45 minutes against Aston Unity in 1940.

When West Bromwich Dartmouth met Old Hill on 1st August 1942 a collection was made for Eric Hollies who had moved to the Dartmouth from Old Hill. The collection raised £13—8s—6d, a significant sum in those days when the maximum wage Clubs were permitted to pay was £4 a match. Eric announced he would hand it to the Red Cross and a spectator then made it up to £20.

The League arranged a number of Representative games during the war years against Coventry and District Cricket League, Coventry Works Sports Association, The London Counties and the West of England. These games raised over £800 for war charities, one game at Dudley in 1943 attracting 4,000 paying spectators.

In 1945, with threats to the civilian populace receding as the war in Europe was drawing to a conclusion, the clubs voted to restart the Second Division. Aston Unity and Moseley, still with no home venue, were unable to field a side but other clubs found it useful in rebuilding playing strength and club interest.

Extra Cover 1940—1945

20.7.40   Smethwick 89
            Kidderminster 295, Tom Goddard 140, with eleven 6's and nine 4's.

24.8.40   Kidderminster 177 G.S. Tomkinson 74
            West Bromwich Dartmouth 180—5 Reg Perks 71, T. Goddard 5—58. With Reg Perks bowling flat out, he had to have six fielders on the boundary in front of the wicket when bowling to G.S. Tomkinson.

| 13.6.42 | Kidderminster 223—9 G.S. Tomkinson hit 50 including 3 sixes off first three balls he received. Old Hill 112 |

13.6.42 Kidderminster 223—9 G.S. Tomkinson hit 50 including 3 sixes off first three balls he received.
Old Hill 112

4.7.42 Moseley 128—3 in rain restricted game
Kidderminster 116—9 Four Kidderminster wickets fell in last 7 balls and last man Ken Loney who had changed had to go out to bat in suit, collar and tie.

15.5.43 Aston Unity 82
Walsall 83—6 having recovered from 5 wickets for 6

5.6.43 Mitchells and Butlers 53 D. Mayer 9—25
Walsall 19 R.H. Cotton 6—5 C. Grove 4—11

6.5.44 Walsall 41 A.E. Thomas 5—6 bowled 14 overs off which only 2 scoring shots were made
Old Hill 96—6

3.6.44 Stourbridge 63
Moseley 61 lost last 4 wickets for 1 run C.S. Elliott 4—33 S. Grainger 6—28

16.6.45 Old Hill 273 H.C. Edwards 99. J.B. Eley 54. C.H. Palmer 43. F.A. Gross 5—94
Mitchells and Butlers 231 F.A. Gross 75. C.B. Harbage 49. A.E. Thomas bowled 32 overs and took 5—90. Mitchells last wicket fell off the last ball of game.

1945 Danny Mayer left Walsall having taken over 250 wickets in 1941—1945

11.8.45 West Bromwich Dartmouth 149
Kidderminster 16 E. Hollies 7—5 A.A. Perry 3—10

Second Division

6.8.45 Mitchells and Butlers 70
West Bromwich Dartmouth 63 from 57—2

League Positions 1940—1945

First Division

	1940	1941	1942	1943	1944	1945
Aston Unity	9	9	9*	9	10	9
Dudley	4	10	8	8	2	5*
Kidderminster	3	3	2	6	5	4
Mitchells & Butlers	5	4*	4	5	3	5*
Moseley	7*	7	9*	10	9	10
Old Hill	1	2	6	2	4	2
Smethwick	6	6	7	7	7*	3
Stourbridge	10	4*	5	3	7*	5*
Walsall	7*	8	3	4	6	8
West Bromwich Dartmouth	2	1	1	1	1	1

* Position held jointly

Second Division Champions
1940—1944 No competition
1945 Dudley

Highest Club Scores in Period

Aston Unity	229–6	v	Moseley	(A)	1945
Dudley	306–7	v	Smethwick	(H)	1940
Kidderminster	315–1	v	Mitchells & Butlers	(A)	1940
Mitchells & Butlers	271–5	v	Old Hill	(H)	1943
Moseley	224–6	v	Old Hill	(A)	1944
Old Hill	286–5	v	Mitchells & Butlers	(A)	1943
Smethwick	291–6	v	Aston Unity	(A)	1940
Stourbridge	249–3	v	Kidderminster	(A)	1941
Walsall	240–7	v	Mitchells & Butlers	(A)	1945
West Brom. Dartmouth	298–4	v	Moseley	(H)	1942

Lowest Club Scores in Period

Aston Unity	35	v	West Brom. Dartmouth	(A)	1945
Dudley	30	v	West Brom. Dartmouth	(H)	1945
Kidderminster	16	v	West Brom. Dartmouth	(A)	1945
Mitchells & Butlers	46	v	Stourbridge	(H)	1942
Moseley	23	v	West Brom. Dartmouth	(A)	1941
Old Hill	37	v	Dudley	(A)	1942
Smethwick	46	v	Mitchells & Butlers	(H)	1940
Stourbridge	40	v	Smethwick	(H)	1940
Walsall	19	v	Mitchells & Butlers	(H)	1943
West Brom.Dartmouth	59	v	Mitchells & Butlers	(H)	1940

Individual Performances

Highest Scores

Aston Unity (W.E. Houghton)	125	v	Moseley	(H)	1945
Dudley (W.E. Merritt)	197	v	Smethwick	(H)	1940
Kidderminster (C.A. Humphries)	158*	v	Mitchells & Butlers	(A)	1940
Mitchells & Butlers (H.O. Kirton)	147*	v	Old Hill	(H)	1943
Moseley (F.R. Santall)	151	v	Mitchells & Butlers	(A)	1940
Old Hill (R. Dovey)	122*	v	Mitchells & Butlers	(A)	1943
Smethwick (V.J. Holloway)	137*	v	Mitchells & Butlers	(H)	1943
Stourbridge (G.A. Fitton)	123*	v	Dudley	(A)	1942
Walsall (R. Howorth)	110*	v	Moseley	(A)	1940
West Brom. Dartmouth (W.E. Jones)	150*	v	Moseley	(H)	1942

* Not Out

Best Bowling

Aston Unity (J. Lamb)	8–37	v	Stourbridge	(A)	1943
Dudley (W.E. Merritt)	10–59	v	Aston Unity	(H)	1940
Kidderminster (R.T.D. Perks)	9–55	v	Dudley	(A)	1942
Mitchells & Butlers (F.A. Gross)	9–56	v	Moseley	(H)	1944
Moseley (S. Watts)	8–22	v	Walsall	(A)	1944
Old Hill (W.E. Hollies)	10–21	v	Mitchells & Butlers	(H)	1940
Smethwick (G.A.E. Paine)	8–35	v	Dudley	(H)	1940
Stourbridge (A.E. Davies)	8–23	v	Moseley	(H)	1941
Walsall (J.H. Mayer)	9–25	v	Mitchells & Butlers	(H)	1943
West Brom. Dartmouth (W.E. Hollies)	9–25	v	Smethwick	(H)	1945

Aston Unity

1946–1959 – THE POST WAR YEARS

Administration

With the war over, life in 1946 began to assume some peacetime normality as players and officials came back from active service. The League meetings returned to the City centre at the White Horse Restaurant, Congreve Street. The effects of shortages of supplies were still being felt in 1947 and 1948 when the Hon. Secretary was advising clubs to place early orders for equipment whilst he applied to the Board of Trade for clothing coupons for umpires' coats!

1947–1948 was to mark a major change in the administration of the League. At the instigation of 'Rusty' Scorer, the 1948 President, the League Clubs agreed to the formation of an Advisory Committee. The object of the formation of this Committee was to create a small forum to investigate and recommend ways of projecting the League to the public, to enquire into all matters affecting policy, welfare and entertainment and to make recommendations thereon to the League Clubs. The League Clubs ensured, however, that the Committee should act in an Advisory capacity only so that the principle of decision by each club having one vote should be maintained. It was agreed the Committee should consist of five club representatives with the Hon. Sec., ex officio.

The members of the Committee were divided into areas for representation, the first members being H.W. Homer, Old Hill, also representing Walsall and West Bromwich Dartmouth, G.S. Tomkinson, Kidderminster, also representing Stourbridge and Dudley, C.C. Goodway, Smethwick, also representing Mitchells and Butlers, H.F. Hill, Aston Unity and R.I. Scorer, Moseley.

At the instigation of the Clubs, the Advisory Committee subsequently made recommendations relating to general policy matters, revisions in rules, applications for reinstatement of professionals to amateur status and made arrangements for League representative matches, Champions v Rest and the League Annual Dinner.

In 1953, it was agreed that one member should retire annually to be replaced by a member of a club not represented, the retiring member being allowed to offer himself for re-election.

The formation of the Committee reduced the number of ordinary meetings the League needed to arrange. In 1956 it was agreed that irrespective of any meetings convened by the Committee, the League should hold a General Meeting in June in addition to the Annual General Meeting and that a meeting could be held on demand of any two clubs.

The long serving Hon. Secretary and Treasurer, John A. Lones, and his Assistant, W.T. Clarke, retired in 1950 after 30 years of dedicated service. They were succeeded by Ken Spooner as Hon. Secretary and Treasurer and J.H. Gaunt as Assistant Hon. Secretary. In 1954, the post of Assistant was changed to that of Hon. Secretary of the Umpires Sub-Committee.

Admission charges to grounds were fixed in 1947 as 1/- unreserved and 1/6 reserved with 6d all in for Second Division games. This was revised in 1955 to 1/- unreserved, 2/- enclosure. In 1957 half price admission for ladies was not agreed to.

Match Balls

For season 1946, the war-time provision relating to one new ball at the start of First Division games and a reconditioned ball for Second Division was retained. From season 1947 a new ball at the start of each innings was agreed for the First Division.

In the Second Division a new ball at the start of the game applied for seasons 1948—1953, after which a new ball at the start of each innings was ruled.

Engagement of Professionals

At the Annual General Meeting in November 1948, it was agreed to delete the requirements for professionals to be available to coach two nights a week. This led to the possibility of Clubs employing their professional on a match basis only thus widening the scope of talent available, and reducing the cost to clubs. The League further stipulated that professionals had to be nominated at the Annual General Meeting.

In 1950 it was ruled that no professional could be reinstated twice as an amateur but this provision was withdrawn in 1959 when it was further agreed that any reinstated player should, after five years service in the League, be considered an amateur and not a reinstated player. This proviso was useful for clubs in view of a ruling agreed in 1957 that Clubs be allowed to sign only one professional and two reinstated players. From 1953, all players applying for registration were interviewed by the Advisory Committee.

Two significant relaxations of rules relating to professionals which led to greater implementation of the League's objects to support County Cricket were the decisions in 1953 for definition of professionals to apply only to players over 18 and a further relax-ation in 1958 when the age was lifted to 21. This released a number of young professionals to play in sides who already employed a professional. Some players immediately affected were John Elliott and Brian Brain, Kidderminster, Ron Headley, Jack Sedgley and Norman Gifford, Dudley, Peter Richardson, Stourbridge, Dennis Amiss, Smethwick, Dick Devereux, Walsall and Brian Glynn, West Bromwich Dartmouth and many others since.

A further significant relaxation in 1954 was that a player employed as a groundsman would not be classified as a professional.

Playing Regulations

In 1956 the League introduced a regulation that wickets were not to be watered after Thursday and in 1957 Clubs were to provide adequate wicket covers. 1958 saw deletion of the Instruction giving the captains the option of playing a second innings in the event of a game finishing before 5.30 p.m.

The Playing Scene 1946—1959

No side was to dominate the post war cricket, West Bromwich Dartmouth being the most successful with four titles, the others being distributed amongst the other clubs except Old Hill, Stourbridge and Walsall who only managed to get to second place.

Kidderminster

Kidderminster were the first side to benefit from the return of players from the War when they secured the Championship in a rain restricted season in 1946. Ray McInlay, Harry Moule, Cedric Sanders and Alec Wyers were rejoined that season by Harvey Perry, Norman and Gerald Humphries (captain) and professional Eric Herbert. "Laddie" Outschoorn from Ceylon, who had spent 3½ years in a Japanese Prisoner of War Camp, came into the area and scored freely for the club in this one season. Kidderminster thus broke West Bromwich Dartmouth's run of five successive title wins and the Dartmouth had to be content with second place. Kidderminster also won the Second Division to give promise of a successful future but their only other success in the First Division in the period was to be in 1950. This success provided a fitting climax to a year celebrating the centenary of the Kidderminster Club's formation. In that year the formidable Arthur Wellard added power to the batting and bowling. Arthur joined the ranks of bowlers taking ten wickets in an innings on 3rd June 1950 when he took 10—33 as Stourbridge were dismissed for 78. Kidderminster were only defending a score of 138 after Bill Andrews had taken 7—57. Arthur Wellard's contributions that season were backed up by outstanding batting by Alec Wyers, Cyril Harrison and captain Harry Moule who had his best season with the Club.

With Harry Moule and Alec Wyers in fine form, batting second in 1950 was no handicap to Kidderminster. In three of the games they batted second and topped 200 to win, losing only four wickets in the process.

17.6.50   Moseley 202—6 dec. J.R. Mainwaring 77. D.F. Harris 51. A.W. Wellard 5—59.
Kidderminster 203—3. H.G. Moule 112 n.o.

8.7.50   Smethwick 200 A.O. Hill 67. J. Sewter 4—37
Kidderminster 201—0 H.G. Moule 103 n.o. A. Wyers 91 n.o.

5.8.50   Dudley 218—6 dec. W. Hicklin 66. A.W. Wellard 4—92
Kidderminster 219—1 H.G. Moule 119 A. Wyers 92 n.o.

Gerald Humphries, Philip Dexter, Trevor Larkham, George Morris and Jim Sewter all made timely contributions to the 1950 success.

Then followed a period of rebuilding in the 1950's as the older players retired and Peter Heard, Peter Harris and others joined to form the basis of a successful side to move into the 1960's.

Mitchells & Butlers

Mitchells and Butlers won the League in 1947 and then again in 1954. Batsman Stan Mitchell, wicket-keeper Fred Hughes and spinners George Bullock and Howard Lilley were members of both Championship sides. Stan was a consistent batsman from 1946 and throughout the period. Although he did not emulate the prolific scoring of Harry Kirton or Arthur Fletcher, Stan could always be depended upon to put together a reasonable score and finish with around 300—400 runs a season.   Professional Alf Pope was the chief wicket taker in 1947, backed up by Dickie Jones, Bob Cotton and Freddie Gross, then in his 17th. year with the Club.   Freddie also made a good contribution with the bat.   Stuart Workman, in his first season as captain, scored most runs and he and Stan Mitchell had good support from 'Pip' Clarke and George Bullock.   Stan Silk another good long playing servant of the Club, kept his place in the side with useful lower order batting and by dint of his fielding. Harry Kirton had an indifferent season but the 1947 title cele- brations included a presentation to him by the Club of a wireless set and electric clock to mark his 25 years service.   His record read: 353 innings 75 n.o., 189 highest, 13641 total runs, 32 centuries. Average 49.03.

On 22 May 1948, Alf Pope had a mixed experience against Aston Unity.   Unity batting first were 18—6, Alf having taken 5 wickets for only 6 runs.   Billy Wood later struck him for two sixes and four fours in one over to lead a Unity recovery to 100 all out. Billy Wood 59, Alf Pope 6w.   Mitchells eventually won by 5 wickets. The Mitchells' championship success in 1954 was matched by their second eleven who won the Second Division neither side losing a game.   Bert Nutter who had joined the side from Northants that season added his all-round prowess to that of Arthur Fletcher, the batting back up being Stan Mitchell, Trevor Elias, Geof Faulkener, Ray Powell and Bob Murrell (Captain).   The bowlers Dean Johnston, Roy Wenman, George Bullock and H. Willey.   Although they did not lose a match they only won six which was one less than the two sides below them in the table.   The other twelve matches being drawn, they only won the title by a margin of one point.

Arthur Fletcher, a former Lancashire League cricketer, had joined the Club in 1949 and gave magnificent service with bat and ball for sixteen seasons.   At one time during the 1954 season, it looked as if he might break the League record for runs scored in a season and, although he did not do so, his 773 runs and 23 wickets had much to do with the team's success.   In all, he was to score around 600 runs a season in 12 seasons.

Mitchells' first match of the 1954 season was also Moseley's first in the League at their new Robin Hood Stadium.   Mitchells batted first and demonstrated that the new wicket was playing well by scoring 205—8.   Arthur Fletcher 79, Geoff Faulkener 49, Stan Mitchell 33, Sid Ramanand 5—45.   Moseley set off well with David Heath 41, Barry Seymour 16, Ken Wyatt 41 to take them to 108—2 but this became 122—5 and then the last five wickets fell to Bert Nutter and Howard Lilley with no addition to the score.   Bert Nutter finished with 5—35, Howard Lilley with 2—30.   Mitchells won with only two minutes to spare!

Apart from the two title successes the club had fluctuating fortunes in the First Division which was surprising for their Second Eleven won their Division 6 times in the fourteen years, indicating a strong reserve strength.   One of the younger players to make the grade in the first eleven in the 1950's was leg spinner and future captain, Derek Robinson.

West Bromwich Dartmouth

West Bromwich Dartmouth continued to be a major force and

were 'dubbed' the 'Yorkshire of the Birmingham League'. They won the League in 1948, 1953, 1955 and 1958 and only dropped out of the first three on three occasions.

Their strength in the late 1940's was built around their outstanding players from the war years, Eric Perry, Georgie Dodd and Tom Stanley together with newcomers Fred Allen, Leslie Croom and professionals Harold Pope and Alf Gover. Derief Taylor, who was to become an excellent youth coach for Warwickshire, had one season as professional in 1951.

On 5 August, 1946, Walsall were dismissed for 48, F. Allen 8−16 and amidst great excitement Dartmouth scraped a victory by one wicket − Eric Perry 20, Frank Bailey 7−25. Walsall then exercised their right to a second innings but this was inconclusive Walsall scoring 63−3 dec. and Dartmouth 36−2. This was played in front of 2000 spectators. In the 1949 season a special bus service was needed to handle a crowd of over 4000, Dartmouth won handsomely, 240−6. E. Perry 50, New Zealander Don Taylor 89, Walsall 92, R.S. Patterson 42, F. Allen 6−25 including a hat trick.

The team was rebuilt in the early 1950's with the introduction of Tom Bevins, Roy Parker, Ronnie Williams, Ben Badal, Australian John Cordner, and John Seddon, Johnny Allen to team up with Leslie Croom, Ted Dimbylow and professional Peter Greenwood. Peter Greenwood's bowling at Smethwick on 20 June 1953 deserves mention. The Dartmouth team had been dismissed for 121, Arthur Booth 6−36. Smethwick were coasting to victory at 80−3 when Peter took six wickets for no runs in fourteen balls, including a hat trick, and Smethwick were all out for 114.

In 1954 Dartmouth surprisingly finished bottom of the table, a position sandwiched between two championship successes. The reason lay in a complete breakdown of the batting, for in 8 of the 15 games played they could not muster 100 runs, leaving no margin for their bowlers Peter Greenwood, John Seddon, Jock Cordner and Ron Williams, who had bowled them to success in the previous season. The batting was weakened by the absence of Ben Badal and West Bromwich Albion's manager, Vic Buckingham, and a loss of form by Tom Bevins and Les Croom. Old rivals, Walsall, were one of the sides to take advantage of the temporary loss of form by Dartmouth dismissing them for 54 and 38 to win both games. In the second of these, on 24 July 1954, George Bull made his first team debut for Walsall and took 8−22.

1955 saw the introduction of "Danny" Livingstone, Charles Daniels and Bert Millichip, the present Chairman of the Football Association, into the batting line up and a new professional, Bert Shardlow, who dominated the League bowling performances by taking 91 wickets in the season. Dartmouth won 11 of the 18 games. Bert had left before the 1958 success but Eric Hollies had decided to retire from the first class game and joined the Club to team up with fast bowlers Tom Pritchard and Rufus Browne. This ensured that the batting of Roy Parker, Gerry Summers, Ron Williams, Al Scott and the wicket keeping of George Tolliday was matched by good bowling to bring the 1958 success.

Walsall

Walsall did not manage a title in the period so could not claim the £200 left in 1942 by the late Billy Preston to purchase mementos for members of the first eleven, who in the first ten seasons after his death, were to win the Championship. They nearly made it in 1949 but finished one point behind Aston Unity. Walsall took second place in 1953, 1954 and 1955 and again in 1958. In 1949 and again in 1953 and 1954 they finished only one point behind the leaders. In each of these seasons the title was not decided until the last matches of the season. In 1949, although Walsall won their last game Aston Unity drew to get the one point needed. 1953 was the most frustrating for, having finished their fixtures two points clear at the top of the table, they had to await the result of the West Bromwich Dartmouth versus Stourbridge game played the following week. Dartmouth won by 3 wickets after a tight game to get 3 points to win the League by one point.

Walsall had five stalwarts through nearly all the period. Batsmen Bobby Patterson, John Wootton and Eric Waite, all rounder Malcolm Fenton and wicket keeper Mac White. Jack Hight, George Lowbridge, Roy James and Geoff Whitehouse supplemented the batting in the first part of the period and Frank Bailey the bowling. The second period saw the introduction of long serving batsman Jimmy Ashwell and bowler Gil Gregory, Jock McShane, Albert Hunt, Clive Hammonds and Dennis Dewsbury. Outstanding professionals were George Paine, 1947 part 48, Frank Smailes, 1949—51, Alf Valentine 1952—54 and Dennis Cox, 1958—9.

The keen Walsall supporters had plenty of excitement if no titles. George Paine earned his match fee in two games against Moseley, in each of which he and Bobby Patterson shared a partnership of 157 and George performed well with the ball.

24.5.47 Walsall 249—4. G.A.E. Paine 126. R.S. Patterson 53
         Moseley 131. G.A.E. Paine 6—70. E. Wright 53.

2.8.47   Moseley 205—8 dec. G.A.E. Paine 5—68
         Walsall 206—4. G.A.E. Paine 110 R.S. Patterson 55.
         The 206 was scored in 93 minutes.

Home supporters who had left the Walsall ground on 5 August 1950 in the belief that their heroes had beaten Moseley yet again must have been surprised when they opened their newspapers to find the game was a draw. Moseley batted first and scored 161, Bob Mainwaring 56, Frank Smailes 8—42. The scoreboard unfortunately showed only 158 when the innings closed so, when Walsall were 159—9 (Malcolm Fenton 48, George Paine (now with Moseley) 5—35) the players and umpires left the field. The mistake was pointed out by the scorers and the teams went out to bowl the three balls remaining in the last over which was being bowled by George Paine. The players were in various forms of dress — pin stripes, braces, coloured shirts, collars and ties. With only one wicket left, Walsall could take no chances and Malcolm Fenton was unable to score off George Paine's three balls so the players trouped off with a draw as the result.

Gilbert Gregory gave consistent bowling support to the professionals and the Moseley fixture was again to feature on 23 August 1958 when he took 8—18 to dismiss Moseley for 49 in reply to Walsall's 107. It brought his total wickets in season to 60, a postwar Walsall club record. He also featured as a batsman when he hit six fours off 7 balls to snatch a victory against Kidderminster in June 1957.

Dudley

For four seasons, 1951—1954, Dudley brought together a famous international duo when they signed George Headley as professional to partner Bill Merritt who had just been reinstated as an amateur having served as professional from 1946. George Headley had been known as "The black Bradman" but locals considered this was not a true title for they said that, whereas Bradman compiled his record scores by steady and undemonstrative batting, George created his with flair, enthusiasm and excitement. He certainly brought these qualities to the League breaking the batting record for a season when he scored 922 runs in 1951 to beat the previous record of 878 shared by his partner Bill Merritt (1940) and Harry Kirton (1935). George went on to score 2897 in only 4 seasons.

With George and Bill and young Jack Breakwell as brilliant all-rounders backed up by batting of Harry Thomas, Eddie Breakwell and Bill Hicklin and the bowling of Bill Goodreds and Frank Golding, it is surprising that they only managed to win one championship in the four years, and that in 1952. The reason seems to lie in their inability to force victories on their good batsman's wicket for in both 1951 and 1954 they drew twelve of their 18 games. Such was the interest created by the Dudley side that when they played at Walsall on 30 June 1951 over 3000 spectators ringed the ground, including the Mayors of both Walsall and Dudley Boroughs. They saw a high scoring game.

Dudley 242—5 G.A. Headley 111. H. Thomas 73. W.E. Merritt 28
Walsall 217—3. M. Fenton 71 n.o. T.F. Smailes 58 n.o. J.C. Ashwell 43.

On 23 August 1952 the Headley/Merritt combination featured in a rout of Mitchells and Butlers to bring the championship in style to Dudley. Dudley had scored 253—1 George Headley 169 n.o. Harry Thomas 62 n.o. Mitchells batted for a draw and were 101—4 and then lost their last six wickets for no runs! Bill Merritt took 5 wickets, including a hat trick, Bill Goodreds the other. Derek Robinson 0 not out.

When George Headley left after the 1954 season Dudley dropped to bottom place in 1955 but recovered to win the title again in 1957 with Reg Perks as professional. George Headley had been replaced by his son, 17 year old Ron Headley, who was destined to become also a West Indian Test cricketer. Ron was to feature prominently in the League for many years when he left the County scene. Bill Merritt and Tom Palmer had also retired, to be replaced by Ron Smith, Tony Sherwood and 18 year old Jack Sedgley who, like Ron Headley, was to be a leading player with league clubs.

Having made sure of the Championship in 1957, Dudley were to fail against the redoubtable Bert Latham on 28.8.57. Moseley scored 188—4 D.P. Ratcliffe 48 D.M.W. Heath 47 W.A.K. Wyatt 48 n.o.
When the last over started Dudley needed four to win with 3 wickets in hand. Bert Latham took 2 wickets with his first two balls and with the next ball the last man was run out, to give Moseley an unexpected victory.

In May 1959 the two promising youths, Jack Sedgley and Ron Headley, were to record their first centuries in the League in high

A rare occurrence – Geo. Headley bowled.

scoring games.

16.5.59   Dudley 240—1 dec. off 43 overs. J.B. Sedgley 107 n.o.
R.G.A. Headley 51. Alan Spencer 66 n.o.
Moseley 230—3 off 55 overs. D.M.W. Heath 142 C.L.
Malhotra 82 putting on 222 for the 2nd wicket.

142 was the highest score made by David in his League Division One career.

23.5.59   Dudley 259—2 off 47 overs. R.G.A. Headley 119.
A. Spencer 82 n.o. J.B. Sedgley 38.
Aston Unity 257—9 off 46 overs. H. Ramanand 91.
J.M. Kennedy 38. M. Wilson 37.

Ron Headley was to score another century — 139 n.o. out of a Dudley total of 193—6 against Stourbridge on August 15 1959.

Aston Unity

Aston Unity spent nearly all the period in the lower positions in the table, apart from 1949 when they did surge from tenth in 1948 to become Champions and in 1951 when they again climbed from the depths to finish third. Jack Hossell, a familiar figure in highly coloured blazer, was a popular all-rounder in the Aston Unity side for the whole of the period. He played for Warwickshire in 1939 and 1946 and 1947 and captained the Unity Championship side in 1949. Much of the credit for this isolated success must go to professional Morris Nichols who had this one year with the Club in which he took 69 wickets. Ted Eames and Ken Gilson provided variation to the attack whilst Ken Gilson, Alf Woodroffe, Bill Lovering together with Jack Hossell scored the majority of the runs, backed up by Eric Ripley, Geoff Stubbings, Ray Sparkes and Dennis Hodgetts. Dennis Taylor had a good year behind the stumps catching fifteen and stumping 11.

Morris Nichols best performance occurred on May 21 1949 at Smethwick. The Unity batted first and scored 150, Jack Hossell 43, Eric Ripley 34, Ted Eames 28. Norman Downes 5—56. John Oldham 4—52. Smethwick struggled against the pace of Nichols but Ronnie Pearson held them together with a determined innings of 52 until he too fell to the paceman. When Cyril Goodway came in as last man to join N. Lorraine, twenty four were required to win, as great tension and excitement ensued. The two batsmen added 22 until Lorraine was bowled by Morris Nichols to give Unity victory by one run. Morris finished with 9—48. Ric Hunt in his twenty fourth year in the first eleven took the other wicket. No cricket enthusiast could desire a more enjoyable or sportsmanlike game, was the verdict of the day!

Presenting the championship trophy at the end of the season was a proud moment for League President Mr. A.E. Morgan, a member of Unity since 1914, and the first Unity member to have held that office in the League.

Dick Pollard joined Unity as professional in 1950 and with Ted Eames bowling at his best in season 1951, the club managed third place but apart from Alf Woodroffe and Ted Whitehead the batting lacked the consistency to get into top place. Frank Mitchell served as professional from 1953 until 1956 and in the 1950's, Roy Bent, David Roberts, John Kennedy, Rex Wallbank, Bob Furley, Barry Hodder and Terry Riley were among new players, together with the Ramanand brothers, Sid and Harry. Norman Ingram

Cyril Goodway, Ken Spooner (Secretary), H.E. Mitchell (President) with League Championship Cup, 1951.

demonstrated his loyalty and attachment to the Club, turning in good second eleven performances and pulling his weight in the first eleven when called upon.

Smethwick

Cyril Goodway's efforts to bring the first ever championship to Smethwick were crowned with success in 1951 when they held off a late challenge from Kidderminster.

The season started badly when Smethwick lost the first two games against Aston Unity and Old Hill. Against Unity they were dismissed for 54, professional Dick Pollard taking 6—18 Ted Eames 4—32. Unity scored 50 in the first hour, Jack Hossell 27, and then took half an hour to muster the 5 needed to win, finishing at 55—6. Arthur Booth, Smethwick's slow left arm professional took 5—18, having left his Borough Council elections in Lancashire to make his debut for the Club. Quick bowler John Oldham, Norman Downes, and Ray McHenry added variation to the bowling. The responsibility for batting rested primarily on Bernard Rowley, John Oldham, Ron Pearson, Frank Fielding, Ray McHenry, Harry Parish, Cyril Goodway and A.O. Hill.

With two games left to play at the end of the season Smethwick were only one point ahead of Kidderminster and the old disruptive force, rain, was in the air. Smethwick at home to Stourbridge were rained off with Stourbridge 78—1. Kidderminster meanwhile had rattled up a quick 161—1 in 34 overs, Harry Moule 77, Alec Wyers 42, Cyril Harrison 40 not out, to leave themselves 39 overs to dismiss Aston Unity. Despite a 50 from Ted Whitehead, Unity lost 8 wickets for 84. With the worried Smethwick players on one end of the telephone Alf Woodroffe, the Unity captain, gave them a commentary on the last few minutes and Smethwick were relieved to hear that Kidderminster were unable to clinch victory.

These results left the two sides still one point apart with only one game to play. Smethwick, anticipating a win, obtained an extension of their licence for the next two Saturdays, one to celebrate winning, the other for hosting the Champions v The Rest. Kidderminster suggested that they make alternative plans to put the beer barrels on a train to Kidderminster. In the event there was no problem for Smethwick beat Moseley by 4 wickets whilst Kidderminster had the worst of a drawn game v Old Hill. The scores at Moseley were:

Moseley 178—9 dec off 60 overs. N.T. Parker 57. D.F. Harris 33 n.o. A. Booth 4—59. J. Oldham 3—45. N.C. Downes 2—40.
Smethwick 180—6 off 51.3 overs. H. Parish 63 n.o. J. Oldham 34.

Harry Parish chose a good day to make his best score of the season and he and Cyril Goodway were chaired from the field. They then all returned to Broomfield, together with members of the Combined Services side who were playing at Edgbaston to take advantage of Smethwick's bar extension.

The following season, Smethwick were involved in another title decider on the last match of the season. Having just failed by one point to be contenders themselves, they met Stourbridge who held a one point lead over Dudley. Stourbridge, batting first, were dismissed for 104. Arthur Booth 7—24. John Oldham 2—39.

Smethwick won by 4 wickets at 105—6. Ronnie Pearson 34. Dudley had won their game to win the title and by this win Smethwick overtook Stourbridge who slipped from top to third place.

Tom Pritchard turned out for Smethwick as professional for one season in 1946. In a game against Moseley he took 6—48 as Moseley were dismissed for 167 and then he and Ron Pearson hit 90 in 19 minutes to take Smethwick to a seven wicket victory. Tom finished the game off by hitting 3 successive 6's and a 4 Pritchard 63 n.o. Pearson 49 n.o.

On 21 June 1947 Bernard Rowley had made his debut in the First Division of the League and scored 100 not out for Smethwick against Kidderminster. This was to mark the start of a long, fruitful and dedicated career in the League for Smethwick and later Old Hill. Bernard is considered by his contemporaries to have been one of the finest league players, a player who could easily have made the grade in first class cricket. In this first season he was already drawing attention not only with his batting but also in that aspect of the game which raises the level so much — good fielding. His outfielding and long accurate throws from the boundary were much appreciated by all pundits of the game. George Headley considered Bernard to be of Test Cricket standard.

On 26 June 1948, a record crowd of over 3000 saw Smethwick win an exciting match against West Bromwich Dartmouth by one wicket.

West Bromwich Dartmouth 97. Norman Downes 5—27.
Smethwick 99—9 the last pair Norman Downes 10 n.o. and Peter Carswell 6 n.o. winning the game for Smethwick after Wally Bridgman refused to give Peter 'run out' because Wally had been knocked over by a fielder running to the wicket. Wally said since he was flat on his back he could not see the wicket broken! Norman Downes collected many wickets with his left arm spinners, later to become an an umpire and President of Smethwick.

On 25 May 1957 Walsall suffered a hat trick by Smethwick bowlers in both Divisions, N.C. Downes and Des Green.

Div.One.   Smethwick 205—8 dec. B. Rowley 56
           Walsall 125. N.C. Downes 6—33, taking 6—10 including
           hat trick in his last 3.5 overs.

Div.Two.   Smethwick 183—7. G. Bayley 94
           Walsall 171 E.J. Waite 59, Des Green 4—24, including
           hat trick.

The following month, two fine bowlers the League has fielded, Cedric Sanders and John Oldham, had a field day when Smethwick met Kidderminster.

Smethwick 77 Cedric Sanders 7—30
Kidderminster 62 John Oldham 7—22 the last 5 for 9. Cyril Goodway catching 4 and stumping 1.

As the 1950's drew to a close Roy Freeman, Trevor Jones and Gwyn Benson joined the Smethwick ranks and in 1959 a young man destined to become an international star — Dennis Amiss made his debut in the Smethwick first team.

Stourbridge

Stourbridge just failed to win the League in 1952 when they

lost their last game against Smethwick, as mentioned earlier. In 1948 they had their second best season up to that time in terms of wins when they won ten matches, they had only bettered this in their championship year of 1919. The ten wins, however, only brought them second place in the table behind West Bromwich Dartmouth, who had 12 victories.

In the 1948 season, when Ronnie Bird and Jack Breakwell joined professional Bill Andrews, Stourbridge started the season in grand style winning their first five games only to lose the sixth to eventual champions West Bromwich Dartmouth. They turned the tables in the return encounter but Dartmouth had built up a five point lead which Stourbridge were unable to close. Stan Grainger, Arthur Fitton, 'Ginger' Taylor played at the start of the period, to be succeeded in the 1950's by Peter Taylor, Mike Thompson, Martin Horton, Derek Richardson, Derek Russell, George Mills, Clive Bourne and Ron Jones. Norman Whiting returned to the club in 1953 after a six year spell with Worcestershire to perform well with the bat and pick up wickets with his off spin. John Bloomer continued to distinguish himself as wicket keeper and batsman. On 12 July 1947, he hit the first century on Aston Unity's new Hillcourt Ground in a Stourbridge victory. Louis and Geoff Harper provided steady batting but the side lacked sufficient big guns to match the more successful sides.

Stourbridge did, however, nourish big guns of another calibre for following their introduction of Don Kenyon to the cricket public Stourbridge included in their 1950 and 1951 sides another player destined for Test Cricket, 18 year old Peter Richardson. In 1950, although he had only had eight innings, he scored 519 runs to finish with an average of 103.8. In 1959, when he had established himself as an England opener, Peter Richardson played for the Club against Smethwick in front of a large crowd. Smethwick batted first, scoring 174—7 dec. Ray McHenry 51. Peter 103 n.o. then delighted the crowd to steer Stourbridge to a seven wicket victory. Jock Livingston scored 31, Norman Whiting 23. Peter then moved away from the area to qualify for Kent.

In 1958, professional Jock Livingston had brought his own brand of exciting cricket, scoring 817 and 752 in 1958 and 1959 respectively. Stourbridge thus made up for their lack of titles by producing entertaining cricket.

Old Hill

With players of the calibre of Bert Edwards, Ron and Harold Dovey, Jack Edwards, Jack Gilbert, C.W. Daniels and wicket keeper Arthur Coley to back up successive professionals, Arthur Thomas, Don Taylor, Peter Jackson and Charlie Grove, it is surprising to find that Old Hill did not win a title in the period even though they generally managed to finish in the middle of the table.

Their batsmen did not find Kidderminster in a relaxed August Bank Holiday mood in 1947 for almost before the holiday crowd had paid for their tickets Old Hill were 6 wickets down for 8 runs, Colonel J.W.A. Stephenson the former Essex and England player having taken 5 of them. E.J. Bayliss with 19 and Jack Edwards 18 prevented a debacle and Old Hill struggled to 69. Stephenson only taking one more wicket. The Old Hill stalwarts on the grassy banks had no time for their tea and cakes before Albert Thomas took three Kidderminster wickets in his first over but Harvey Perry was not one

Bert Latham in action

of them and in his own imperturbable and immaculate way he steered Kidderminster to 70—7 scoring 34 of the runs himself.

In 1951 on 16 June, Old Hill were to feature in a match at Dudley which could be dubbed an 'umpires nightmare'. Early in the game an umpire signalled a six when the ball hit the sight screen within the boundary and later in the innings corrected it to four. Old Hill went on to score 197—6 Bert Edwards 66 Ron Dovey 53. When the last ball of the match was bowled Dudley score stood at 197—6. Lionel Hickin, the Dudley captain, hit the ball towards mid-on and he and his partner Bill Merritt ran. Bill Merritt collided with bowler Peter Jackson, recovered, and ran on but had not reached the crease when his wicket was put down. The umpire at that end gave him not out on the ground that he had been obstructed so Dudley claimed the run. The other umpire then said that he had called 'Dead Ball' as soon as the obstruction occurred but did not know whether the batsman had crossed at the time. The umpires then drew stumps and as there was doubt about the result the match was referred to the M.C.C. who ruled that the result should be recorded as a draw.

At the end of 1958 season Old Hill's Bert Edwards and Jack Edwards — no relation — left the side. Bert retiring to become a Life Member of the club and Jack moved from the district. Since the club had been formed in 1884 there had always been an Edwards playing, tracing back to Billy Edwards, Bert's father, a founder member of the Club.

Jack Gilbert also left the club in the 1950's but Mike Bradley, Harry Moule and Terry Grainger joined Ron and Harold Dovey and in 1959 professional Harry Kelleher to carry the team into the 1960's.

Moseley

When cricket records are discussed Bert Latham of Moseley must hold a unique place. In the 1946—59 period he not only took all ten wickets in an innings on two occasions but also against the same side and on their home ground — the unfortunate side being Kidderminster.

The first occasion was on 22 May 1954. After a rain delayed start, Moseley staggered to 136—7 declared in 55.2 overs, leaving Kidderminster just under 2 hours batting. The scorecard of the Kidderminster innings read:

H.G. Moule		b. Latham	32
R.S. Lucas	c Thompson J.	b. Latham	2
C.S. Harrison	c and	b. Latham	0
H.O. Crosskill	lbw	b. Latham	16
D.H. Naylor	c Thompson J.	b. Latham	16
W.T. Larkham	c and	b. Latham	5
G. Darkes		b. Latham	0
G.T. Morris		b. Latham	6
W. Booton		b. Latham	0
R. Morris	not out		0
C.J. Sanders	c Heath J.	b. Latham	0
		Extras	3
		Total	80

87

	o.	m.	r.	w
H.J. Latham	10	2	37	10
R.B. Abell	5	0	28	0
R. Bonell	4	0	12	0

Harry Moule held out until the score was 73 when a beauty of a ball bowled him.   The last 5 wickets fell for 7 runs.   Bert missed the hat trick when on three occasions he took two wickets in two balls.

The repeat performance came only three years later on 11 May 1957.   On this occasion Kidderminster batted first, again on a damp wicket.

Their scorecard this time reading:

G. Rathbone	b. Latham	13
N. West c Thompson J.	b. Latham	1
P. Harris c Thompson J.	b. Latham	0
R. Morris	b. Latham	12
W.T. Larkham	b. Latham	18
W. Booton	b. Latham	0
P. Booton not out		4
G.A. Longmore	b. Latham	0
A.D. Talbot	b. Latham	0
G.T.O. Wilson	b. Latham	4
C.J. Sanders	b. Latham	0
	Extras	3
	Total	55

	o.	m.	r.	w.
H.J. Latham	16	5	29	10
N.T. Parker	6	3	6	0
R. Bonell	9	6	17	0

Moseley won by 9 wickets.

Bert Latham had joined Moseley in 1953 having been invited to the Club by David Heath when they had met some time before in an RAF representative match, whilst doing National Service. Described as one of the fastest bowlers ever to have played in the League, he had a spell with Warwickshire from 1955 to 1959 but a knee injury forced him to give up playing at that level.   He was to play in the League over 25 years in which time he took over 1000 First Division wickets.

Bert's success was achieved by attacking the wickets with fast good length deliveries.   The two ten wicket feats are examples of his accuracy with twelve bowled, one Lbw, four wicket-keeper cathces, one catch in the gully and two caught and bowled.

After the war, Moseley had struggled to rebuild their side with Dennis Harris, Barry Seymour, Bob Mainwaring, Rusty Scorer and Cecil Addleman doing most of the work during which time with the help of George Paine they had only once managed to lift themselves into the top half of the table finishing second in 1950.   Later in the period with Bert Latham and fellow bowlers Roy Abell, Roy Bonell, batsmen David Heath and George Jakeman and wicket keeper Jim Thompson joining long serving Cecil Addleman, Ken Wyatt and Norman Parker a new side was built to take the title to Moseley in 1956 and 1959.

The 1956 title, the first for 18 seasons, was achieved in David Heath's first season as captain.   Then 24 years of age David probably became the youngest player to captain a championship

DUDLEY CRICKET CLUB
CHAMPIONS, BIRMINGHAM & DISTRICT CRICKET LEAGUE.
SEASON 1952.

Back Row: J. Keeling, R. Wright, J. Hickman, T. Roberts,
K.J. Corbett, Ald. J.H. Molyneux, W.H. Atkins.
Centre Row: D. Tanfield, J.C. Pearson (Chairman), W. Hicklin,
B. Hemmings, A.J. Fry, F.W. Golding, K. Burns, E. Breakwell,
W.H. Edwards, H.R. Winchurch (Hon. Secretary).
Front Row: H.A. Thomas, T.R. Palmer, W.A. Goodreds,
W.E. Merrit (Capt.), G.A. Headley, J. Breakwell, H.G.Groves.

side. The success in 1959, when Moseley had been joined by Chaman Lal Malhotra and Peter Horne, will have a special place in the Club's history for it also celebrated the first season on the present splendid ground.

Two of the League's foremost exponents in the art of spin bowling demonstrated their craft on the occasion of Moseley's last game at the Robin Hood Stadium. Eric Hollies took 6—36 as Moseley were all out for 143. David Heath 33. Roy Abell then eclipsed Eric's performance with 6 wickets for 2 runs in only 7.3 overs as Dartmouth tumbled to 55 all out having been 51—2 before Roy entered the attack. A fitting climax to end the era.

Extra Cover 1946—1959

1946	Eric Hollies, playing for Warwickshire took all 10 wickets for 49 in Nottinghamshire's first innings — 7 bowled, 3 Lbw.
28.6.47	Smethwick 209 R.M. Pearson 62 B.R. Taylor 8—73 Stourbridge 107 N.H. Whiting 23 N.C. Downes 7—20 Norman Downes took 4 w for 2 runs in his last 4 overs
15.5.48	Walsall 223—9 dec. G.A.E. Paine 52 J.C. Wootton 58 Aston Unity 223—8 A.L. Cox 71 with 3 wanted to win off last ball W.A.C. Wood run out attempting 3rd run.
28.5.48	Walsall 127 — were 117—2 then 6 'ducks' C.J. Sanders 5—28 J. Holroyd 4—37 Kidderminster 130—2 R.E. McKinlay 52
26.6.48	Aston Unity 85 W.E. Merritt taking 6 w for 2 runs including 4 in 4 balls Dudley 86—3
26.5.51	Aston Unity 129 A. Woodroffe 53 Walsall 84 R. Pollard 6—32 E.A. Eames 4—37 G.R. Lowbridge scored 68 of Walsall's 84
17.5.52	Kidderminster 194—5 H.G. Moule 50 Aston Unity 19. 7 'ducks' Extras 6. West Indian H.W.K. Lobban 7—9
27.6.53	Kidderminster 194—8 H.G. Moule 60 Aston Unity 194 Lost last 3 w for 0 runs in last over
7.6.54	Smethwick 40 Roy Abell, then a fast bowler, 6—26 Moseley 41—4

In 1956—57 Season Chaman Lal Malhotra (Moseley 1959, Mitchells & Butlers 1960—61) scored 502 n.o. for Mehandra College (Patiala) v Government College (Rupar). The highest individual score made by a Birmingham League cricketer.

Highest Club Scores in Period

Aston Unity	257—9	v	Dudley	(H)	1959
Dudley	259—2	v	Aston Unity	(A)	1959
Kidderminster	258—4	v	Aston Unity	(A)	1950
Mitchells & Butlers	270—5	v	Dudley	(H)	1950
Moseley	245—7	v	Old Hill	(A)	1951
Old Hill	278—6	v	Moseley	(H)	1946
Smethwick	249—7	v	Kidderminster	(H)	1950
Stourbridge	240—4	v	Moseley	(H)	1953
Walsall	249—4	v	Moseley	(H)	1947
West Brom. Dartmouth	263—6	v	Aston Unity	(A)	1948

League Positions 1946–1959

First Division

	19 46	47	48	49	50	51	52	53	54	55	56	57	58	59
Aston Unity	10	9	10	1	8*	3*	9	10	9	9	9*	9	9	7*
Dudley	4	3	3	6	8*	5*	1	4*	5	10	3*	1	8	4*
Kidderminster	1	6*	8	7	1	2	8	3	4	7	9*	5	10	2
Mitchells & Butlers	3	1	5*	10	5*	8	10	4*	1	3	8	7	5*	10
Moseley	9	8	7	5	2	7	6*	7	3	4*	1	3	3*	1
Old Hill	6*	5	5*	8*	4	5*	6*	8	7*	4*	2	8	7	3
Smethwick	5	6*	4	4	5*	1	2	4*	7*	6	6	4	5*	7*
Stourbridge	6*	10	2	8*	8*	9	3	9	6	8	3*	10	3*	4*
Walsall	8	4	9	2	5*	10	4	2	2	2	7	6	2	9
West Bromwich Dartmouth	2	2	1	3	3	3*	5	1	10	1	5	2	1	4*

* Position held jointly

Lowest Club Scores in Period

Aston Unity	19	v Kidderminster	(H)	1952
Dudley	39	v Old Hill	(A)	1946
Kidderminster	48	v Mitchells & Butlers	(A)	1949
Mitchells & Butlers	59	v Moseley	(H)	1956
Moseley	36	v West Brom. Dartmouth	(A)	1958
Old Hill	42	v West Brom. Dartmouth	(A)	1951
Smethwick	40	v Moseley	(A)	1954
Stourbridge	34	v West Brom. Dartmouth	(A)	1948
Walsall	48	v West Brom. Dartmouth	(H)	1946
West Brom. Dartmouth	33	v Smethwick	(H)	1954

Individual Performances

Highest Scores

Aston Unity (J.M. Kennedy)	130 v	Mitchells & Butlers	(A)	1959
Dudley (G.A. Headley)	169*v	Mitchells & Butlers	(A)	1952
Kidderminster (H.G. Moule)	135*v	Stourbridge	(H)	1947
Mitchells & Butlers (E.A. Watts)	152 v	Dudley	(H)	1950
Moseley (D.M.W. Heath)	142 v	Dudley	(A)	1959
Old Hill (J.D.B. Edwards)	138*v	Smethwick	(H)	1951
Smethwick (B. Rowley)	122*v	Mitchells & Butlers	(A)	1949
Stourbridge (P.E.Richardson)	123*v	Mitchells & Butlers	(A)	1950
Walsall (T.F. Smailes)	129 v	Mitchells & Butlers	(A)	1950
West Brom. Dartmouth (E. Perry)	155 v	Aston Unity	(A)	1948

*Not Out

Best Bowling

Aston Unity (M.S. Nichols)	9–48 v	Smethwick	(A)	1949
Dudley (W.E. Merritt)	9–63 v	Smethwick	(H)	1946
Kidderminster (A.W. Wellard)	10–33 v	Stourbridge	(A)	1950
Mitchells & Butlers (D. Johnston)	8–23 v	Aston Unity	(A)	1953
Moseley (H.J. Latham)	10–29 v	Kidderminster	(A)	1957
Old Hill (W. Lee)	8–19 v	Dudley	(H)	1946
Smethwick (J. Oldham)	8–28 v	Walsall	(A)	1958
Stourbridge (R. Howorth)	8–30 v	West Brom. Dartmouth	(A)	1954
Walsall (G. Gregory)	8–18 v	Moseley	(H)	1958
West Brom. Dartmouth (B. Shardlow)	9–30 v	Kidderminster	(A)	1955

Second Division 1946–1959

Second Division Winners

1946	Kidderminster	
1947	Moseley	
1948)	Mitchells & Butlers	
1949)		
1950)	Moseley	
1951)		
1952	Mitchells & Butlers	
1953	(Old Hill (Stourbridge	
1954)	Mitchells & Butlers	
1955)		
1956	Dudley	
1957	Smethwick	
1958	Mitchells & Butlers	
1959	Walsall	

Highlights

8.5.48	Old Hill 138 Aston Unity 138 F. Willetts 6−27 Result − Tie
12.6.48	Moseley 88 Jack Bannister 5−18. Described as a 'promising fast bowler with a good line and length' − attributes to be much in evidence in his career with Warwickshire. Mitchells & Butlers 91−5
24.7.48	Smethwick 166 R. McHenry 50 R.L. Evers 7−61 Kidderminster 166 H. Morris 54. Result − Tie
14.8.48	Moseley 178 16yr old schoolboy David Heath 80 Smethwick 81 H.A. Tyler 6−15 and 5 W for 0 runs in 7 balls including hat-trick
21.5.49	West Bromwich Dartmouth 107 Old Hill 13 17yr old Barry Hatfield 6w−8 runs
18.8.51	Mitchells & Butlers 159 Walsall 159 Result − Tie
1953	Bank Holiday weekend Les Jones, Walsall, scored 103 n.o. v Dudley then 123 n.o. v West Bromwich Dartmouth.
26.6.54	Aston Unity 169−7 J.R. Sparkes 102 n.o. Dudley 115−2 14yr old Ron Headley 30.
24.7.54	West Bromwich Dartmouth 205−5 D.F. Robinson 50 C.A. Armstrong 53 Smethwick 19 'Veteran' Bob Cotton 7−15
13.8.55	Walsall 277−1 J. McShane 89 G. Taylor 160 − scored 256 for first wicket − a club record Stourbridge 123 D. Dewsbery 5−43
27.8.55	Old Hill 171 Kidderminster 135 − Playing the bottom club, with a game in hand, Kidderminster lost last match and the championship
5.5.56	Kidderminster 199 G. Bridgford 92 Old Hill 20 G. Lacey 5−7 F. Williams 4−8 Some revenge for Kidderminster after last seasons last match defeat
2.6.56	5 West Indians played for West Bromwich Dartmouth!
7.7.56	Dudley 226−5 17 yr old Jack Sedgley 103 n.o. Kidderminster 156
10.5.58	Kidderminster 133 West Bromwich Dartmouth 133 Result − Tie
27.5.59	Dennis Amiss in Smethwick 2nd XI
27.6.59	In match between Kidderminster and Dudley Jim Sewter (the present Worcestershire scorer) was given out hitting the ball twice when he hit ball back to bowler. − Probably in high dudgeon, when bowling, he ran out batsman backing up.

1960–1974 – THE BONUS YEARS

Administration

The League suffered a great loss in 1963 when the Honorary Secretary and Treasurer Ken Spooner died just as the season opened. Jack Williams volunteered to fill the temporary vacancy and was formally elected to the post at the 1963 Annual General Meeting. To reduce the growing work-load on the Hon. Secretary, Mr. M.F. White was appointed Treasurer in January 1965 and David Bryant, Assistant Hon. Secretary, in 1970.

In 1970, the League appointed delegates to the recently formed Warwickshire and Worcestershire Cricket Associations in membership of the National Cricket Association which had been formed in 1968. The formation of this national body had thus brought the realisation of the 1879 dreams that had prompted Harry Brettell to form the Birmingham Cricket Association. Harry Brettell would, no doubt, have been delighted to know that Leslie Deakins, the Secretary of Warwickshire County Cricket Club and a strong supporter of the League and indefatigable worker for all levels of cricket, was involved in the formation of the National Cricket Association and became one of the first members of the Executive of the Association. Mr. Deakins' work for the League was marked by his election as President of the League in 1982 when he became one of the few Presidents who had not previously held an Executive post or played in the League.

Between 1964 and 1974, the League received a total of £9500 in generous annual grants from the Warwickshire County Cricket Supporters' Association. Each year the money received was distributed to assist member clubs in special projects and came as a welcome boost when the income from the gates was negligible. In 1970 Kidderminster took only £72 'gate' against expenses of £3626 and, to survive, clubs were entirely dependent on members' subscriptions and money raised by social events. Apart from the latter rounds of the Challenge Cup, the League was no longer the source of public entertainment that it had been in earlier years. This lack of support came, not from any lowering of standards of play but from social changes. More families had cars and could enjoy days away, there were more and longer holidays, television attracted static watchers whilst the more energetic had greater opportunities to take part in other interests. A new word became more commonplace – sponsorship – as sport endeavoured to find sources of financial support. First class cricket was to introduce sponsored cricket in the Gillette Cup in 1963, The John Player League in 1969, and the Benson & Hedges Trophy in 1972 – all games in which a positive result was achieved in one day – a source of entertainment to prove popular with the public!

League Clubs began to obtain sponsors for their games and,

whilst Kidderminster unsuccessfully urged the introduction of limited over cricket, the League made more conservative changes by limiting the overs for the side batting first to 60 in 1969 and then to 55 in 1972.

A special and pleasant event took place on 10 March 1972 when the League made a presentation to R.I. 'Rusty' Scorer to mark his 80th birthday and his 60 years continuous service to the League. He had been honoured earlier by being elected President for his fourth term, having previously held the post in 1948, 1953 and 1963. The presentation took the form of a Silver Salver inscribed by one person from each member club in the League, together with the names of the Advisory Committee, the President of the M.C.C., the Secretary of the M.C.C. and his great personal friend, R.E.S. Wyatt.

As Chairman of the Advisory Committee 'Rusty' Scorer had been a strong driving force in the post-war years, using his influence and administrative ability to spread the name of the League beyond the Midlands by prevailing upon leading figures of the day to attend and speak at League dinners and arranging representative games against notable sides such as Sir Julian Cahn's XI. During the 1914—18 war he was awarded the Military Cross. In the Second World War from 1942—46 he organised week long Birmingham Cricket Festivals at Edgbaston. These Festivals were only able to take place due to the perseverance of Rusty who overcame rationing and war-time restrictions, Ministry Regulations and material shortages to make a desolate ground fit to house the 140,000 spectators who attended during the Festivals and raised nearly £10,000 for Charity. For his war time charity work he received a personal letter of appreciation from the Prime Minister, Winston Churchill.

In 1934 when the Moseley Club was in desperate financial straits he used his influence in his other sporting interest, Rugby, to persuade two teams of distinguished players to play in a match to raise money for the Club and, not only that, he staged it at Villa Park the home of Aston Villa Football Club. Twenty years later he was to fire everyone with such enthusiasm that the club were able to obtain, lay out, and build the splendid ground that now carries his name — 'Scorers'.

Engagement of Professionals

In 1961, the League opened up the opportunity for professionals to return to amateur status by deleting a rule that prevented a player from twice being re-instated and by ruling that a reinstated player who had played for five years as an amateur could then be considered as an amateur.

The 1958 amendment to Rules raising of the age to 21 before being considered in the League as a professional was further expanded in 1971 by the League ruling that each Club could play one contracted County player between ages of 21 and 24 in addition to the professional and contracted players under 21. This enabled the County Clubs to loan out more players for League experience.

The M.C.C. definitions of 'professional' and 'amateur' were completely revised in 1963 and introduced a definition of 'paid player'. This led to similar alterations in the League Rules and a part of old cricket tradition was ended.

Playing Regulations

In 1964 the interval between innings was extended from 15 to 20 minutes and the following season the start of play from 2.30 p.m. to 2.15 p.m.

The most significant change for many years was the introduction, in 1970, of 20 overs to be bowled in the last hour into the "Laws of Cricket". This was adopted by the League and, as in other levels of cricket, it improved the playing conditions in the last hour. No longer were there disputes on the calling of time or the slowing down of over rates. Moreover the spectacle was removed of fielders striving for victory rushing to change positions at the end of an over to try to get in another one, only to have the umpire who was 'walking in at his normal pace' call 'Time', on reaching the wicket.

Points System

In an endeavour to arouse more interest, a system of bonus points for fastest scoring rate was introduced in 1962 coupled with no points for a draw. The revised law was soon proved to have imperfections for at the start of the season Kidderminster and Stourbridge were the only sides to play both of their opening games and the League Table read Kidderminster 8 points, Stourbridge 4 points, Moseley 1, the rest 0 — 'a flying start' for Kidderminster which led eventually to a League title. Furthermore, the bonus point could be won even if a side lost so teams that won by getting the opposition out in a few overs could find the opposition got the bonus. With no point for a draw, one of the sides who may have figured in a high scoring draw got no points. These slips were remedied in 1963 when the point for a draw was re-introduced and a bonus point could only be gained by a side who won or drew, and to clear another difficulty, bonus points could only be awarded if the side batting second received 20 overs unless they had won or were all out.

The Playing Scene 1960—1974

The enthusiasm which had brought a new ground for Moseley and the Championship in 1959 was to carry the Club to seven titles in the next fifteen years, with only three seasons out of the top three. West Bromwich Dartmouth won three times, Kidderminster once and shared twice, Walsall won once and shared once. Old Hill and Smethwick each won once.

The introduction of the bonus point for the faster scoring rate brought a change in tactics as captains elected to bat second on winning the toss. This was because the side batting first, unless they were bowled out, usually received more overs than the side batting second. The captain of the side batting second thus had the option, which he often took, of not chasing runs for a win but batting for a draw and scoring enough runs to gain the bonus point. This led to an increase in the number of drawn games and often end of match excitement as batsmen scrambled for the last few runs for the bonus point.

Moseley

The batting strength of Moseley was built around David Heath, Neal Abberley, John Gough, George Jakeman, Barry Fletcher, David Kench, Terry Devenport and Bert Latham with Ian King in the 1960's and John Taylor and Dick Chase in the 1970's. Bowling was in the more than capable hands of Bert Latham's quickies and Roy

Five Members of 6 Moseley Championships 1956, 59, 61, 63, 64 & 67
R.B. Abell, J.W. Thompson, D.M.W. Heath, H.J. Latham, G. Jakeman.

Abell's spinners, Brian Barrett aiding the quick attack and Jim Andrew the spinning partnership. The late 1960's saw Steve Rouse and Trevor Jones joining the attack and in 1973 Gordon 'Red' Harrys. The wicket keeping was in the hands of Jim Thompson, succeeded in 1969 by John Taylor from Essex, who added powerful batting to his excellence behind the sticks.

1961 saw the Club win the First and Second Division titles. Both sides then beat the Rest of the League sides and, to crown a remarkable season, the Moseley Seconds won the League Challenge Cup.

Moseley's chief rivals in this season were West Bromwich Dartmouth and their meeting on 15 July was crucial to the Dartmouth's chances of overhauling their rivals. Rain delayed the start until 4.00 p.m. Moseley put into bat, struggled against the bowling of Frank King and Derek Pearson and batted for 61.3 overs scoring 176—7, John Gough 77. This left Dartmouth time for only 16 overs batting and no chance of victory. The 16 overs were academic, and Dartmouth registered their protest by scoring only 12—0.

Four years later, almost on the anniversary, the 17 July, the Dartmouth took their revenge by batting for 94.4 overs scoring 220—9. David Gale 92, Roy Parker 53 n.o. Jim Andrew bowled 40 overs, Bert Latham 31. Moseley were left with 15 overs in which they scored 56—0 but the scores were now settled and the captains shook hands as they left the field.

A major factor in Moseley's success in the late 1950's and the 1960's was the outstanding captaincy by David Heath who gathered and blended together good individual players into a fine side. On the field he was an astute reader of the game, making opponents work hard for their runs and bringing the same dedicated approach to his batting so that he was an accomplished opening bat finishing well up in the scoring table each season. His performances brought him an invitation from the County Club in seasons 1949 to 1953. David has taken a prominent place in Club and League affairs, becoming President of Moseley and has acted as Chairman of the League Managment Committee since its formation in 1978. He served one year as President of the League in 1979 and has been honoured by the Presidency in the Centenary Year. In 1987, he was appointed General Secretary to Warwickshire C.C.C.

1963 and 1964 saw further Moseley title successes, in each season of which Bert Latham and Roy Abell took 100 wickets between them. When the last match of the 1964 season came Moseley were four points in the lead and needed one point to be clear leaders whilst second club Kidderminster needed to win and obtain the bonus point to stand a chance of sharing the title. In the event, Moseley met Dean Johnston at his most penetrative and were all out for 59, Mitchells and Butlers winning by four wickets. Kidderminster, meanwhile, were struggling to beat West Bromwich Dartmouth's 219 (B.T. Glynn 68, Roly Jenkins 32, Roy Tattersall 4—48) and were eventually all out for 119 (Basil D'Oliveira 36, Roly Jenkins 3—20, R. Turner 4—26) so Moseley stayed champions, despite their defeat. The two teams occupied the same League positions in 1967, when neither lost a game. Although Moseley won seven, Kidderminster only managed four wins. Drawn games were a feature of the season, fifty nine of the 90 games finishing in this way. This may have been due to a lack of penetration in the League bowling but Moseley had Jim Andrew and Roy Abell at the top of the bowling averages to ensure their success.

Moseley beat off old rivals West Bromwich Dartmouth to win the title in 1969 and 1970, but could not hold off their other challengers Kidderminster, who in 1973 managed to share the title. The two sides were neck and neck during the season and once again the decision was left to the last game. Moseley, leading by 3 points, needed two points to win the title, whilst Kidderminster needed a win. This Kidderminster achieved by beating Walsall when batting in bad light. They scored 138—8 (Steve Johnson 40 Ernie King 29) to beat Walsall's 137 (David Smith 5—32 John Aldridge 4—44) Moseley, meantime, had the worst of the game against Aston Unity. Unity scored 165 (H. Yarnold 40, Steve Rouse 5—47) but Moseley could only muster 116—8 to share the title. Unity's bowling successes that day were Geoff Jackson 4—42 and Harold Turner, who was eventually to become Moseley's captain, also 4—42.

Aston Unity

Aston Unity did not achieve any title successes and their last season at Hillcourt in 1972 saw their fortunes at the lowest ebb when they finished at the bottom of the table, having managed only one win and three bonus points. This was unexpected for the previous season they had challenged the champions, West Bromwich Dartmouth, to such an extent that Dartmouth had to win their last match to keep the Unity in second place, only two points behind. The Unity's misfortune followed them to their new ground at Bassetts Pole when their groundsman Ken Boak was killed in a road accident only days before the ground was opened. Ken had formerly been Warwickshire's groundsman and had served Unity for over fifteen years.

Roy Bent, Barry Hodder and David Roberts played throughout the period to be joined in the mid 1960's by batsmen Howard Yarnold, Colin Price, Robert Ingram and fast bowlers Geoff Jackson, Wilf Puffett, Les Cooke and spinner Alex Thornhill. Roy Bonell, Maurice Wade, Bob Furley and Jack Hossell had shared the wickets in the early years, Ian King, Terry Riley and Jack Hossell the batting.

Colin Price made his debut on 18 August 1964 in a memorable match against title chasers Kidderminster which Unity won despite a tremendous effort by Basil D'Oliveira;

Aston Unity scored 214—9 Colin Price 68, Mike Boyle 64 n.o. and Jack Hossell 42. Basil D'Oliveira 5—82.

Kidderminster 198 Basil D'Oliveira 109 in 87 minutes Geoff Jackson 4—50 Roy Bonell 3—51. Les Cooke 3—19.

This started a long career for Colin as a backbone of the Unity batting, extending to the present day, during which time he has not missed a First Division game. Unity and Kidderminster took part in a memorable high scoring match on 6th August 1967 with Kidderminster again striving for the title. This match ended with Kidderminster wanting two to win off the last ball but finished with the scores level:

Aston Unity 245—7 in 64.5 overs bowled in three hours Colin Price 70, David Roberts 88, Trevor Larkham 4—66

Kidderminster 245—2 off 45 overs, Peter Harris 83. Richard Pearcey 68 n.o. Tony Smith 48 retired hurt.

Jack Hossell retired from the side at the end of the 1964 season but still maintained close links with the League, serving on the Advisory Committee until 1977. Jack's retirement ended an era during which Jack and his father had played in the League for the Club for nearly 50 years, Jack himself starting in 1929. He was a forcing left hand bat and bowled insidious slow left arm and had a spell with Warwickshire C.C.C. in 1946 and 1947. In the 1939 season in the League he scored over 400 runs for Unity in four weeks including two centuries and a 97. He captained the Unity Championship side in 1949. He was respected by all his contemporaries as a fine gentleman and player and still applies his knowledge to the benefit of the Warwickshire Club as a co-opted member of the County Club Committee.

Mitchells and Butlers

The distinction of being the first person to score a thousand runs in a season was earned in 1961 by Alan Townsend. Alan had retired from first class cricket with Warwickshire the previous season and joined Mitchells & Butlers as professional. He scored 1102 runs with an average of 84.76 and took twenty one wickets in a prolific season in which his team mate Arthur Fletcher scored over 500 runs and took 27 wickets. With Dean Johnston, Colin Stringer and John Kain also in the wickets and Chaman Lal Malhotra, Frank Bridges, and Stan Mitchell in the runs, the side went the season without losing a game to finish runners up to Moseley. They did, however, inflict a heavy defeat on the champions on 22 July 1961.

Mitchells & Butlers 240—3, Alan Townsend 134 n.o. (his highest of the season) Chaman Malhotra 52 Brian Barrett 3—60.

Moseley 73 David Heath 25 Albert Wright 5—48 John Kain 5—22.

As if to emphasise that his achievement was not a "one off" Alan scored 1008 runs in 1970 and confirmed his place in League history for no other batsman topped the thousand in the days of 18 match season. The 1970 total was a near thing for he needed just 12 runs when Mitchells met Kidderminster in the last match of the season. There was rain in the air but Mitchells batted first and when he was out for 20 he received generous applause on his return to the pavilion. The game was later abandoned just after Kidderminster had started their reply. Alan was renowned in cricket for his pleasant demeanour, sportsmanship and brilliant close to the wicket fielding. He stepped down from the first eleven after the 1973 season but continued to contribute his skills as coach and second team player. He still acts as coach for youngsters in the County with his message to them that cricket is a game to be enjoyed.

Arthur Fletcher left Mitchells to become professional at Walsall in 1966, but Derek Robinson continued to ply his craft with bat and ball throughout the period when he was also a popular captain. Trevor Elias, Stan Mitchell, John Fitton, Colin Stringer and Dean Johnston made up the side in the early 1960's with Winslow Howard, Ken Porter and John Lumb later bringing fresh faces into the batting, John Weston, Alan Townsend Jnr., and evergreen Eric Hollies into the bowling. Peter Tresham taking over the wicket-keeping from long-serving Fred Hughes. David Ratcliffe, Ray McHenry, Alan Millichamp, Syd Headley, Ray Carter and professional Charlie Barnett also had spells with the club. The period, however, was to bring no championship honours to Mitchells and 1969 was a season without a win. Stourbridge were the victims of two fine opening stands by Mitchells:-

2nd July 1960 Stourbridge 206—9 in 52 overs Derek Russell 56. George Mills 52. Arthur Fletcher 4—45

Mitchells & Butlers 207—1 in 35.1 overs. Charlie Barnett 115 n.o. Arthur Fletcher 87

27 July 1963 Mitchells & Butlers 230—0 Alan Townsend 125 n.o. Arthur Fletcher 102 n.o.
Stourbridge 178—5 Derek Russell 103 n.o. There were, thus, three not out centuries in this game — a League record.

Stourbridge

Stourbridge could not claim any title in the period but, following their tradition of giving promising young players an opportunity, they were to introduce to the League cricket Douglas Slade, Peter Robinson, David Stewart, Brian Richardson, John Inchmore, Paul Pridgeon, Brian Brain and two players who were to become famous internationals, Glen Turner (New Zealand) and Imran Khan (Pakistan).

Doug Slade, who was later to have an excellent career in the League with West Bromwich Dartmouth, made a telling debut on 9 July 1960 when he took 8—35 against Dudley. Brian Brain was another to impress on his debut when in his first game on 1 May 1965 he took 5—35 against Smethwick and followed this with 8—18 to enable Stourbridge to dismiss near rivals Kidderminster for 89 and register a ten wicket success. Glen Turner made a quiet entry into the League as a 19 year old who took no risks but this dedication to building up his technique was to pay off as he created new records in his First Class career. Even at this early stage he compiled 107 not out against Kidderminster on 26 August 1967 and in the season scored 314 runs and took 15 wickets.

Two amateurs were also to hit the headlines, Roy Snow and Mike Wooldridge the latter taking a wicket with his first ball in League cricket, against Smethwick, on 12 May 1973, when he finished with 5—53. Roy Snow joined the ranks of the ten wicket-takers on 21 May 1966 when he took 10—41 to dismiss Aston Unity for 106. His efforts proved to be in vain for Stourbridge collapsed to 79 all out against the bowling of Les Cooke 6—21 and Roy Bonell 2—24. Roy's membership of this Unity side thus meant that he had the unique experience of playing in three matches where ten wickets in an innings were taken by a bowler for he had been a member of the Moseley sides in 1954 and 1957 when Bert Latham had his two successes.

Stourbridge had a period of rebuilding in the late 1960's only Martin Hill, David Cowin and Norman Whiting being regular members throughout most of the period. The side hit the absolute low in 1968 when they finished the season having no wins or bonus points. The club fortunes improved in the early 1970's with the arrival of Keith Wilkinson, Alan Richardson, Roger Hargreaves, Dave Collins, Tex Whitehouse, Mike Wooldridge and Frank Wright. On 20 June 1970, they had the satisfaction of being the first side to beat Moseley since August 3 1968 and this in unusual circumstances. On the way to the ground one of the cars broke down and four players were late arriving. Stourbridge took the field with seven men, Norman Whiting wearing batting gloves acting as stand in

wicket-keeper.   Moseley lost a wicket without a run being scored
and were eventually dismissed for 90.   Alan Richardson, who had
left Moseley because he was unable to get a regular place in the first
eleven took 7—33.   Stourbridge then scored 91—0, David Stewart
59 n.o., Keith Wilkinson 23 n.o.

Kidderminster

Stourbridge themselves lost all their ten wickets to one bowler
on 11 May 1968 when Dave Smith of Kidderminster took 10—18 off
only 9.2 overs.   Dave took the last five wickets in six balls including
the hat trick, Stourbridge collapsing to 43 all out in reply to Kidderminster's 163—7 declared.   Dave had joined Kidderminster the
previous season and together with John Aldridge, Paul Roberts, Ray
Carter and veteran Trevor Larkham was to bowl Kidderminster to a
joint title with Moseley in 1973.   The batting that season was
dominated by Peter Harris, Stephen Johnson, Roy Barker, Ernie
King and Godfrey Lamb, making his first team place with good
middle order batting and excellent wicket-keeping.   Peter Harris
and Trevor Larkham were also members of the Championship sides
of 1962 and in 1966 when the title was shared with Walsall.   The
opening partnership of Peter Harris and Peter Heard in those years
was one of the most prolific enjoyed by the Club and contributed to
the Club's success in the period.

In 1962 the supporting batsmen were Tony Smith, David
Bennett, Paul and Bill Booton.   The bowling attack was spearheaded
by Fred Rumsey with Roy Tattersall, Mike Evers and Trevor
Larkham in support.   Roger and Chris Newman and Jim Yardley
had taken over the role of supporting batsmen in 1966 with John
Aldridge, Len Beel and that man again — Trevor Larkham, taking
most of the wickets.   When things got tight at the end of the season
Roy Tattersall was brought back, having retired the previous season,
and responded with eight wickets in his two matches including three
in the last over he was to bowl in the League.   1966 also saw Peter
Harris score 763 runs in the season to beat a club record of 733 held
since 1910 by Stanley Gethin.

Peter continued in great form the following season to score
867 runs to beat his own club record.   Ernie King, Kevin Griffiths,
David York, Tony Burkes, Richard Perry and Mike Hopkins came on
the scene during the period.   Ernie proved himself a valuable acquis-
ition to the team with his exciting play and his excellent club spirit.

In 1964 Basil D'Oliveira, qualifying for Worcestershire, teamed
up to share the bowling with Roy Tattersall and the batting with
Peter Harris and Peter Heard.   Basil scored 706 runs in the season
and took 43 wickets.   After 13 games Kidderminster led the table,
but lost two and drew 3 of their last five games, and finished second
to Moseley.   In two of the draws they had 9 of the opponents
wickets down and one loss was against Aston Unity who had
previously only won one game all season.   They had the satisfaction
of recording an emphatic win over champions Moseley on 11 July.
Moseley 60 H.J. Latham 60 B. D'Oliveira 5—25 P. Mountford 4—17.
Kidderminster 61—1.

Richard Perry, son of Harvey Perry, had a good day on 24 July
1971, when he reduced West Bromwich Dartmouth from 40—1 to
47—6, taking five wickets in ten balls finishing with 6—21.

Kidderminster were the kings of close title finishes in the

period for, in addition to the two last match deciders referred to in the Moseley account and the shared title with Walsall, their outright win in 1962 was obtained in a grandstand finish to the season when they met challengers, Smethwick, in the last match. Holding a two point lead, a draw was sufficient, and winning the toss they batted for 81 overs to score 267—4. Peter Harris 121 not out, David Bennett 62 not out. Smethwick with no hope now left, had time for only 31 overs to be bowled but scored 170—6 Dennis Amiss 59, Bernard Rowley 56. The Kidderminster preparations for celebration brought laughter to the Kidderminster Court when their application for an extension to their bar licence was tabled as being required for: "After the lazy cricket match of the season".

Smethwick

Smethwick had to wait another six years until 1968 for their title win in the period although they finished second in 1962, 1965 and again in 1974 when they once again kept up their challenge until the last match of the season. On this occasion West Bromwich Dartmouth gained the one point they required from their game with Mitchells and Butlers to finish one point ahead of Smethwick who had crushed Walsall by eight wickets after dismissing them for 51 Paul Junkin 6—24 Tim Hawkes 4—17.

Smethwick's success in 1968 was founded on five outstanding all rounders Bernard Rowley, Gwyn Benson, John Oldham, Ravindera Senghera and Paul Junkin with the batting of Graham Warner and Roy Freeman, the batting and wicket keeping of Roy Walton and the bowling of Tim Hawkes. Dennis Amiss and John Jameson played early in the period until they won their places in Warwickshire's first eleven and Dave Derricott, Tim Binks, Errol Simms, Neville Moore joined towards the end of the period to form the backbone of the sides of the future. Tom Pearsall and Brian Richardson had a spell with the club in the period, one innings of 115 by 17yr old Brian Richardson being described by Walsall's veteran Jack Hight "as one of the finest in many a long year".

Cyril Goodway had hung up his boots at the end of the 1961 season, his last game being as captain and wicket-keeper of the Rest of the League versus Champions Moseley. When the last ball was to be bowled Moseley wanted three runs to win and Cyril carefully set his field only for Bernard Rowley to bowl a seamer wide of the leg stump the ball going for 4 byes well wide of Cyril's outstretched hand, Cyril's exclamation is not to be recorded!

Four extras were to prevent Dennis Amiss getting his first century in the League on 20 May 1961. Stourbridge had scored 201—9 dec. George Mills 77. Jock Livingston 57 and with Smethwick on 198—2 and Dennis on 99 the winning runs came off extras, a disappointment for the young starlet who was to score a century of centuries in his First Class career.

Dudley suffered two heavy defeats at the hands of the young Smethwick batting line up. On 10 July 1965 Smethwick scored 172—3 Bernard Rowley 62 n.o. Dudley were dismissed for 29 (Geoff Hampton 12, Tim Hawkes 4—15 and Rudolph Cohen 6—13). Rudolph, a West Indian, was to come to England from Jamaica the following year as replacement for Lester King in the West Indian touring party but did not play in a Test. On 1 July 1972 Tim Hawkes was again effective against Dudley who were all out for 58, their last five wickets falling for 3 runs, all leg byes.   Tim Hawkes taking 7—15.

Dudley

Dudley were to finish runners up to Smethwick in 1968, their highest League position in the period.   That season saw Harry Kelleher join as professional from Old Hill and they came close to success with Dennis Breakwell joining up with namesake Jack Breakwell, Frank Golding, Roy Barker, Gerry Kendrick, Ken Kelmere, Geoff Hampton, Tex Whitehouse and Bob Silvester.

On 10 August that season they dismissed Kidderminster for 24 with Harry Kelleher taking 8—10 including 4 wickets in his last over.   Two weeks previously they had won an exciting game against Mitchells & Butlers when off the last ball of the match Tex Whitehouse had hit the six runs required for victory.   George Dews had a three year spell as professional from 1962—64 but even his proficiency with the bat could not make up for the lack of a really penetrating bowler and with home games played on an excellent batting pitch, Dudley occupied a lowly league position.   The signing of Tom Graveney, whilst he qualified for Worcestershire, gave a boost to attendances and interest in 1961.   On his debut at Kidderminster he scored 72 and with Harry Thomas getting a century Dudley declared at 222—5.   Kidderminster rose to the challenge and at 181—0 with thirty minutes left victory was in sight but Frank Golding stepped in with a hat trick finishing with 5—64 as Kidderminster failed by just 4 runs.   Peter Heard 96, Peter Harris 81.

Dudley had an opportunity to share in championship celebrations in 1970 when they handsomely beat Moseley who wanted a win to be sure of the title.

Dudley scored 130—9 Gordon Wilcox 32 n.o. David Cook 5—55. Bert Latham 4—36., but Moseley collapsed to 39 all out Brian Brain playing his first game for Dudley taking 7—22.   After the game, Moseley heard that their championship contenders, West Bromwich Dartmouth, had also lost so Dudley were at least allowed to share the champagne.

Dudley had many changes of personnel during the period but club men whose names appear from season to season were Club Chairman Ron Smith, Jack Breakwell, Frank Golding, Gerry Kendrick, Ken Kelmere, Don Jones, Bob Silvester, Dick Adey, then towards the end of the period Mel Green, Alan Cattell, Tony Willis, and Alan Grace, youngsters who were to give good service to their team and the League in the future.

Old Hill

Old Hill won the title in 1960, only losing one game in the process, to Smethwick, when Bernard Rowley took 7—41 to dismiss them for 142 after Harry Kelleher had taken 7—31 to limit Smethwick to 197.   Harry Kelleher, paceman turned off spinner, had a splendid season with the ball taking 51 wickets and he was ably backed up by Mike Bradley, Don Hall and Ron and Harold Dovey. Harry Moule, in his twenty first season in the League, had his best season ever, scoring 624 runs and enjoying good support from Mike Whitney, Ron Dovey, Terry Grainger, Jimmy Bunn and Don Jones whilst Harry Kelleher and Harold Dovey supplemented their bowling with useful scores.   Their best win was against Moseley. Old Hill scored 156, Harry Moule 74, but then dismissed Moseley for

OLD HILL C.C.
B'HAM & DISTRICT CRICKET LEAGUE CHAMPIONS 1960

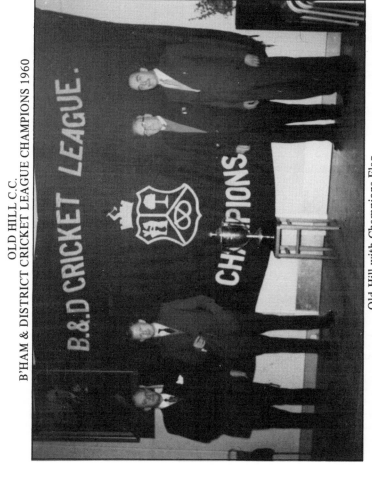

Old Hill with Champions Flag

Bert Homer, O.H. Chairman, Ron Dovey, Captain, Vic Price, O.H. Sec., Bert Edwards, O.H. President.

58 Harry Kelleher 6—13, Don Hall 4—9.   David Sturman, Jimmy Bunn, Roy Keeling, Brian Bullingham, Jack Sedgley, Geoff Eley and Don Jones played through most of the period with Tom Pearsall, Peter Bagley, Don Guest, David Woodhouse, Alan Head, David Cooper and Steve Thompson.

Bernard Rowley moved over from Smethwick in 1971 to act as professional until 1974.   He kept up his outstanding all round performances and took over the coaching after the Club had suffered two disastrous seasons in 1969 and 1970 when they only won one game.   Bernard, Tom Pearsall and Jimmy Bunn were consistently in the runs but the side did not have the flair to force good positions into victories and were unable to rise from the bottom half of the table in the later years.   The Club had, however, taken a lead in promoting youth membership which augured well for the future.

Walsall

Walsall shared the title with Kidderminster in 1966 and won it outright in 1972.   In the 1966 season there was a preponderance of drawn games, the two title holders being the clubs with the most bonus points, the position at the top being:—

	P	W	D	L	B.P.	Total
Walsall	18	4	13	1	12	37
Kidderminster	18	4	12	2	13	37
Moseley	18	5	12	1	8	35
Dudley	18	4	12	2	7	31
Old Hill	18	4	12	2	7	31

56 of the 90 games played finished as draws.   When the last games of the season were played, Walsall and Kidderminster were equal points with Moseley only two points behind so once again competition for the title was fiercely contested to the end.   Moseley were unable to beat Dudley and Walsall and Kidderminster both drew and obtained the bonus point.   Walsall won the toss against Smethwick and were restricted by tight bowling of Bernard Rowley, 7—42 to 168—9 in 65 overs.   Smethwick started disastrously losing four wickets for 27 runs to the bowling of Gilbert Gregory and Dennis Dewsbery.   Even 46 not out from Bernard Rowley was not enought to deny Walsall the important bonus point Smethwick finishing at 96—7.   Walsall then had to await the result from Stourbridge who were locked in an exciting battle with Kidderminster. Kidderminster had declared at 169—6 in 50 overs, Peter Heard 62, to give themselves time to dismiss the bottom club who had no wins and only three bonus points to their credit.   They met unexpected resistance, Stourbridge finishing with 165—9.   Martin Hill 52, but this was off 55 overs so Kidderminster thus gained the bonus point and shared the title.

The Walsall side which achieved the success included Arthur Fletcher who had accepted an invitation from the Club to leave Mitchells & Butlers to act as professional.   Always a difficult batsman to dislodge he dominated the batting in which Dick Devereux, Phil Beddow, Mike Greenhough also starred, with good support from Philip Brown, Terry Hope and wicket-keeper Les Rolinson. Gilbert Gregory, Terry Hope, Dennis Dewsbery and Trevor Davies took the bowling honours.

Walsall's confirmation as champions in 1972 again depended on the last matches but in this case their rivals Moseley, who were one point behind, lost to Kidderminster and a Walsall victory over Mitchells & Butlers gave them a clear lead of five points. Walsall had a good playing record, winning ten of the eighteen games with seven home wins out of nine the other two being rained off. This title success followed a season when they had finished bottom having not won a game. The improved change of fortune can certainly be attributed to a strengthening of the bowling attack with the debuts of Alan Hodgson, Richard Boothroyd and Dennis Breakwell in support of Dennis Dewsbery, Paul Bailey and Tony Durose who had joined the Club as professional the previous season. Roger Bender, Trevor Aston, Ian Watson, Philip Brown, Derek Nicholls and Mike Greenhough provided the batting strength. Trevor Aston having his best season with the bat was unfortunate to miss the deciding match because of illness but was promised a share of the champagne!

In 1960, Walsall introduced to the League a 17yr old Walsall Grammar School boy, David Brown, who was to become a Warwickshire and England Bowler and Manager of the County Club. Having already taken wickets in the Second Division he won his place in the first eleven. On August 1 of that season he was to feature in an unusual incident. Bowling at West Bromwich Dartmouth he collided with batsman Ron Williams who made no attempt to complete a second run and was run out despite a protest. The home crowd showed their disapproval. The incident had occurred off the last ball of an over but when the next batsman came in the umpire had omitted to call 'over' and David bowled another four balls making a ten ball over.

Walsall and West Bromwich Dartmouth were to figure in an event of a different nature on the 8 August 1970. Walsall Second eleven were dismissed by West Bromwich Dartmouth Second eleven for 50 a score which Dartmouth soon exceeded for the loss of only one wicket. Barrie Middleton, Walsall Second eleven wicket-keeper, then returned to Walsall to see how the first team were faring. The first team wicket-keeper, David Hughes, had been carried off the field and sent to hospital with a head wound after colliding with a Dartmouth batsman Jon Fellows-Smith, who was avoiding a throw by Derek Nicholls, who was making his debut in the First Division. The Dartmouth captain, David Gale, agreed to let Barrie Middleton take over as substitute wicket-keeper and he celebrated the unexpected promotion by taking three catches, one a diving left hand catch on the leg side. Dartmouth replying to a Walsall score of 125 were dismissed for 89. Dennis Dewsbery dismissing Roly Jenkins Dartmouth's last man with the last ball to be bowled. Tony Durose finished with 6—53. Barrie described this day as the greatest day of cricket in his life. Derek Nicholls became a leading all-rounder and captain of the Club.

In 1973 Graham Yallop sampled League cricket with Walsall and was so impressed that he returned for a season in 1975 and scored 1152 runs. A bat he used is mounted in the Walsall pavilion. Graham was soon to become an Australian Test Player and captain.

West Bromwich Dartmouth

Following their success in the 1940's and 1950's West Bromwich Dartmouth were still to continue to be a strong side, winning titles in 1965, 1971 and 1974 and finishing second on four other occasions. In 1965, the leading batsmen were Jon Fellows-

Smith, Jack Hyams, Alan Morton, Tony Lee, Roy Parker and wicket-keeper batsman Ron Williams.   Bowling was in the hands of Roly Jenkins, George Cummings, Roger Turner and Bob Bates whilst David Gale and Frank King were effective all-rounders.   Roly Jenkins, Jon Fellows-Smith and David Gale were still leading performers in the 1971 side when Ron Miller, Brian Brain, Rufus Browne and Jim Cumbes joined Roly in the attack.   Jim Millichip, Roger Newman, Alan Neal, Duncan Fearnley and Mike Edmundson were the new names in the batting line up.   Duncan Fearnley became Chairman of Worcestershire and was instrumental in signing up Ian Botham for the County in 1987.

Alan Neal, Rufus Browne, Mike Edmundson and Jim Millichip remained to take part in the 1974 success together with Mike Pryce, Doug Slade, Australian Robert Jefferey, David Humphries, Tony Waheed, Rob Jones and bowlers Peter Bradley, David York, and Mustapha Khan.   Peter Bradley put in a match winning bowling performance on June 8 1974.   The Dartmouth, playing Aston Unity, had been dismissed for only 113 when Peter, in twenty overs, took 9—32 as all the Unity batsmen were out caught for a total of 46, the last four bats getting 'ducks'.   Ron Miller had gone one wicket better against the Unity on 29 June 1968 when he took 10—46 in a Unity total of 130 to become the second bowler to achieve the feat in that season, Dave Smith of Kidderminster having taken 10 the previous month.

Reference to bowlers would be incomplete without the mention of wiry and wily Roly Jenkins.   He was loaned to Stourbridge as professional in 1938 but recalled by Worcestershire and only played a few games for Stourbridge.   He returned to the League in 1963, at the age of 44, to play for West Bromwich Dartmouth and for eleven seasons continued to puzzle batsmen with his leg breaks and googlies.

On his first match on his return Roly took 5—51 against Moseley and in all took 477 wickets.   On 11 July 1970 Old Hill were moving along nicely at 86—2.   Roly had not got a wicket but he then struck, taking 6 wickets in nine balls including a hat trick and changed a 0—39 average to 7—39 by the time Old Hill had been dismissed for 104.   For five seasons 1967 to 1971 he was partnered by Roland Miller the ex-Warwickshire slow left arm bowler and with these two in tandem the opposition could be sure to face at least twenty five overs in an hour.   With Roly in the side Roland Miller had to become 'Ronnie'.   Roly was renowned for his repartee and many young batsmen on being dismissed were consoled by, "Never mind, lad, I only bowl one of those every season!"

Extra Cover 1960—1974

14.5.60   West Bromwich Dartmouth 149 from 68—9 F. King 63
           Rufus Browne 14 n.o. A. Wright 5—32
           Mitchells & Butlers 124—6. B. Sinclair 70 n.o.

12.8.61   West Bromwich Dartmouth 156—9 R. Williams 49 G.
           Blyth 6—58
           Stourbridge 25   J. Sedgley 11 D.B. Pearson took 8
           wickets for 9 runs.

2.6.62   In a Kidderminster versus West Bromwich Dartmouth
           match, Fred Rumsey, Kidderminster fast bowler, left
           the field after taking two wickets.   On his return the

West Bromwich Dartmouth 1970

R. Newman, R. Browne, L. Staines, P. Parsons, J. Cumbes, R. Miller, T. Rider (Scorer)
R. Jenkins, S.A. Neal, D. Gale, J.P. Fellows-Smith, K. Kelmere.

109

umpires refused to let him bowl since 'he had been resting'. Umpires afterwards admitted they were wrong. This event anticipated the more recent Law changes precluding a fielder from bowling until he had been back on the field for the period he was off, if greater than 15 mins.

26.5.62   Dudley 218—3 G. Dews 120 n.o.
Walsall 218—8 K. Girkin 93
Four Walsall wickets fell to run outs as they scampered for the runs.

7.7.62   Moseley 150 N. Whiting 5—45
Stourbridge 103 P. Robinson 70. N. Whiting 18. R. Abell 6—41. 7 'ducks'.
Report said 'Enough ducks to start a poultry farm.'

23.5.64   Smethwick 109 T. Hope 6—22 was 5—3. P. Brown took 4 catches at 1st slip.
Walsall 110—1.

1.5.65   Walsall 39. H.J. Latham 6—12. R.B. Abell 2—5. P. Beddow 18
Moseley 43—1

28.5.66   Dudley 190—6 R. Barker 111 not out (19 yr old)
Kidderminster 188—7. D. Bennett 52.
With 3 wanted to win and when everyone thought there was one more ball, the umpire called 'over'. The Kidderminster scorer ran on the field with his book but the umpire was adamant that six balls had already been bowled.

15.7.67   Aston Unity 176—7. T. Riley 57. R. Fradgley 3—27. G. Turner 3—44
Stourbridge 177—1. D. Cowin 83 n.o. D. Russell 46. G. Turner 36 n.o.

12.8.67   Stourbridge 33. J. Andrew 6—5 including one hit for four.
Moseley 34—1

21.6.69   West Bromwich Dartmouth 203—7. A. Neal 66. L. Staines 41 n.o.
Aston Unity 162—8. D. Roberts 40. P. Levenger 34. R. Miller 4—49. R. Jenkins 3—75.
Aston Unity hung on for a draw against the spin twins with their last man Les Cooke padded up ready to come in even though he had his arm in a sling after a mishap during the Dartmouth innings.

15.8.70   Stourbridge 63. D. Stewart 21. A. Head 6—20. S. Screen 4—42
Old Hill 64—6. G. Eley 14. B. Bullingham 13. C. Hoppitt 3—17
Old Hill's first win since 3.8.68

16.6.73   Mitchells & Butlers 160 W. Howard 51. A. Durose 5—31
Walsall 153. M. Scott 64. A. Townsend (Jnr.) 4—61.
Winslow Howard, acting as deputy wicket-keeper, caught 5 and stumped 1 batsman. When batting he skied a ball and set off for the pavilion but when the

chance was not taken he dashed back to the crease to avoid being run out.

League Positions 1960–1974

First Division

	19 60	61	62	63	64	65	66	67	68	69	70	71	72	73	74
Aston Unity	9	5*	10	8*	9	6	9	10	8	4	5*	2	10	4	9
Dudley	8	9*	9	10	10	8*	4*	8	2	3	5*	4*	9	7*	7
Kidderminster	6	8	1	3	2	8*	1*	2	9	7	3*	9	3	1*	3
Mitchells & Butlers	4*	2	5*	5	3	3*	6	5*	7	8*	8	3	7	7*	8
Moseley	3	1	3*	1	1	3*	3	1	5	1	1	7	2	1*	6
Old Hill	1	7	3*	4	6*	10	4*	5*	6	10	10	4*	6	7*	10
Smethwick	4*	4	2	6	8	2	7	4	1	5	5*	8	8	10	2
Stourbridge	10	9*	5*	7	6*	5	10	9	10	8*	9	6	4	6	4
Walsall	7	5*	8	8*	5	7	1*	5*	4	6	3*	10	1	5	5
West Bromwich Dartmouth	2	3	5*	2	4	1	8	3	3	2	2	1	5	3	1

* Position held jointly

Highest Club Scores in Period

Club	Score		Opponent		Year
Aston Unity	245–7	v	Kidderminster	(H)	1967
Dudley	262–6	v	Mitchells & Butlers	(A)	1964
Kidderminster	267–4	v	Smethwick	(H)	1962
Mitchells & Butlers	(248–2	v	Stourbridge	(H)	1961
	(248–3	v	Kidderminster	(A)	1962
Moseley	249–4	v	Stourbridge	(H)	1963
Old Hill	242–4	v	Kidderminster	(H)	1963
Smethwick	242–6	v	Kidderminster	(H)	1961
Stourbridge	230–7	v	Old Hill	(A)	1972
Walsall	243–6	v	Stourbridge	(H)	1970
West Brom. Dartmouth	274–5	v	Smethwick	(A)	1961

Lowest Club Scores in Period

Club	Score		Opponent		Year
Aston Unity	39	v	Mitchells & Butlers	(A)	1968
Dudley	29	v	Smethwick	(A)	1965
Kidderminster	24	v	Dudley	(A)	1968
Mitchells & Butlers	68	v	Dudley	(H)	1963
Moseley	39	v	Dudley	(H)	1970
Old Hill	49	v	Stourbridge	(A)	1963
Smethwick	43	v	Mitchells & Butlers	(A)	1972
Stourbridge	25	v	West Brom. Dartmouth	(H)	1961
Walsall	39	v	Moseley	(H)	1965
West Brom.Dartmouth	65	v	Dudley	(A)	1968

Individual Performances

Highest Scores

Aston Unity (M.S. Cook)	138	v	Old Hill	(H)	1965
Dudley (G. Dews)	136*	v	Aston Unity	(H)	1962
Kidderminster (P.M. Harris)	138	v	Smethwick	(A)	1966
Mitchells & Butlers					
(A. Townsend)	136*	v	Smethwick	(H)	1969
(G.S. Warner)	136*	v	Stourbridge	(A)	1973
Moseley (D.M.W. Heath)	136*	v	Dudley	(A)	1965
Old Hill (J.B. Sedgley)	122*	v	Kidderminster	(A)	1973
Smethwick (B. Rowley)	127*	v	Kidderminster	(H)	1961
Stourbridge (M. Hill)	120	v	Walsall	(A)	1970
Walsall (R. Bender)	118	v	West Brom. Dartmouth	(A)	1972
West Brom. Dartmouth					
(R. Williams)	127*	v	Old Hill	(H)	1965

* Not Out

Best Bowling

Player	Figures		Opponent		Year
Aston Unity (G.K. Jackson)	8–19	v	Dudley	(H)	1973
Dudley (H.R.A. Kelleher)	8–10	v	Kidderminster	(H)	1968
Kidderminster (D. Smith)	10–18	v	Stourbridge	(A)	1968
Mitchells & Butlers (R.Legg)	8–19	v	Aston Unity	(H)	1968
Moseley (P. Morgan)	8–36	v	Dudley	(A)	1972
Old Hill (H. Dovey)	9–38	v	Kidderminster	(H)	1960
Smethwick (B.Rowley)	7–15	v	Stourbridge	(A)	1967
Stourbridge (R. Snow)	10–41	v	Aston Unity	(H)	1966
Walsall (K.J. Aldridge)	9–20	v	Aston Unity	(H)	1961
West Brom. Dartmouth					
(R. Miller)	10–47	v	Aston Unity	(H)	1968

Second Division 1960—1974

Second Division Winners

1960	Walsall	1969	Moseley
1961	) Moseley	1970	West Bromwich Dartmouth
1962	)	1971	Kidderminster
1963	West Brom. Dartmouth	1972	)
1964	Aston Unity	1973	) West Bromwich
1965	West Brom. Dartmouth	1974	) Dartmouth
1966	Moseley		
1967	) Walsall		
1968	)		

Highlights

29.7.61   Walsall 159
            Moseley 147
            With Moseley at 100—2, skipper John Heath gave Tom
            Pritchard (ex-Warwickshire paceman) permission to leave
            early and Moseley suffered their first defeat of the
            season, only batting 10 men.

25.8.62   Moseley won the title when they beat Mitchells &
            Butlers in the last match with both sides on the same
            number of points.
            Moseley 161 G. Thompson 48, J. Heath 30 n.o. R.
            Talbot 4—57.
            Mitchells & Butlers 123. R.E. Murrell 21, G.S. Mitchell
            34. B. Barratt 4—58. P. Morgan 3—31.

16.5.64   Moseley 142
            Old Hill 142 Tie. Old Hill recovered from 81—8 then
            the last man was out off last ball.

10.7.65   Old Hill 22. Roger Turner 7—8, Rufus Browne 3—12
            West Bromwich Dartmouth 26—0

17.7.65   Moseley 48 Bob Bates 5—9. Bob Sherriff, Moseley
            opener batted 2½hrs for 7 n.o. Rufus Browne was twice
            called by umpire Norman Downes for throwing — Rufus
            went on at the other end and was called again. He
            finished off the over under-arm, bowling a wide in the
            process.
            West Bromwich Dartmouth 49—2.

24.7.65   Smethwick 119 Bob Bates 6—42
            West Bromwich Dartmouth 121—8
            With the ground unfit Mike Simms and Alan Mackenzie
            went to Handsworth and purchased ex-army blankets at
            14/11 each to mop up pools of water so a start could be
            made at 4.00 p.m.

5.7.69   Kidderminster 120 were 89—0 when Paul Bailey took
            8—7 to finish 8—33
            Walsall 121—3 Roger Bender 58 not out.

13.6.70   In a match against Dudley, Roger Hamilton Brown,
            Aston Unity, was given out caught at the wicket. When
            he had reached the pavilion he was recalled only to be
            bowled next ball.

30.6.73   Moseley 132 Phil Beddow 5—46
            Walsall 84   Peter Morgan 9—22

Smethwick

1975–1987 YEARS OF CHANGE & NATIONAL SUCCESSES

Administration

The first major change was the decision in 1975 to enlarge the League by the admission of teams from Warwickshire and Worcestershire County Cricket Clubs. This necessitated lengthening the playing season and alterations to the League Rules to allow the County sides to play contracted players on their staffs, unlike in 1894 when only three professionals were permitted to play for Warwickshire Club and Ground.

Further changes in Club membership were enforced by the resignation of Worcestershire after the 1976 season, their replacements Duport after the 1981 season and Dudley following their tragic loss of their ground after the 1985 season. These changes gave opportunity for Worcester City in 1982 and Coventry and North Warwickshire in 1986 to join the League and extended the sphere of influence of the League on local cricket.

In 1976 the League also followed the lead of other sports organisations by seeking forms of sponsorship and came close to entering into an agreement with a foreign car manufacturer. Although the proposition was attractive it did not receive unanimous support from all the clubs at the centre of the British car industry and plans for the agreement were dropped.

In 1985 a group sponsorship was arranged with British Telecom who made a payment to each club, except the County Club, in exchange for the mounting of an advertisement board on each ground. The County Club was not included on account of their own commercial activities in this field.

A major change in the Administration was made in 1977 when the Advisory Committee was disbanded to be replaced by a Management Committee. Over the years the Advisory Committee under the Chairmanship of its founder 'Rusty' Scorer, had served the League economically and well but it had no place or function in the Rules of the League and it was felt by the Clubs that the time was opportune to create a committee with designated functions. The League Rules were amended to give effect to the formation of a Management Committee comprising six elected members together with the League President, President elect, Honorary Secretary and Honorary Treasurer. Its areas of responsibility for the day to day running of the League are now defined in the Rules and include the provision to adjudicate on matters of dispute.

The Management Committee faced such a dispute in 1985 when Greg Matthews, a former member of Old Hill and a member of the touring Australian Test side, was included in the Old Hill side when not required to play in the Test side. Greg scored 93 in a win against Moseley. The Management Committee ruled that he was ineligible and a League meeting supported the Committee and Old Hill were instructed to replay the game and had points deducted.

Jack Williams who had served as Hon. Secretary for thirteen years expressed his wish in 1977 to retire from the post and was succeeded by David Bryant the present holder of the position.

In 1983 the League took a step towards increasing the publicity it received by creating a new post of Publicity Officer, the post being filled with enthusiasm by John Allen, a long serving member of the West Bromwich Dartmouth Club. John captained the Dartmouth Second Eleven side to championships in 1963, 1965 and 1970.

Playing Time and Points

In 1981 the points for a win were increased from 3 to 5 and for a tied match from 1½ to 2½.

The growth in interest in limited over cricket in the seventies and eighties in both First Class and club cricket brought calls for similar arrangements in the League and, starting in 1983, fifty overs matches were introduced. Unlike most other competitions the League did not adopt the idea that games should be a purely win or lose situation and retained the award of points for a draw. The League also stipulated that no bowler should deliver the ball underarm. What would Billy Hollies have thought of this?

The points system was adjusted in 1983 to 10 points for a win, 6 for a side scoring most runs in a drawn game, 2 for the side scoring fewer runs in a drawn game, 5 for a tie where scores are level in an equal number of overs and 3 for a match abandoned before both sides had completed a minimum of 25 overs. To complement the change to 'overs' cricket an Instruction to Umpires was added giving the criterion for the judgement of a 'wide'.

For 1985 further amendments were made to allow a side declaring its innings to be able to use the overs not used in addition to the 50 overs allocated when they took the field. In 1984 the points for an abandoned match were reduced to 2. The need for the first of these amendments was highlighted by a game on 1st September 1984 when Warwickshire amassed 369—5 in their 50 overs against Walsall having been unable, according to the Rules, to declare. The reduction in points from 3 to 2 for an abandoned game was to remove the anomaly of sides in an abandoned game being able to obtain one more point than a side which had finished with fewer runs in a drawn game.

In 1975, with the season extended, provision was included for certain games at the beginning and end of the season to start and end 30 minutes before 'normal time' for the season and in 1976 'normal time' for start of play was changed from 2.15 to 2.00 p.m. The 1984 and 1985 last match championship deciding games were affected by failing light and provision was made in 1986 for each AGM to decide which games were to be started and finished one hour or half an hour earlier than the 'normal time'.

Slow Over Rates

The malaise of slow over rates affecting Test and County cricket had spread by the 1980's into the League cricket and in 1983

116

the League Rules made provision for umpires to report incidents of slow over rates. From 1984 a penalty was introduced of one point for each over bowled after a three hour limit or for restricted over games where the limit was to be based on 3½ minutes per over. This rule saw an improvement in the over rate as fielding captains kept one eye on the clock. The pressure on umpires was increased for, in addition to their normal duties, they now had to record and make allowance for any unforseen delays but in accord with their dedicated service to the game they have taken this duty in their stride and applied their jurisdiction in keeping with the spirit of cricket. Three clubs lost points in 1984, none in 1985 but in 1986 points deducted cost Warwickshire the title when losing five points in this way, mainly because of a proliferation of no balls, they finished one point only behind the champions, Walsall.

Overseas Players

Whilst the Test and County Cricket Board debate and legislate on the number of overseas players appearing in the County sides, similar problems have arisen in club cricket as a growing number of proficient overseas players seek experience in the English cricket scene. Such players can be retired first class cricketers who have always joined in the English game but numbers are now swelled by overseas professionals, players on cricket scholarships, players on exchange scholarship arrangements with County Clubs and players on extended holidays — all seeking to develop their talents and at the same time hoping to attract the notice of English County Clubs. High quality young performers who have played in recent years include Graham Yallop and Greg Matthews from Australia, Graeme Hick from Zimbabwe and Brian McMillan a South African. Graham Yallop became captain of the Australian side whilst Brian McMillan returned for a season contracted to Warwickshire. It is pleasing to note that Graeme Hick, quickly a popular member of the Kidderminster side has decided to dedicate his career with the object of being accepted eventually as an English player. Since 1986 he has been delighting spectators at Worcestershire matches with his free-scoring batting. In 1986 season he became the youngest player to score 2,000 runs in a season in First Class Cricket breaking a record previously held by Len Hutton.

The number of overseas players was beginning to limit opportunities for young local talent and in 1986 a rule was introduced to the effect that Clubs could play one nominated overseas player only. The term 'overseas' was to apply to an overseas national who had not been fully resident in the U.K. for two years prior to the season in which he wished to play. For 1987 the rule was tightened further to ensure that only one overseas player could play irrespective of whether he was a Club player, Paid player or Contracted player.

Wicket Covers

From time to time the League had stressed the need for clubs to provide wicket covers and, indeed, most clubs had done so even though good covers can be expensive and on club grounds always difficult to maintain and store. On open grounds they could also be subject to vandalism. In 1980, the League Rules stipulated that provision of covers was mandatory.

Practice During Games

In 1980, an Instruction to Umpires was issued banning practice once play had begun. This was a re-introduction of the rule which had been deleted in 1950. The rule had formerly been introduced in 1900 after spectators had been hurt by a ball hit from a practice net.

Objects of the League

The Objects of the League were stated in a new form in 1986.
"Objective
To promote that which is best for the development of cricket within the geographical area of the League. High standards of performance, sportsmanship and playing facilities whilst preparing the best young players for County Cricket."

Awards

In 1977 Norman Downes offered a diamond ring value £1000 to any bowler taking ten wickets in the First Division and a £500 ring for a similar feat in the Second Division. Neither award was claimed but a number of players benefited from Norman's contribution of a crate of two dozen bottles of beer to the 'Man of the Match'.

Jock Livingston instigated in 1978 an annual award of three cricket bats to young players. The Management Committee was to nominate one player from the annual game League Junior XI v Coventry League, the other two to under 21 players selected from nominations submitted by the Clubs. The first winners of these awards were Martin Wright, Moseley, Bob Dyer, Aston Unity and Steve Bill, Warwickshire.

Playing Scene 1975—1987

League clubs were to gain National distinction in the 1980's by winning the National Cricket Association Trophy on five occasions. Moseley won in 1980, Old Hill in 1984, 1985 and 1987 and Stourbridge in 1986. These successes achieved against the best nationwide opposition have confirmed the high standard of cricket enjoyed in the League which has been described by Mushtaq Mohammad as the strongest competition.

Batsmen who quickly took advantage of the extra League matches from 1975 to enable them to join the 1,000 run makers in a season were Graham Yallop, (Walsall), 1152 runs and C.L. Price (Aston Unity) 1093 runs. These both achieved the feat in 1975. Doug Slade (West Bromwich Dartmouth) did not need the extra games in 1978 when he passed the thousand mark in only fifteen innings to finish, after 20 innings, with a record of 1407 runs, with the most centuries (7) ever recorded in a season. It was to be another six seasons, 1984 before the thousand was again attained this time by Graeme Hick, (Kidderminster), 1234 runs and Ian Stokes, (Moseley) 1236 runs.

Kidderminster

Kidderminster were the first side to carry off the championship in a twenty-two match season winning the League in 1975 and having another good season to finish joint runners up to Walsall in 1976. Peter Harris, Peter Jones, Stephen Johnson, Godfrey Lamb, Roy Barker, Keith Wood and newcomer Colin Hemsley provided the batting strength. John Aldridge, Derek Oliver and Peter Jones took most wickets with help from all-rounder Colin Hemsley and energetic Ernie King. The side was decimated after the 1976 season when Roy Barker, Peter Jones, Peter Harris and Colin Hemsley left to join Duport and Stephen Johnson and Derek Oliver left. The reformed side with Godfrey Lamb, Ernie King, John Aldridge, Peter Radburn, Tim Oakley, John Rose, Derek Telling, Brian Cowley, Geoff Hayes and Dr. Hugh Bradby did well to hold on to a middle of the table position. With further changes the next best position was third place in 1984 when stalwarts Godfrey Lamb, Peter Radburn and Brian Cowley were stimulated by the arrival of 18 year old Graeme Hick on a cricket scholarship with Worcestershire. Graeme broke the club batting record and the hearts of most of the opposition bowlers. Unfortunately for Kidderminster, his exploits with the bat led to his call up by Worcestershire towards the end of the League season and the club's title hopes foundered. Other players who had also joined the side were Mike Wilkinson, Damian Jones, David Stephens, Delvin King, Peter Iddon, Paul Proctor, Horace Palmer and Geoff Parry whilst Club Secretary Graham Capper moved in from the second eleven to pick up wickets. Graeme Hick made an auspicious start to his League career when, in the first match of the 1984 season, he was instrumental in Kidderminster recording a good win against Mitchells and Butlers.

Mitchells and Butlers 205–6 M. Green 50. G. Warner 68
Kidderminster 206–4 P. Proctor 62. G.A. Hick 80

Two weeks later he was to record the highest score for Kidderminster in the First Division, the highest since W.E. Merritts 197 in 1940.

Kidderminster 309–4, G.A. Hick 182 n.o. (19, 4's 3, 6's.) M. Wilkinson 83
Moseley 159–7, B. Hylton 51 n.o.

By the end of the season he had scored 1234 runs and was presented with a silver salver by the Club in recognition of a new club record. He also received a 'Primary Club' tie to mark one first ball dismissal.

Worcestershire

Worcestershire's short spell in the League meant a call up of a number of their players already with Clubs in the League. Ravindera Senghera from Smethwick, Keith Wilkinson and Paul Pridgeon from Stourbridge, and Paul Roberts from Kidderminster, joined Ivan Johnson, Rodney Cass, Barry Jones, Cedric Boyns, Norman Whiting, Gordon Wilcox, Phil Neale, Ian Rutherford, Carl Bates and P. Westaway to form the backbone of the players to call upon. With their small playing staff they had to supplement contracted players with local club players to field a side and in the two seasons fielded over forty players. Their problems were also aggravated by having to use an alternative venue to the County Ground in order to fit in with County fixtures. Phil Neale, to become Worcestershire's captain, scored two successive centuries in 1975 in what were probably the club's best performances in the League.

26th July 1975 Dudley 174–9 I.N. Johnson 2–27
Worcestershire 175–2 P.A. Neale 102 n.o. B.J.R. Jones 36

2nd August 1975 Moseley 222–8 J.F. Taylor 71 P.A. Pridgeon 3–40 I.N. Johnson 3–54 C.N. Boyns 2–21
Worcestershire 226–3 P.A. Neale 146 n.o. B.Jones 39

Owing to a Worcestershire transport problem the latter match started 15 minutes late with Worcestershire only fielding 7 men for a time. The 1976 season was marked by Worcestershire's success in the Benson and Hedges Competition when they reached the Final only to lose to Kent. On the 17th July, the day of the Final, the County were due to meet Kidderminster at Kidderminster. The Club were anxious to share the day with all their staff but were unable to agree a mutually acceptable alternative date with Kidderminster. The League ruled that the game should be played. In the event Worcestershire did not field a side and Kidderminster, who had turned out for the game, were awarded three points. This conflict of fixtures was the first to arise in the League's history but was to become a more regular occurrence with the success of Warwickshire, Moseley, Old Hill and Stourbridge in National Competitions so that re-arrangement of fixtures for such an event has become an accepted practice. The same dispensation has not applied when the local soccer sides have reached the Football Association Cup Final as Coventry and North Warwickshire found in 1987.

Walsall

Walsall were the 1976 champions and were to repeat their success in 1980, 1982 and 1986. In each of the seasons they kept their supporters on tenterhooks until the last matches of the season. On September 4th 1976, they met championship contenders West Bromwich Dartmouth at Gorway, holding a one point lead. The game started badly for Dartmouth who had to shuffle their batting order because players had been delayed on the motorway. Richard Boothroyd compounded their problems by twice taking two wickets in one over to finish with 6—35 as Dartmouth struggled to 100, David Humphries making top score with 29. Dartmouth fought back and, with six wickets down for 67 and Doug Slade with four wickets, Walsall were rescued by a masterly knock by Nick Archer, who compiled a neat 31 not out to bring victory by 3 wickets, the winning runs coming from four overthrows. 1980 was not so traumatic. An eight wicket win against bottom club, Duport, was enough to maintain a two point lead over Old Hill. Moseley had to be overcome in 1982 to hold off a challenge from Mitchells and Butlers. Walsall's hero on this occasion was Mushtaq Mohammad, the Pakistani Test star, as the scorecard shows:—

Moseley 149 A Moles 38 M.Mohammad 3 —35 D. Nicholls 2—20 R. Archer 3—42
Walsall 150—5 recovering from 36—4, M. Mohammad 66 n.o. D. Shipp 37, S. Coley 3—38, P. Davis 2—37.

In season 1986, the leadership in the last month passed from Coventry and North Warwickshire to Moseley, then to Walsall, and from them to Warwickshire, whilst Stourbridge had sufficient games in hand to overtake them all. Walsall, having lost in this period to both Coventry and Warwickshire, thought their chance had gone but, when the results came through on the last day, all the contenders had faltered and a Walsall win at Worcester City saw them scrape home by one point with 132 points to Warwickshire's 131.

This win was achieved as a result of a courageous declaration by skipper Derek Nicholls. With Walsall on 189—3 off only 44 overs he declared to give his bowlers six extra overs to dismiss Worcester City. John Moore and Bob Whitehouse 54 not out having batted well for Walsall. Worcester were dismissed for 97 in

49.4 overs, Dilip Doshi taking four early wickets and Richard Boothroyd polishing off the innings with the last four wickets for five runs when Worcester seemed set to hold out. Although they had won the match Walsall still had to await news from the Warwickshire and Stourbridge games. On hearing that they had won the title they rushed back to share in the celebrations at Gorway. Meanwhile the first intimation of their success which reached Gorway was the arrival of Bert Latham, the League President, with the Cup.

Bert had spent all afternoon awaiting the outcome of the three games and by the time it was known it had been too late to make the journey to Worcester.

The Walsall stalwarts in all these successes were Derek Nicholls, Nick Archer, Phil Brown and Richard Boothroyd, with Terry Rawlinson and Tom Pearsall stepping up from the Second Eleven from time to time from 1977. Mike Greenhough, Trevor Aston, Alan Conway and Hamilton Jones, Tony Durose and Bob Sylvester were additional members of the 1976 side. The back up to the long serving club men in the 1980 and 1982 successes was provided by Roy Virgin, John Aldridge, John Golightly, Peter Whitehead, Des Shipp, Richard Archer and in 1982 by Mushtaq Mohammad, Andy Gibbens, Australian Malcolm Dolman and Chris Parr.

Roy Virgin was an extremely popular club man from 1978 to 1983, his immaculate batting contributing 4041 runs in League games in the period with 851 in the 1980 success.

The back up to the long serving club men had completely changed by 1986, newcomers being Steve Jenkinson, John Moore, Lawrence Smith, Nick Marsh, Lloyd Tennant, Andy Mackleworth, Bob Whitehouse and the fine bowling of Indian Test Star Dilip Doshi. Dilip could be depended on to bowl twenty-five tight overs in each game and topped the League wicket-takers with 75 wickets in the championship year, following up 69 in the previous season. The 75 was the highest for the club since Danny Mayer took 79 in 1943. A further success which augurs well for the future of the Walsall Club has been the number of winning sides the Club have fielded for three years running 1984—1986 inclusive in the National Cricket Association Under 15 Competitions. Wayne Law and Ashley Perry are two such youngsters who have won First Team places in 1987.

Stourbridge

Stourbridge put themselves in the forefront of the League's Centenary Celebrations by winning all three Divisions in 1987, having won the National Cricket Knock Out Competition in 1986. As that season drew to a close they had looked certain candidates for the League title but the excitement of a Final at Lords probably affected their League performances, for they faltered in the crucial final games of a tightly contested climax to the season. Stourbridge had no such problem in 1987 clinching the title with two matches to spare. The season had been disrupted by bad weather four weeks being completely washed out, but they creditably notched up thirteen wins out of the eighteen games played.

The 1987 season did not open too well with an early defeat in a low scoring match at Old Hill on May 16th. Having dismissed Old Hill for 96 they were shot out for 78.

Old Hill 96 Mushtaq Mohammad 41 Gordon Smith 4—40, Stuart Lampitt 5—38
Stourbridge 78 Stuart Lampitt 43 Mark Frost 7—47, Andy Webster 3—29

A convincing win against Aston Unity at the end of May then set off a winning sequence which secured the title and included a notable victory against Walsall.

Walsall 200 Nick Archer 64, Lawrence Smith 39, G. Smith 3—67
Stourbridge 201—5 David Banks 55 n.o., Chris Tolley 41 n.o. Dilip Doshi 3—78

The 1986 and 1987 successes were achieved by sides with a useful blend of youth and experience which brought together the best side Stourbridge had enjoyed for many years. The experience was provided by Gordon Smith who had joined the Club from Dudley to seal up one end with a steady and accurate spin attack, Graham Saint, wicket keeper from Smethwick and batsman Harshad Patel from West Bromwich Dartmouth.

Gordon Smith captained the 1986 side and David Banks took over for 1987 to blend together Australian Ross Stephen, Tony Lea, Jonathon Wright, Stuart Lampitt, Chris Tolley, Mike Brewer, Paul Fox, G. Haynes, C. Houghton-Smith and Club President Barry Corbett. It was fitting that Barry who gave the club many years service and financial assistance should be at the wicket when the run was scored which secured the Championship.

Another club stalwart to join in the celebrations was Dave Collins, for many years the club wicket keeper and in 1987 Club Secretary. In the early 1980's, Dave had given encouragement and coaching to a young wicket keeper prodigy Phil Whitticase, who was signed by Leicestershire in 1984 having joined Stourbridge when he was barely big enough to see over the pads!

Other players who served the club over the period were Roger Hargreaves, Frank Wright, Keith Wilkinson, Bob Sidaway, Mick Wooldridge, Alan Richardson, David Burrows, Steve Brookes and opening bat Martin Hill, whose consistent batting was missed when he left the district. In the same period, Chris Derham, David Grosvenor and George Bentley had spells in the First Eleven. Simon O'Donnell the Australian Test Player turned out in the 1986 season.

Two of Stourbridge's best performances in the late 1970's were achieved against the Warwickshire sides in 1978 and 1979. On 26th August, 1978 the top of the table Warwickshire side visited lowly Stourbridge, needing just one win to make sure that their big lead in the table was invincible. Stourbridge, batting first, were reduced to 48—4 but John Inchmore 41, Frank Wright 21 and Martin Hill 29 saw them through to respectable 169—9, Richard Savage taking 5—50. Paceman John Inchmore 4—24 and Steve Brookes 5—30 soon had the young Warwickshire side in trouble and they were all out for 95, with Extras 28, top score. It did however, take the Stourbridge attack 35 minutes to prise out the last pair, Ian White and Steve Bill. To crown this Stourbridge had no difficulty removing the Warwickshire batsmen at Edgbaston the following June when they dismissed them for their lowest score in the League, 49.

Warwickshire 49 Andy Lloyd 19 Greg Watson 5—13 Martin Saunders 4—25
Stourbridge 50—5 Gladstone Small 2—5

Stourbridge – Winners of Younger Trophy 1986

J. Huband, G. Haynes, P. Fox, J.P. Wright, K. Jones, G. Saint, D. Collins, M. Rowley (Scorer)
C. Tolley, S. Lampitt, D.A. Banks, G. Smith (cpt.) H. Patel, M. Brewer, A. Lea.

To add to their triple success in the League in 1987 their Under 16 side won the Alpine Trophy to bring to a close the most successful season in the Club's history.

Old Hill

Old Hill were to achieve a title in 1983 after occupying the runners up position in 1977, 1978 and 1980.   They then capped these successes by winning the National Cricket Association Knock Out Trophy in two successive seasons, 1984 and 1985 and again in 1987.

Such notable national success can only be achieved by a strong all round side, playing with enthusiasm and backed up by a good club spirit.   This the Old Hill Club has in good measure and opponents can always be assured of a hard fought contest.

Keith Wilkinson, who moved to the club from Stourbridge in 1977, became a strong influence in the side with his consistent batsmanship allied to a flair for captaincy, which brought the best out of his team.   Roy Keeling, Peter Bagley, Alan Brookes and Graham Stockley featured throughout the period, with Bernard Rowley, Tom Pearsall, David Nutt, Ron Headley, John Swinburne, Nigel Smith, Steve Thompson, Dave Flavell and long-serving Geoff Eley in the late 1970's.   The 1980's saw the introduction of Cedric Boyns, Steve Walker, Colin Hemsley, Phil Oliver, Frank Watson, Mark Frost, Andy Webster, Bob Lanchbury, Steve Derham and international stars Greg Matthews and Mushtaq Mohammad. Mushtaq had been instrumental in the title success of Walsall in 1982 and moved to Old Hill to repeat the act in 1983 when Old Hill led for most of the season, except for a short spell when Dudley, the eventual runners up, took over.   Old Hill signified their intentions when, in the first two weeks of May 1983, they demonstrated bowling strength against West Bromwich Dartmouth and batting strength against Walsall.

7th May West Bromwich Dartmouth 72 in 25 overs G. Parker 25 P. Bagley 9—19 J. Day 1—23
Old Hill 73—2 K. Wilkinson 49 n.o.
14th May Walsall 252—6 S. Mohammad 66 S. Jenkinson 61   D. Nicholls 56 n.o.
Old Hill 256—5 M. Mohammad 104 n.o.   G. Matthews 49   C. Hemsley 44 D. Nicholls 3—43

In the season Greg Matthews created a new club record when he scored 937 runs.

In 1977 Old Hill pressed the champions Aston Unity to the last game of the season and featured in two high scoring games against Smethwick and Mitchells and Butlers.

21st May 1977 Smethwick 251—1 N. Moore 141 T. Binks 93
Old Hill 253—4 R.G.A. Headley 112 n.o. R. Keeling 42

4th June Old Hill 253—2 K. Wilkinson 162 n.o. R. Biddle 45
Mitchells & Butlers 103 W. Howard 41 G. Warner 35 J. Swinburne 5—16 B. Rowley 4—40

A year later on 10th June 1978 Old Hill's batting strength carried them to a notable victory over Aston Unity:—

Aston Unity 239—7 H. Yarnold 91 P. Junkin 60
Old Hill 240—1 K. Wilkinson 126 n.o. R.G.A. Headley 74 n.o.

124

OLD HILL
WILLIAM YOUNGER CUP 1984

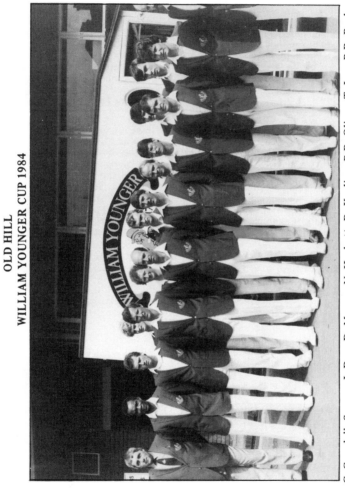

C. Cowdell, Scorer, J. Day, D. Mayne, N. Hackett, R. Keeling, P.R. Oliver, T. Lea, P.R. Bagley, R.G.A. Headley, F. Watson, C.N. Boyns, C. Hemsley, K.W. Wilkinson, A.E. Brookes, G.A. Stockley, S.A. Walker.

West Bromwich Dartmouth

West Bromwich Dartmouth were unable to achieve a title in the period, the longest lean spell since the pre 1930 period. The Club were nevertheless always in contention for League honours finishing second on four occasions, 1975, 1976, 1981 and 1985. In 1975 and 1985 they lost close title deciders against the eventual champions, Walsall and Moseley respectively. In the first, they were handicapped when their batting order had to be shuffled due to players being held up on the motorway. In the second, when led for the season by David Steele, they needed to win at Moseley. Moseley batted first and scored 197—6 Ian Stokes 54 Bob Milne 44. Dartmouth responded in fine style with Paul Humphries 71 and Harshad Patel 31 sharing an opening stand of 107. The light was, however, failing and as wickets fell new batsmen could not cope with the bowling of Simon Coley, Andy Moles and Brian McMillan, and Dartmouth could only muster 183. By the time the game finished the scorers were unable to determine how the last wicket fell.

Alan Neal was a dependable opening bat until he left to join Aston Unity in 1985 but he and Douglas Slade had formed a powerful opening partnership in the 1970's. Doug Slade broke all league batting records in 1978 when he scored 1407 runs with 7 centuries average in 20 innings of 117.25. His overall record in the League with Dartmouth was exceptional, with over 6,500 runs and 270 wickets in nine seasons. Doug Slade, Alan Neal and bowler Carlton Christie had support in the 1970's from batsman wicket-keeper David Humphries, batsmen Mike Edmundson, Barry Abel and Martin Schepens and bowlers Terry Spencer, Max Field, Tony Waheed and David York. These were succeeded by batsmen Harshad Patel, Gary Parker, Coshic Patel, Dr. Hugh Bradby and Abid Din and bowlers Geoff Edmunds, Ian Denning and John Wootton. Vanburn Holder had one season in 1981 taking 58 wickets but bowling 182 no balls!

Geoff Edmunds captained the side in 1984 and played a captain's part in the attack, taking 63 wickets with his best performance at Smethwick when he helped dismiss the home side for 71. After an opening stand of 37 Geoff put himself on and in 13.4 overs took 7 wickets for 8 runs, the last 4 for 0. Dartmouth won by 8 wickets. Smethwick had featured in another collapse the previous season. Dartmouth, batting first, had recovered from 94—5 to score 243—8 Mark Scott 76 Geoff Edmunds 37, then Smethwick were all out for 167, their last four wickets falling in 8 balls. Barry Matthews was the successful bowler taking 3 for 5 in his last over.

Smethwick

The frailty in depth of Smethwick's batting and a need for more penetration in the bowling, accounted for Smethwick's lack of success in this period.

The club still provided plenty of entertainment and surprises for their members especially in May 1978. On the 13th May Smethwick were dismissed by Moseley for 159 after being 102—2, Neville Moore 64, David Derricott 41 n.o. Bert Latham taking 5—45 including 3 in 4 balls. Moseley in reply were 110—1 when Neil Penton also took 3 in 4 balls for Moseley to collapse to 150 all out. Harold Turner 71, Rob Milne 30, Neil Penton 5—26, Tim Hawkes 2—31. At home to Warwickshire, on 29th May, Smethwick went into tea facing a visitors total of 241—6 declared, Gary Thomas

Doug. Slade 1978
Birmingham and District Cricket League

Inns.	N.O.	Runs	Highest Score	Average
20	8	1407	118 N.O.	117.25

54, Andy Lloyd 42, Phil Oliver 46, Errol Simms 5—81. Refreshed by the tea, Neville Moore crashed a quick 76 then his partner Guy Thompson 81 not out and Tim Binks 80 not out carried on the good work to take Smethwick to an exciting victory by nine wickets 242—1 in only 45.3 overs.

In June 1981 it was Kidderminster's turn to be surprised. A total of 243—4 seemed safe after Godfrey Lamb 94 and David Stephens 56 had added 124 for the 4th wicket. Neville Moore and Tim Binks were this time dismissed for 23 and 24 respectively but Bippin Patel 94 not out, Neil Penton 37, and Derek Kallicharran 33 not out saw Smethwick to 245—5 and a win by 5 wickets. Derek Kallicharran is a younger brother of West Indian Test Star Alvin Kallicharran.

Long serving players in the period were Neil Penton, Tim Binks, Dave Derricott, Tim Hawkes, Abid Din, Peter Rose, Guy Thompson, Graham Saint, Mike Satchwell, David Bastable, Neville Moore, Errol Simms and Carlton Green. John Jameson returned to play for one season in 1977, before becoming a First Class umpire.

Changes in the playing strength in the 1983—4 seasons saw the entry of Gerry Smith, Winslow Howard, Greg Watson and the attractive stroke player Amarjit Kaypee. Roy Freeman, a member of the 1955 side, could still, in 1979, pick up three catches in a defeat of Mitchells and Butlers.

Mitchells & Butlers

Mitchells and Butlers were only once to get into the reckoning for championship honours. That was in 1982 when they finished second, being held off by Walsall winning their last match as Mitchells beat Stourbridge to maintain their challenge to the end. Gary Thomas, a youngster with the club before he became a prolific scorer with Warwickshire in the League, rejoined the club that season to add skill and dependability to the batting of Graham Warner, Mick Green, Tony Willis, Paul Venness and Winslow Howard. John Weston, Darren Shorter, Kanak Patel took most of the wickets, assisted by Paul Venness, Mick Stocker and John Corbett. Long serving Derek Robinson, together with Peter Tresham, Geoff Parker and Earl Harris, left the first eleven scene in the early 1980's, whilst in the following years, Tom O'Donnell, Joe Benjamin, Ivan Hutchings and John White joined the playing strength together with Neville Moore from Smethwick.

Both Gary Thomas and Neville Moore celebrated their first appearance against their old clubs with reminders of their batting prowess, although each time they finished on the losing side. On 1st May 1982 Gary Thomas scored 114 not out in a Mitchells total of 254—3 against Warwickshire. Warwickshire, however, totalled 257—5 with Dennis Amiss scoring 71 and Simon Wootton 76. On 12th May 1984 it was Neville Moore's chance to face his old club, Smethwick. Neville crashed 125 in his inimitable style in a Mitchells total of 213—8. Smethwick responded with 216—8, David Westwood 99 just failing to get his first century.

Mitchells featured in a splendid win against Warwickshire at Edgbaston in May 1976. Batting first Mitchells scored 257 aided by a swashbuckling innings of 150 by 'Alf' Masood which included 4 — 6's and 26 — 4's and ranks as one of the most exciting League innings seen on the ground. Peter Lewington with 5—56 and David Hopkins 4—81 returned bowling analyses which were good in the circumstances. Warwickshire's batsmen were soon in trouble facing the bowling of Peter Walker 4–33, and John Weston 4–32 (4–1 at one time) and were all out for 114, David Smith 28.

Graham Warner, who joined Mitchells in 1973, has contributed over 500 runs each season, in immaculate style, and also brought excellent sportsmanship to the game and dedicated undemonstrative enthusiasm. On 28th May 1977, he led Mitchells to a splended win at Kidderminster.

Kidderminster 245–4 Geoff Hayes 111 not out, his maiden century, Ernie King 54
Mitchells and Butlers 247–3 Graham Warner 120 not out, Geoff Parker 62.

Aston Unity

Aston Unity finished the 1970's in style, winning the title in 1977 and finishing second in the following two seasons. The 1980's saw a dramatic slump in their fortunes as they slipped to be bottom of the table in five of the last six years. Colin Price is the only player whose name appears in the scorebook in every season. In the 1977 success he was joined by batsmen Robert Ingram, John Gough, Tony Butler, Mike Edmundson with support from Howard Yarnold, Mike Dolby and John Kennedy. Geoff Jackson, Geoff Ward, Peter Moran and all rounder Paul Junkin took the wickets, to bring success. The opposition only socred more than two hundred runs on two occasions, thus relieving the pressure on the Unity batsmen. The bowlers came to the rescue of the side in a crucial match at Walsall. Unity only scraped 85 against Tony Durose 6–47, and Derek Nicholls 4–15. When Walsall replied Paul Junkin 5–41 and Geoff Jackson 4–31 set Walsall on the slide and dismissed them for 85 also, the game finishing on a knife edge as the last two Walsall wickets fell at that score. The 1½ points obtained for the tie were the margin by which Unity finished clear leaders over Old Hill. On the last day of the season with a win needed against West Bromwich Dartmouth, the other challengers for the title who strengthened their side by bringing back Paddy Clift, the Unity bowlers again ensured an emphatic win achieved by nine wickets:–

West Bromwich Dartmouth 96 Ghulam Sherali 47 n.o. Paul Junkin 3–21, Geoff Jackson 4–25, Peter Moran 3–26
Aston Unity 97–1 Tony Butler 47, John Gough 27 n.o.

As the 1980's progressed, a number of new faces appeared, Steve Bayliss, Ivan Hutchings, John Peace, Chris Callaghan, Chris Davies, Gordon Harrys and Alan Watton, but the side could not settle into any rhythm, with the constant change of faces which normally accompanies lack of success.

On 30th May 1981, a Unity bowler again dominated a game at Walsall. Unity were all out for 120, Derek Nicholls 4–51, Mushtaq Mohammad 3–26. Gordon 'Red' Harrys then took 9–42 in 21.3 overs to dismiss Walsall for 105, Roy Virgin 29, Mushtaq Mohammad 26. On the first match of 1983 'Wooden Spoonists' Aston Unity scored 113–5, Ivan Hutchings 29, Chris Callaghan 20 n.o. and in a rain restricted match dismissed champions Walsall for 76, Phil Brown 28. This success was not to be a portent of better times for Unity, for they did not win again until 23rd June 1984 when they beat Smethwick.

Smethwick 206–6. P. Conway 100 n.o. I. Irvine 39
Aston Unity 209–6. I. Hutchings 50, M. Miles 50 C.L. Price 58 n.o.

In 1985, Alan Neal the veteran West Bromwich Dartmouth batsman and 1986 President of the League, joined the club following on the arrival of Errol Simms from Smethwick. With a number of promising youngsters including Craig Price, Jared Connop, Garry Steer and Andy Stevenson together with new players David Abell, Peter Davis, and Andy Samuels the Club look forward to an improvement in their fortunes.

Dudley

Dudley's playing fortunes were the reverse of those of Aston Unity, for they rose from the bottom of the table in the late 1970's to win the title in 1981. This success could be attributed to the return of Ron Headley to his first League Club after an absence of 21 years. Following their poor showing in the League in the 1970's Dudley, in 1980, invited Ron to leave Old Hill and take over as professional to coach and blend together a generally young side which contained a leaven of experience provided by Gordon Smith, Mel Green and Alan Richardson. In the 1981 success, Gordon Smith provided the guile in the slow bowling, taking 61 wickets backed up by Chris Green, whilst all-rounder Joe Benjamin provided an enthusiastic fast assault backed with support from John Aldridge, Ralph Oakley and all rounder Aren Singh. The batting was in the capable hands of Ron Headley, Alan Smith, Mel Green and Steve Henderson with useful contributions from Alan Grace, Philip Page and Bob Crossland. Dudley's success was ensured when, with two weeks to go, they emphatically defeated West Bromwich Dartmouth, their nearest challengers, completing a run of 6 wins. Their most comprehensive win of the season occurred on 11th July.

Dudley 205−8, Aren Singh 107 n.o. Alan Warner 4−71
Mitchells & Butlers 77, Joe Benjamin 4−29 John Aldridge 3−30, Gordon Smith 3−14

Gordon Smith, who first appeared in Dudley's side in 1960, had a good start to the season in 1978. Dudley batting first at Moseley were all out for 103, Alan Grace 49. Moseley were 59−2 when Gordon took 6 wickets for 1 run for Moseley to finish 73 all out. Gordon taking 7−13 off 10 overs. He followed this up in 1979 by reducing Kidderminster from 40−1 to 101 all out, his contribution being 8−11. Dudley won this game by 6 wickets.

Players to feature for Dudley in the late 1970's, who did not share in the 1980 success, were long serving Gerry Kendrick and Don Jones with Bill Hicklin, Bob Barlow, Ken Price, Tony Willis, John Lampitt and Dick Macey. New-comers to the side from 1981 being T. Hagger, Mike Moseley, Bill Kelleher, Stuart Lampitt, Mark Frost, Simon Kimber, Andy Pearson, Mark Sedgley and in Dudley's last season Brian Barrett, professional Peter Lee, and wicket-keeper Jason Robinson. The revitalisation of the club started in the 1980's was, however, to be terminated by the subsidence caused by old limestone workings. This left the club with no ground and no option but to resign from the League, after a membership stretching back to 1893, a decision very much regretted by the member clubs.

Moseley

Moseley were another side to have a lean time as the 1970's closed, dropping to ninth place in 1979 as long serving players David Heath, Roy Abell, Keith Jones and Dick Chase withdrew from the first eleven and Gordon Harrys left to join Aston Unity. Mike Cheslin, Harold Turner, Basil Hylton, Jack Watts and Peter Davis teamed up with Bert Latham, John Taylor, Bob Milne and Nick Perrin to take the side into the 1980's.

The new era started well, with Moseley, in 1980, becoming the first League side to win the National Cricket Association Knock Out Trophy.

With the introduction of Ian Stokes, Malcolm Eustace, Earl Harris, Neil Devenport, Andy Moles, Simon Coley and later Graham Plimmer and in 1985 the return of Gordon Harrys, the side under the leadership of Harold Turner achieved championship honours in 1984 and 1985. In these two seasons they had effective assistance from South African all rounders, Craig Norris, 1984 and Brian McMillan, 1985, who were in England on cricket scholarships.

Ian Stokes, as opener, laid the basis for the batting in 1984, scoring 1236 runs in the season with six centuries. Andy Moles, Jack Watts, Craig Norris and Basil Hylton were the other major contributors. The bowling department was led by Craig Norris, Simon Coley, Harold Turner and Andy Donner, whilst Graham Plimmer proved an efficient successor to the expert wicket-keeper John Taylor. The 1985 side saw Brian McMillan take over Craig Norris's mantle as all rounder. Bob Milne and Earl Harris featured in the batting averages and Gordon Harrys added aggression when sharing the opening attack with Simon Coley.

In both 1984 and 1985 there was a nail-biting climax to the season. On 8th September 1984, Moseley needed to beat Warwickshire to be sure of the title whilst the other title chasers, Worcester City and Kidderminster were locked in battle at Worcester. The games aroused the attention of Radio West Midlands who provided the commentaries and up to date scores of both games. As the tension mounted a following programme was cancelled to give extended coverage of the exciting climax to the season. Warwickshire, prompted by a score of 144 from Geoff Tedstone and a quick 44 from Wayne Matthews soon made it clear that, barring a mammoth score, all Moseley would get was a draw. Warwickshire scored 287–6. Harold Turner opened with Ian Stokes and although they scored 45 and 49 respectively they were never up with the scoring rate and had to settle for a draw at 165–4. Eventually news came through from Worcester that bad light had stopped play and Moseley were declared as champions. Bad light again virtually decided the 1986 title when Moseley beat West Bromwich Dartmouth, as described under the Dartmouth account.

When Moseley met Aston Unity on 2nd July 1977, a minutes silence was observed during the tea interval as a tribute to Alex Thornhill who had died suddenly during the previous month. Alex was a playing member of the Moseley Club from 1975, having previously played for Aston Unity from 1969–1974.

On 15th May 1982, Bert Latham took 3–53 against Warwickshire to bring his total wickets in the First Division to 1,000. Bert had the additional satisfaction of taking the wicket on the Edgbaston ground, the home of the County Club for which he had played and always supported. Andy Moles' consistent batting from 1982 to 1986 earned him a contract with Warwickshire in 1986.

Duport

When Duport took the place of Worcestershire in the First Division in 1977 they accepted that it would not be good enough to promote their Second Eleven, even though they had performed creditably in that Division. Consequently Duport signed up a number of players from other clubs led by Peter Harris, Peter Jones, Roy Barker and Colin Hemsley from Kidderminster and Frank Wright from Stourbridge, with Robin Hobbs, the former Essex leg spinner, joining as professional. The side with Magan Patel, Jayanti Patel, Gordon Wilcox and fast bowlers Nigel Wilson and John Buttress finished ninth in the table. Keith Jones, the former Middlesex player, then moved from Dudley to replace Robin Hobbs as professional and the side was supplemented by Dick Macey, S. Ledgister, Dave Webb and A. Richards but after finishing bottom of the table from 1979—1981 the Club resigned from the League. A notable day in their short period in the League was 22nd July 1978 when two of their batsmen scored a century.

Duport 248—3 H.G. Wilcox 119 S. Ledgister 105
Smethwick 189—8 P. Rose 54 N. Wilson 5—48

Then, on Sunday 31st August 1980, they met National Knock Out champions Moseley in a fixture re-arranged from the 23rd when Moseley had won the National title at Lords. Duport were dismissed for 83, Andy Donner 7—17, but fought back to dismiss Moseley for 54, John Buttress 7—29, and register their first win in two seasons.

Worcester City

Worcester City were voted into the League to replace Duport in the 1982 season and quickly made an impression when they were able to hold a strong Old Hill side.

Old Hill 251—5 M. Weston 138 C.N. Boyns 33
Worcester City 188—6 D. Slade 78 D. D'Oliveira 47 D. Mayne 5—60

The following week they were to beat Kidderminster.

Kidderminster 194—7 E. King 50. D. King 51 n.o. G. Parry 5—50
D. D'Oliveira 2—29
Worcester City 196—2 D. Slade 82 n.o. D. Walker 47

Doug Slade was to again be a League success with bat and ball and with Damian D'Oliveira, Derek Walker, Geoff Parry, Trevor Davies, Trevor Riddings, Steve Watkins and John Elliott, it is likely that they would have pressed the leaders more closely had all rounder Ian Rone been able to play instead of being side-lined by an injury in the first game. Worcester's challenge for the championship in 1984, faded in the bad light of the last game against Kidderminster. In that season, although Doug Slade had retired and Damian D'Oliveira was full-time at Worcestershire, the side included New Zealander Pat Hounsell, a prolific scoring batsman, Paul Bent, Phil Newport, Steve McEwan and Colin Groves. Two memorable games in 1984 were against Aston Unity and Moseley.

28th May 1984
Worcester City 164—4 P. Newport 60, I. Rone 58 n.o. G. Harrys 2—50
Aston Unity 23, M. Chapman 6 n.o. P. Newport 6—10, S. McEwan 4—9

7th July 1984
Worcester City 231—6, P. Hounsell 56, S. Watkins 70, I. Rone 45, C. Norris 3—58
Moseley 231—6, I Stokes 115, M. Eustace 49, D. Walker 2—51,

S. Watkins 2—3

When Worcester City met Aston Unity in the return fixture, on 11th August 1984, the Unity gained revenge with an unexpected victory, a slip by Worcester which may have cost them the championship.

Worcester City 185—6, G. Inglis 58 n.o. C. Groves 67 n.o.
Aston Unity 189—2, I. Hutchings 63 n.o. C.L. Price 75

Pat Hounsell and Worcestershire's Phil Newport were not available after the 1984 season. The Club finished in 11th place in the table in seasons 1985—87 as they rebuilt the side with Eddie Nicholson, Shaun Lloyd, Mel Brooker, David Goodall, S. Cairney and S. D'Oliveira joining Ian Rone, Colin Groves, Steve McEwan, Paul Bent with David Humphries taking over captaincy in 1987.

Warwickshire

Warwickshire entered a strong side in the League in 1975 with Neal Abberley, Geoff Humpage, Phil Oliver, Keith Jones, John Whitehouse, David Smith and Mel Wood featuring in the batting and Keith Gardom, Haisham Khan, Peter Lewington and Mel Wood the main bowlers. As with every season since, the sides showed many changes whilst the County coaches, Alan Oakman and Neal Abberley, ring the changes during the season as players are called up for standby or duty with the County, come for trial or fall victim to fitness in the six day a week fixture list.

In a club side, a long run in the team generally indicates good performances and good club service but in the Warwickshire side it means a long run on the fringe of the County side. A number of players who have been outstanding performers in the League have not eventually been retained by the County as they have been replaced in the County coaching scheme by younger players. A few such players have been batsmen Gary Thomas, Robin Dyer, Simon Wootton, Kassim Ibadulla, Rob Yapp and Wayne Matthews. Bowlers not retained have been David Hopkins, David M. Smith, Simon Sutcliffe, Willie Morton, Stephen Wall and all rounders Gordon Lord and Chris Lethbridge. Players who have made the County side whilst doing well in the League include Geoff Humpage, Andy Lloyd, John Claughton, Gladstone Small, Asif Din, David Thorne and Geoff Tedstone and also Chris Maynard who moved to Lancashire.

1986 and 1987 saw the introduction of Tim Munton, Adrian Pierson and a number of young new faces. Promising performances have come from Jason Ratcliffe, David Percival, Eddie Milburn, Gary Steer, Rob Weir, Gareth Williamson and Neil Smith, son of Warwickshire's M.J.K. Smith, and the young side performed well to finish runners- up to Stourbridge in 1987.

The side won the League in 1978 and 1979 playing under the captaincy of Gary Thomas. A feature of their success in 1978 was that there was a positive result in nineteen of the twenty games played. Two others were rained off. The side won 14 and lost 5, the same number of losses as Stourbridge, who finished joint 7th. This is a good indication of the positive attitude of the side who went for a win sometimes at the expense of a loss. It is interesting to note a change in 1980 when the side lost no games but only won 5 and finished 3rd in the table.

A crucial result in the 1978 season occurred on 5th August when Warwickshire, Aston Unity and Old Hill were locked together at the top of the table. Warwickshire met Aston Unity at Edgbaston. Put into bat, Unity were all out for 46, David Hopkins taking 6—19. With storm clouds gathering, Gary Thomas and John Claughton scored the required runs to finish the game by 4.15 p.m. Heavy storms broke over the area and Old Hill rang up to find out how their contenders were faring and were dismayed to find Warwickshire had grabbed the points. Old Hill did all they could to resume their game but to no avail and Warwickshire had established a lead which they did not lose. Aston Unity eventually finished in second place. In 1982 Dennis Amiss made two appearances in the side. Branded as a South African 'Rebel' he was precluded from playing against the Indians at Edgbaston so turned out at West Bromwich Dartmouth. He opened with Robin Dyer and together they put on 220 in 110 minutes, Warwickshire declaring at a total of 281—1. Dartmouth were not daunted and at 263—6 forced Warwickshire on to the defensive. They then suffered two run outs and the last pair batted out for a draw.

Warwickshire 281—1. D.L. Amiss 115, R.I.H.B. Dyer 138 n.o.
West Bromwich Dartmouth 268—9. S.A. Neal 86, H. Bradby 54, D.M. Smith 4—70

David M. Smith finished the season with 51 wickets, the most taken by a Warwickshire player in the First Division. The side came close to success in finishing joint 2nd in 1985 and second in 1986 and 1987. Leading the table in 1985 with only four games to go, they unexpectedly lost two of them to let in Moseley. In 1986 they were to be penalised five points for slow over rates and finished one point behind the champions, Walsall.

Coventry and North Warwickshire

Coventry and North Warwickshire's first season in 1986 augured well for their future in the League. They were in contention for the championship until three games from the end of the season. Their main strike bowler in the season, Steve Ogrizovic, was recalled to his soccer goalkeeping duties by Coventry City at the end of June, otherwise Coventry may have produced a surprise title success. The Club's loss was the football clubs gain for Steve kept goal in their 1987 Cup Final success at Wembley. Rob Grant, Dave Brooks, Geoff Edmunds from West Bromwich Dartmouth sustained Coventry's bowling attack. Andy Grant, Neil Parker, Graham Davies, Mark Eames and Brian Mills took the batting honours with contributions from Dave Robinson, Dave Hagan, joined in 1987 by Wayne Matthews, Michael Carew, Tim Openshaw and David M. Smith. Barry Flick and Tim Barnby filled the wicket-keeping spot.

Coventry and North Warwicks featured in two tight low scoring games in the 1986 season: —

14 June 1986
Coventry & N.W. 58 Andy Grant 20 Steve McEwan 5—29 Graham Gill 5—25
Worcester City 32 Colin Groves 11 Steve Ogrizovic 8—12 Rob Grant 2—12

23 August 1986
Coventry & N.W. 76 Andy Grant 26 Dilip Doshi 5—38 Richard Boothroyd 4—37
Walsall 70 Nick Marsh 25 Rob Grant 7—31 Dave Brooks 2—7

This sensational win against League leaders Walsall brought Coventry & N.W. back into the championship race but they could not sustain their challenge in the remaining 3 games.

When Coventry and North Warwicks met Aston Unity on 16th May 1987, Coventry F.C. were making their first appearance in the F.A. Cup Final at Wembley. The Coventry and North Warwicks innings was played to a background of cheers from the pavilion as supporters deserted the cricket, for the television, to share in the excitement as their local side beat Tottenham Hotspur F.C. 3 −2, after extra time.

The Unity innings which started as the game at Wembley finished was accompanied by the continuous sound of car horns and celebrations. Despite all the distractions the game of cricket was played out, Coventry and North Warwicks winning. The Unity players later had to find an alternative route home as the City centre filled with excited revellers.

Extra Cover 1975 − 1987

31.5.75	West Bromwich Dartmouth 275−4 Paddy Clift 120 n.o. Mike Edmundson 130 n.o. Old Hill 219−7 D. Cooper 67 n.o. Roy Keeling 52 Jack Sedgley 52 Clift & Edmundson added 225 for the 5th wicket.
31.5.75	Stourbridge 162 Alan Richardson 64 Frank Wright 51 Peter Jones 5−51 from 1−44 Kidderminster 163−0 Colin Hemsley 89 n.o. S. Johnson 71 n.o.
5.7.75	Worcestershire 248−2 K.W. Wilkinson 152 n.o. P. Westaway 45 Stourbridge 104−5 P.Pridgeon 3−33
19.7.75	Bob Willis, Warwickshire and England, played for Warwickshire v Old Hill after injury. He took 3−33
26.7.75	Warwickshire 265−1 Neal Abberley 146 n.o. Keith Jones 103 n.o. Partnership of 254 for 2nd wicket Smethwick 240−9 Neville Moore 74 Ray McHenry 56 Keith Gardom 4−70 M. Wood 3−53 A splendid afternoon's cricket was the verdict.
1976	Dudley did not earn a bonus point during the season.
12.6.76	Mitchells & Butlers 81 Richard Boothroyd 4−33 Walsall 84−7 from 14−3 Bob Sylvester 35 − he hit 18 and was out in one John Weston over
26.6.76	Aston Unity 122 John Kennedy 37 Geoff Edmunds 4−29 Warwickshire 80 were 1−4 Roy Bent taking 3 wickets for 1 run
6.6.77	Warwickshire 70 Terry Rawlinson 8−31 the best League bowling performance against Warwickshire Walsall 71−6 Alan Conway 30
30.7.77	Warwickshire 235−9 Phil Oliver 67 John Claughton 55 Walsall 56 R.A. Smith 6−11 including 4−1 in one over with hat-trick.
8.7.78	Aston Unity 83 Brian Fisher 24 John Weston 4−34

Mitchells & Butlers 45 John Corbett 10, Geoff Jackson 5—24 Paul Junkin 5—14

1979   Duport fail to win a game

5.5.79   Warwickshire 266—0 Gary Thomas 117 n.o. Asif Din 139 n.o.
Smethwick 197—7 Guy Thompson 65 Neil Penton 51

2.6.79   Mitchells & Butlers 45 Mick Green 21 John Aldridge 8—25
Walsall 47—2 Roy Virgin 21

23.6.79   Walsall 192—5 Roy Virgin 82 Nick Archer 33
Moseley 192 Mike Cheslin 71 Nick Perrin 40 n.o. John Aldridge 4—67
Moseley's last man Peter Davis run out off last ball of match so the result a tie — Walsall's second of the season having tied with Dudley on 9th June. Dudley 145—8, Walsall 145

28.7.79   Moseley 176 Basil Hylton 65 Geoff Humpage 4—21 Steve Rouse 5—56
Warwickshire 177—5 Gary Thomas 55 Geoff Humpage 50
Geoff Humpage caught one behind the wickets, took off his pads and Gary Thomas his deputy took two catches off Geoff's bowling.

18.8.79   Aston Unity 107 Paul Humphries 50. Batsmen No's. 3, 4, 5, and 6 all 'ducks', Mike Clinton 3—28 (3 in 8 balls) Simon Burchill 4—65
Stourbridge 83—7

17.5.80   Warwickshire 211—5
Duport 136 Chris Maynard 6 wicket keeping catches

24.5.80   Old Hill 188 Roy Keeling 98 Neil Penton 4—56
Smethwick 156 Neville Moore 58 Cedric Boyns 8—42

14.6.80   When Moseley, League leaders, visited West Bromwich Dartmouth on a rainy afternoon, Dartmouth scorer, Tom Rider, and others purchased blankets and soaked up water off the pitch using a mangle to wring out the water. The game started at 5.00 p.m. and finished just after 9 p.m. Moseley gained a bonus point in a draw with one more than the minimum number of overs bowled. No other side played so points were then valuable but Moseley later fell out of championship race.

21.6.80   Kidderminster 145 were 21—6 Derek Oliver 32 n.o. and Brian Cowley added 65 for last wicket, Steve Brookes 5—64 Simon Burchill 4—38
Stourbridge 149—6 were 69—6 Steve Brookes 45 n.o. Roger Hargreaves 32 n.o.
This game illustrated the swings of fortune that cricket can provide.

12.7.80   West Bromwich Dartmouth 175 were 153—2 Barry Abel 63 Alan Neal 37. John Aldridge did most damage taking 6—3 in one spell to finish 6—50 John Golightly 4—68
Walsall 176—1 Roy Virgin 68 n.o. Tom Pearsall 65

25.4.81	Snow stopped play in all games

25.4.81   Snow stopped play in all games

2.5.81   Old Hill 163 Cedric Boyns 68 Doug Slade 4—38, Phil Burnell stumped 2 caught 1.
West Bromwich Dartmouth 163 Alan Neal 61 Dave Mayne 6—35 (was 2—29)
5 Dartmouth out Lbw
A tie — with umpires kept busy!

3.5.81   Warwickshire versus Mitchells & Butlers scheduled for Sunday play — the first time for a First Division game in the League — Game was not played due to rain!

9.5.81   Stourbridge 127 Mark Scott 44 Chris Derham 23 Peter Radburn 4—41 Horace Palmer 3—23
Kidderminster 124 J. Taylor 30 Steve Brookes 4—46
Kidderminster batted on in bad light to try for victory, 6 of the side were out Lbw so umpires could see!

25.7.81   Old Hill 196—6 Alan Brookes 53 Steve Walker 55 n.o.
West Bromwich Dartmouth 199—7 won with 23 off last over.   Vanburn Holder hitting 60 not out including 5 — 6's.   Alan Neal 52.   Earlier in the season Vanburn hit 54 including 6 — 6's.

25.7.81   Duport v Warwickshire.   Warwickshire fielded for 11 overs before it was noticed they had 12 fielders.   No chances had gone to hand so the umpires decided not to start again!

15.5.82   Ivan Hutchings Aston Unity, age 16 playing Mitchells & Butlers scored his maiden century.   A member of Aston Unity since he was 11.

5.6.82   Stourbridge 229—3 Barry Corbett 108 Ross Stephens 72 Scoring 181 for first wicket
Aston Unity 174—9 Colin Price 65 J.A. Grimshaw took 6—23 from 1—22 and bowled 16 Overs 10 maidens

19.6.82   Smethwick 120 Shahid Mohammad 39
Mel Brooker 8—42 dismissing first four for 6
Kidderminster 121—5 Godfrey Lamb 54

3.7.82   Smethwick 238—7 Shahid Mohammad 57 Neil Penton 44
Mitchells & Butlers 239—4 scored in only 39 overs Mick Green 60 Gary Thomas 130 n.o.

21.8.82   West Bromwich Dartmouth 265—3 Alan Neal 110 n.o.
David Hopkins 119 added 202 for the third wicket
Kidderminster 116—2 Frank Watson 55 n.o.   Godfrey Lamb 31 n.o. when bad light stopped play.

28.8.82   Kidderminster 137 Delvin King 39 Peter Davis 9—70 John Taylor stumped 2 caught 2
Moseley 138—9 Mike Cheslin 38 Harold Turner and Simon Coley added 23 for last wicket to win

6.8.83   Stourbridge 174—9 David Banks 47 John Taylor 42 Mushtaq Mohammad 5—65
Old Hill 178—7 but they were reeling at 77—6 after Greg Watson took 4 wickets for no runs — he finished at 5—50 Alan Brookes 48 and Colin Hemsley 41 n.o. rallied Old Hill.

| 6.8.83 | Kanuk Patel of Mitchells & Butlers dismissed 10 Kidderminster batsmen taking 9—67 and running out the Kidderminster number 10 batsman. |

| 26.5.84 | Aston Unity 77 Colin Price 23, Mick Stocker 6—29 Joe Benjamin 3—29 Mick Green took 6 wicket keeping catches |
| | Mitchells & Butlers 79—8 but were 53—8. Mike Sheldon 12 n.o. John Weston 13 n.o. Gordon Harrys 4—22. |

16.6.84	Stourbridge 250—7 Simon Wootton 103 Jonathon Wright 78 John Golightly 5—67 twice took 2 wickets in 2 balls.
	Walsall 251—7 won off last ball Chris Parr 85 Nick Archer 59 John Moore 51 n.o. W. Linn 4—85
	Two weeks later Walsall were to lose a similar high scoring game
	Walsall 250—5 Nick Archer 96 Lawrence Smith 69 Michael Moseley 4—98
	Dudley 251—3 Mark Sedgley 117 Chris Green 64

7.7.84	Worcester and Moseley featured in a high scoring tie
	Worcester City 231—6 Pat Hounsell 56 Steve Watkins 70 Ian Rone 45
	Moseley 231—6 Ian Stokes 115 Malcolm Eustace 49

| 9.9.84 | Old Hill v Warwickshire re-arranged for a Sunday Warwickshire County side engaged in Nat-West Final on original date lost to Lancashire |
| | Warwickshire 158—4 Geoff Tedstone 72 n.o. Asif Din 40 Warwickshire were progressing well when rain interferred to reduce match to 34 overs. Old Hill needed 20.2 overs only, as former Warwickshire all-rounder, Philip Oliver, smashed 112 n.o. with 5—6's and 16 — 4's for Old Hill to win by 9 wickets. |

| 27.4.85 | Snow stopped play in all games. At Dudley v West Bromwich Dartmouth the snow was swept off the pitch and the game re-started but after a further snow-fall the game was abandoned. Quite an introduction to League cricket for former Test Star David Steele — West Bromwich Dartmouth's professional. |

| 25.5.85 | Aston Unity 123 Colin Price 23 Simon Kimber took last 7 wickets for 15 runs after starting with 0—25 |
| | Dudley 125—6 Andy Pearson 44 |

| 6.7.85 | Warwickshire 269—1 G.J. Lord 117 n.o. K.D. Smith 81 W.P. Matthews 53 n.o. |
| | Dudley all out 150 — were 140—3 M. Corcoran 55 S. Kimber 43 when Gordon Lord took 4 wickets for one run and Willie Morton 3 for 5 — plus 4 no balls. The last 6 batsmen all 'ducks'. |

25.7.85	Stourbridge 121 David Banks 34 Jonathon Wright 21 Frank Wright 21 David Steele 7—62
	West Bromwich Dartmouth 99 Richard Cox 25 Mike Brewer 7—51
	Two bowlers with 7 wickets and a father and son combination for Stourbridge.

| 24.8.85 | Moseley 155—7 Andy Moles 34 Bob Milne 33 |
| | Mitchells & Butlers 155—6 Mick Green 45 Neville Moore |

	32. A tie – Joe Benjamin got 8 off first 3 balls of last over but Mitchells could not get the winning run.
26.5.86	West Bromwich Dartmouth 86 Nigel Heath 25 Stuart Kensitt 5–25 Graham Saint, Stourbridge keeper took 7 catches. Stourbridge 87–1 David Banks 36 n.o. Jonathon Wright 28 n.o.
14.6.86	Moseley 219 Jack Watts 92 and Harold Turner 54 added 63 for last wicket Ricardo Elcock 5–72 West Bromwich Dartmouth 215–7 Mark Plummer 37 John Waterhouse 37
9.8.86	Warwickshire 198 from 178–2 the last 8 wickets falling in 4 overs. Robin Dyer 91 David Percival 54 Rob Weir 4–88 Coventry and North Warwickshire 149 from 94–0 Mark Eames 45 Andy Grant 38 Anton Ferreira 7–34
26.4.87	Smethwick 147 Gordon Lord 7–35 Old Hill 150–4 Colin Hemsley 41 Gordon Lord released by Warwickshire and signed by Worcestershire shows his prowess as left arm spinner.
12.7.87	Kidderminster 229–3 Mark Sedgley 76 Horace Palmer 60 Put on 140 for the first wicket. Warwickshire 231–7 Mark Humphries 7–80 Kidderminster lose despite good performances by three of their players.
1.8.87	Coventry & North Warwicks 262–5 David Robinson 56 Michael Carew 127 Peter Bagley 3–54 Old Hill 251–9 Gordon Lord 70 Mushtaq Mohammad 105 Rob Grant 3–93 A splendid afternoon's cricket as Old Hill chased the huge total and then had to hold out for a draw.
8.8.87	Coventry & North Warwicks 285–6 Wayne Matthews 121 David Robinson 33 Kidderminster 176–3 David Leatherdale 45 Andy Sharpe 62 n.o. Good scores two weeks running fail to bring victory to Coventry.
8.8.87	Old Hill 222–7 Colin Hemsley 34 Alan Brookes 58 Steve Derham 45 n.o. Smethwick 224–6 David Smith 135 Nick Willetts 30 Lowly Smethwick surprise title contestants, Old Hill, thanks to a good knock by David Smith the former Warwickshire opener. This win helped Stourbridge's hold on the top position and made up for a similar surprise victory by Smethwick which had prejudiced Stourbridge's title hopes in 1986.
31.8.87	Old Hill 185–7 Colin Hemsley 67, Mushtaq Mohammad 72 Rob Weir 4–53 Warwickshire 186–2 Jason Ratcliffe 76 n.o. David Percival 41 Paul Smith 47 Warwickshire's first League win at Old Hill since Warwickshire joined the League in 1975.

League Positions 1975–1987

First Division

	19 75	76	77	78	79	80	81	82	83	84	85	86	87
Aston Unity	5	7	1	2*	2	8	8*	12	12	11	12	12	12
Dudley	12	12	12	7*	11	5	1	9	2	5	4	–	–
Kidderminster	1	2*	6	6	7	11	8*	7*	10	3	6	10	8*
Mitchells & Butlers	10	8	11	12	4*	7	10	2	5	8*	10	9	6
Moseley	4	4*	8	7*	9	3*	3	4	6	1	1	5	10
Old Hill	3	6	2	2*	4*	2	11	5	1	4	8	6	3
Smethwick	9	9	5	5	6	10	6	6	4	12	9	8	7
Stourbridge	11	10	7	9*	10	9	5	11	8*	8*	5	4	1
Walsall	8	1	10	9*	3	1	4	1	8*	10	7	1	8*
Warwickshire	6*	4*	4	1	1	3*	7	7*	3	6	2*	2	2
West Bromwich Dartmouth	2	2*	3	4	8	6	2	10	11	7	2*	7	5
Worcestershire	6*	11	–	–	–	–	–	–	–	–	–	–	–
Duport	–	–	9	11	12	12	12	–	–	–	–	–	–
Worcester City	–	–	–	–	–	–	–	3	7	2	11	11	11
Coventry & Nth. Warwicks.	–	–	–	–	–	–	–	–	–	–	–	3	4

* Position held jointly

Highest Club Scores in Period

Aston Unity	269–5	v	Stourbridge	(H)	1984
Coventry & Nth.Warks.	285–6	v	Kidderminster	(H)	1987
Dudley	262–2	v	West Brom.Dartmouth	(H)	1983
Duport	258–4	v	Kidderminster	(H)	1978
Kidderminster	309–4	v	Moseley	(A)	1984
Mitchells & Butlers	295–4	v	Kidderminster	(H)	1984
Moseley	283–9	v	Smethwick	(A)	1984
Old Hill	299–6	v	West Brom.Dartmouth	(H)	1983
Smethwick	280–3	v	Stourbridge	(H)	1977
Stourbridge	271–5	v	Aston Unity	(A)	1984
Walsall	265–6	v	Mitchells & Butlers	(H)	1982
Warwickshire	369–5	v	Walsall	(H)	1984
West Brom.Dartmouth	283–4	v	Aston Unity	(A)	1987
Worcester City	312–4	v	Moseley	(H)	1982
Worcestershire	248–2	v	Stourbridge	(A)	1975

Lowest Club Scores in Period

Aston Unity	23	v	Worcester City	(H)	1984
Coventry & Nth.Warks.	58	v	Worcester City	(A)	1986
Dudley	52	v	Aston Unity	(A)	1977
Duport	54	v	Walsall	(H)	1980
Kidderminster	73	v	Walsall	(H)	1978
Mitchells & Butlers	(45	v	Aston Unity	(A)	1978
	(45	v	Walsall	(H)	1979
Moseley	54	v	Duport	(A)	1980
Old Hill	61	v	Worcester City	(A)	1984
	61	v	Moseley	(A)	1986
Smethwick	69	v	Walsall	(A)	1979
Stourbridge	47	v	Warwickshire	(H)	1976
Walsall	43	v	Coventry & Nth.Warks.	(A)	1986
Warwickshire	49	v	Stourbridge	(H)	1979
West Brom.Dartmouth	48	v	Aston Unity	(A)	1975
Worcester City	32	v	Coventry & Nth.Warks.	(H)	1986
Worcestershire	79	v	Kidderminster	(H)	1976

Individual Performances

Highest Scores

Aston Unity (J. Gough)	129*	v	Warwickshire	(A)	1977
Coventry & Nth.Warks. (M. Carew)	127	v	Old Hill	(A)	1987
Dudley (R.G.A. Headley)	134*	v	Duport	(A)	1980
Duport (K.V. Jones)	124	v	Kidderminster	(H)	1978
Kidderminster (G.A. Hick)	182*	v	Moseley	(H)	1984
Mitchells & Butlers (M.A. Masood)	150	v	Warwickshire	(A)	1976
Moseley (I.W.E. Stokes)	159*	v	West Brom.Dartmouth	(H)	1987
Old Hill (K.W. Wilkinson)	162*	v	Mitchells & Butlers	(A)	1977
Smethwick (N. Moore)	150	v	Stourbridge	(H)	1979
Stourbridge (J.P. Wright)	146	v	Mitchells & Butlers	(A)	1984
Walsall (R.T. Virgin)	124*	v	Warwickshire	(H)	1983
Warwickshire (S.H. Wootton)	159	v	Kidderminster	(H)	1982
West Brom. Dartmouth (M. Edmundson)	130*	v	Old Hill	(H)	1975
Worcester City (D.N.F. Slade)	128*	v	Mitchells & Butlers	(H)	1982
Worcestershire (K.W. Wilkinson)	152*	v	Stourbridge	(A)	1975

* Not Out

Best Bowling

Aston Unity (G. Harrys)	9—42	v	Walsall	(A) 1981
Coventry & Nth. Warks. (S. Ogrizovic)	8—12	v	Worcester City	(A) 1986
Dudley (G. Smith)	8—11	v	Kidderminster	(H) 1979
Duport (J. Buttress)	7—29	v	Moseley	(H) 1980
Kidderminster (C. Hemsley)	9—41	v	Mitchells & Butlers	(H) 1976
Mitchells & Butlers (K. Patel)	9—67	v	Kidderminster	(H) 1983
Moseley (P. Davis)	9—70	v	Kidderminster	(A) 1982
Old Hill (P. Bagley)	9—19	v	West Brom.Dartmouth	(A) 1983
Smethwick (G.G.Watson)	8—51	v	Stourbridge	(H) 1986
Stourbridge (G.G. Watson)	7—28	v	Smethwick	(H) 1979
Walsall (J. Golightly)	8—19	v	Aston Unity	(A) 1980
Warwickshire (D.M. Smith)	7—16	v	Kidderminster	(A) 1983
West Brom. Dartmouth (D.S. Steele)	8—35	v	Stourbridge	(A) 1985
Worcester City (D.B. D'Oliveira)	8—47	v	Walsall	(A) 1983
Worcestershire (C.P. Roberts)	7—53	v	Smethwick	(A) 1975

Second Division 1975—1987

Second Division Winners

1975	Walsall	1981	(Smethwick (Walsall
1976	Warwickshire		
1977	) Moseley	1982	) Moseley
1978	)	1983	)
1979	Walsall	1984	Old Hill
1980	(Walsall	1985	Moseley
	(Moseley	1986	Warwickshire
		1987	Stourbridge

Highlights

1979—81 Phil Beddow captained Walsall second eleven and in 1982 when they finished runners-up to Moseley

15.5.76 Moseley 192—4 M. Heath 104 n.o. D. Heath 41 Father and son put on 91 for first wicket.
Walsall 196—5 Hamilton Jones 104 n.o.

5.6.76 Mitchells & Butlers 176—8 M. Woolfson 76 I Rudge 6—55
Duport 176—8. Duport needed one run for victory off last two balls but two batsmen were run out.

21.5.77 Stourbridge 175—8 P. Radburn 5—62
Kidderminster 179—0 J. Rose 72 n.o. H. Bradby 103 n.o

28.5.77 Walsall 206—7 M. Wilkes 5—85
West Bromwich Dartmouth 207—8 Don Lee hit last ball for 4 to win game.

9.7.77 Old Hill 303—8 with 81 extras 54 byes 18 leg byes 5 wides and 4 no balls.
Some wayward bowling, two deputy-wicket keepers and short boundaries on Colts' ground contribute more to the total than any batsman. D. Flavell 70 n.o.
Warwickshire 269—9 A Babar 75

29.8.77	Warwickshire 269—5 Z. Rusike 80 K. Rattue 94

29.8.77   Warwickshire 269—5 Z. Rusike 80 K. Rattue 94
Aston Unity 266—5 S. Bayliss 69 P. Baker 59 n.o.
B. Fisher 57 n.o.
A Valiant attempt for victory by the Unity.

10.6.78   Moseley 285—3 K. Wright 140 n.o.
Warwickshire 290—6 R. Weston 83 S. Bill 58 n.o.
R.B. Abell 5—92
This was a good win by Warwickshire's youngsters
against the wiles of Roy Abell.

22.7.78   Warwickshire 300—9 C.E. Murray 116 n.o. M.A. Din
52
Walsall 304—8 no batsman scored 50. Barat Jogi and
his brother Navit Jogi added 70 for the ninth wicket
to win the game.

12.5.79   Aston Unity 92 Gladstone Small made impact with
6—11
Warwickshire 94—3

5.7.80   Kidderminster 158 S. Hardwick 77 M. Satchwell 5—32
Smethwick 126—8 P. Westwood 51 K. Porter 5—38
In this game 38 maidens were bowled.

26.7.80   Smethwick 62—2 Roy Abell (Moseley) took his 1000th
wicket in the League before rain stopped play

2.5.81   Dudley 136—8 T. Rawlinson taking all 8 for 62 runs
Walsall 140—6

18.7.81   Stourbridge 178—8 M. Fisher 80
Old Hill 179—9 Won bonus point with calculation taken
to 4th decimal place.

5.9.81   Warwickshire 261—1 J.G. White 106 n.o. S.A.E.Headley
121 n.o.
West Bromwich Dartmouth 190—7 J. Sedgley 75 S.J.
Moseley 5—77

Warwickshire's score compiled at Sandwell Park not on
small Colts ground.

24.4.82   Old Hill 242—3 D. Grosvenor 81 n.o. R. Whitehouse
51 n.o.
Worcester City 60 of which 42 were "Extras"

3.7.82   West Bromwich Dartmouth 239—9 I. Denning 58 A.
Moles 5—56
Moseley 241—2 A. Moles 66 E. Harris 58 n.o. M. Wright
58 n.o.
This was a good win for eventual champions, Moseley,
spearheaded by a fine performance by Andy Moles who
was to make an impact on the County scene when he
joined Warwickshire in 1986.

4.9.82   Walsall visited Moseley for last match of season, needing
a win to share the title with Moseley. Walsall's run
chase was foiled by Veteran Roy Abell.
Moseley 232—6 I. Stokes 75 D. Bowater 53
Walsall 207 S. Starkey 72 R.B. Abell 6—42

11.6.83   Old Hill 111 K. Porter 5—40
Stourbridge 113—9 Alan Cresswell 8—59

18.6.83	Old Hill 157 R.I. Whitehouse 59 Dudley 87 Alan Cresswell 9—35 Two good weeks bowling by Alan
25.6.83	Kidderminster 65 Stourbridge 66—1 Not a good day for Kidderminster's Annual Vice Presidents Day, a big defeat and game over before bar is open!
23.7.83	Kidderminster 173—9 C. Green 8—39 Smethwick 48 D. Oliver 7—15 A match with two good bowling feats.
13.8.83	West Bromwich Dartmouth 276—6 B. Mountford 64 M. Corcoran 67 S. Killworth 54 W.J. Bayliss 5—108 Old Hill 280—8 R. Keeling 103 J. Day 70 C. Christie 5—115 A day not to be a front line bowler
10.9.83	Kidderminster 240—7 E. King 74 B. Pinner 67 Old Hill 85 Paul Weston took all 10 wickets for 38 runs.
19.5.84	Smethwick 143—9 Tied with Worcester City 143
26.5.84	Old Hill 325—6 Roy Keeling 179 J. Day 55 n.o. Dudley 104—8 A. Cresswell 6—33.
28.7.84	Dudley 341—3 N. Willetts 202 n.o. (17yr. old) Moseley 312—8 N. Devenport 80
25.5.85	Warwickshire 175 P. Davis 6—43 Ray Young 5 stumped 1 caught Moseley 182 R. Weir 5—61 M. Bell 4—35
16.8.85	Kidderminster 88 Alan Cresswell again! 8—50 Old Hill 92—2
10.5.86	Aston Unity 118 J. Wootton 7—61 West Bromwich Dartmouth 120—9 Paul Stacey having retired after a blow in the face went to hospital with broken nose and two black eyes, returned when 9 wickets down, and hit his first ball for six to win the game for Dartmouth.
1986	Warwickshire Colts won the title with a side average age of 16½ years under leadership of coach Steve Rouse.
2.5.87	Aston Unity had Peter Davis keeping wicket in the First Division, and his nephew Tony Davis keeping wicket in the Second Division and Peter Davis Junior doing the same job in the Third Division. Peter Davis's brother John, father of Tony and Peter Junior, was also playing in the Division Three Game.
9.5.87	Moseley 257—0, M. Heath 102 n.o. R. Milne 147 n.o. West Bromwich Dartmouth 172 Naheem 75 A good day for Moseley batsmen, for in the First Division I. Stokes hit 159 n.o., so there were three centuries in one day for the Club.

Third Division 1977—1987

Third Division Winners

1977	Walsall		1982	Walsall
1978)	Moseley		1983	Smethwick
1979)			1984	Old Hill
1980	Holy Trinity		1985	Mitchells & Butlers
1981	Kidderminster		1986	Old Hill
			1987	Stourbridge

Highlights

Most wins in a season:—
    16 by Old Hill in 1986 (22 games)
    12 by Moseley in 1979 (16 games)

Undefeated sides in a season:—
    Moseley 1979
    Holy Trinity 1980
    Walsall 1982

Most runs in a season
    661 F. Phipps Holy Trinity   1980

Highest Score
    203 B. Phillips Moseley v Dudley 1983

Most Wickets in a season
    51 J. Bates Coventry & North Warwicks. 1986

Most wicket-keeper dismissals in a season
    22 R. Dawson 1983, 1984

Experienced players who have continued their playing careers to play with and encourage Club youngsters include Brian Barrett and Gordon Brindley, Moseley and Dean Johnston of Kidderminster, all three having been members of championship sides in all three divisions.

Brian Barrett:-   First Division 1961 and 1963.
                     Second Division 1962
                     Third Division 1978 and 1979

Gordon Brindley:- First Division 1970
                     Second Division 1961, 1962, 1966 and 1969
                     Third Division 1978 and 1979

Dean Johnston:-   First Division 1952
                     Second Division 1954 both at Mitchells & Butlers
                     Third Division 1981 at Kidderminster

The captain of the Walsall side in 1982 was Barrie Middleton who had captained Walsall's successful Second Division side in 1975.

West Bromwich Dartmouth

146

CLUB GROUNDS

Aston Unity

In 1889, Unity were playing on a ground in Trinity Road, Aston. The lease of the ground expired in 1908 and the Club moved along the road to a higher site to turn a morass into a cricket field. A substantial house on the site made a splendid pavilion. The field was also used for football but a Minute of a cricket club meeting in 1928, records that the directors had decided to ban football in the future, owing to damage to the outfield.

This valuable freehold plot was partially destroyed by bombs in 1940 and so the club were forced to play all games from 1941—1945 on the opponents' grounds. In 1945, through great efforts of the members led by 'Tich' Hill, a new ground was acquired in Court Lane, Erdington, and for one season whilst this was being prepared the club loaned a ground from the Birmingham Municipal Gas Department in Woodacre Road, Erdington. The new ground in Court Lane was appropriately named 'Hillcourt' in appreciation of the work put in by H.F. 'Tich' Hill, and opened on May 3rd. 1947 with a match against a League eleven.

Big hitting was not appreciated by owners of houses adjoining the ground and, threatened with legal action in 1947, the club had to erect high netting on the boundary. The ground was leased from the Church and the tenancy precluded the provision of a bar so the club purchased a small piece of adjoining ground on which a clubroom was erected.

In 1970, with the tenancy agreement coming to a close, the club launched an appeal in conjunction with the Spartans Rugby Club for the establishment of the present ground at Coppice Lane and this was officially opened on Sunday May 13th. 1973.

The ground has a structural link with the League's formation for the scoreboard was erected at the Trinity Road ground in 1935 in memory of Charles Durban, a great servant of the Club and the League. The board was moved to Hillcourt and then because of planning restrictions, in truncated state, to Coppice Lane. It is presently in need of attention after its long years of service and it is to be hoped that this generation will see the link with the past maintained.

Coventry and North Warwickshire

The Club moved to the ground in 1900 and were able to purchase the ground on generous terms from the Fellowship of Drapers soon after the close of the 1939—1945 war. The facilities are excellent with provision for squash, lawn tennis and hockey, in addition to cricket.

R.E.S. Wyatt the England, Warwickshire and Worcestershire

player was to benefit by playing his early cricket on the fine facilities at Binley Road, arriving from Meriden with his bat and pads tied onto his bicycle.

Dudley

The ground overlooked by Dudley Castle, and in an elevated position giving a panoramic view of the Black Country, was given to the Club by the Earl of Dudley in 1842. In 1878 the Club entertained the first Australian side to visit England. The Club became a registered company and in 1911 the playing area was extended and a spacious pavilion built so that County Cricket could be staged, the first match being on 11th August 1911 – Worcestershire v Gloucestershire. The wicket was favourable to batsmen and in 1914 Warwickshire scored 645–7 F.R. Foster 305 and in 1939 Worcestershire amassed 546–6 v Northamptonshire. In all nearly ninety First Class games were played on the ground.

In 1924 the Club was finding the ground a financial burden and sold it to Dudley Corporation for £3,500 and thereafter rented the facilities.

In 1936, a new scoreboard, generously provided by Mr. Douglas Tanfield the Club Chairman at the time, was erected. The area had been subject to subsidence for some time and in 1978 part of the ground had to be roped off. It is ironic, in a way, to recall that as far back as 1854 a game was played by '22 of Dudley' against George Parr's All England XI in aid of men blinded in the limestone workings, the very workings which were to lead to the demise of the Club 131 years later in 1985.

The ground, with its exposed position, could submit players and spectators to a bleak east wind but nothing could be more cheerless than seeing this centre of nearly 150 years of cricket history in its neglected state.

Handsworth Wood

The ground at Browne's Green was described as having a country aspect with plenty of beautiful trees. The Club built a new pavilion in 1897 but the ground succumbed to the encroachment of development in 1919.

No mention of League grounds would be complete without mention of Barton's donkey. Barton the Handsworth Wood bowler and groundsman kept a donkey to assist on the ground. He had the heavy roller fitted with a geared system so that the donkey could pull it. When rain stopped play a popular past-time of visiting players was to see who could ride the donkey the longest a sport the donkey is reputed to have enjoyed as he threw them off!

Kidderminster

The Club moved to the present ground in 1870, bringing with them the old pavilion from their previous ground. This pavilion, originally a single storey structure, was built on brick piers to provide a dining area but later used as a storage for horse drawn mowers, hand mowers and rollers, together with harness for the horses and special shoes worn over their hooves to protect the turf. This old pavilion now acts as a sight screen when in line with the wicket, and is part of the heritage of the Club.

W.G. Grace played for Kidderminster against 18 of the United

Kidderminster's Old Pavilion

Saxons in 1883 and is recorded as having driven a ball over the house on the West side of the Chester Road. His fee was £10 and a carpet.

The ground was originally rented, but, when the estate came on the market in 1920, Michael Tomkinson purchased the site and, when sufficient funds had been raised by the Club, he sold it to the Club for use for cricket in perpetuity.

In 1927, the scorebox was presented by James Greenwood in memory of his father, for they had both played for the club. The box was modernised in 1980 by Club member Bill Brookes so that the scoreboard operator could operate the numbers from inside instead of out in the open. This would have delighted Frank Bayes who for many years stood outside the box.

The present pavilion was opened in 1925, electricity installed in 1951 and shower baths in 1960. The substantial brick boundary wall was built in 1936 and the lounge was built by subscription and opened in April 1967, the Long Room and tea bar were opened in 1974.

In 1984, the financial standing of the Club was put on a firm footing by the merger of Kidderminster Cricket Club with the Hockey Club and Old Carolian Club to form Chester Road Sporting Club, which aims to uphold the old traditions of cricket and sport on the ground.

The cricket club made history in 1965 when, on conclusion of a televised benefit match between Worcestershire and the Cavaliers, the players turned out for an exhibition of cricket with Dennis Compton batting, Martin Horton bowling. This was filmed by the B.B.C. as one of their contributions to a world wide programme beamed to America to launch the use of the 'Early Bird' satellite.

The ground was used for 88 County games until 1973 and the County made a successful return in 1987.

Mitchells and Butlers

The Club's first ground was sited within the Cape Hill Brewery site and was a small enclosure surrounded by a running track. Boundaries were described by one writer of the day as 'As plentiful as blackberries in August'. A canal feeder to the brewery was a favourite target for batsmen, one batsman hitting three balls into it in one innings in 1923. With extensions to the brewery encroaching on the ground in the 1920's the Club developed the present ground, which was opened in 1930, in Portland Road. The area had previously been used to grow barley to provide some of the malt for the brewery. These new grounds of over thirteen acres were praised for their excellence, providing facilities for tennis and bowls and social activities, in addition to cricket.

The first County game was staged there in 1931 when Warwickshire met Kent and continued to be used for County Cricket until 1961. During the period 1939—1945, the Portland Road ground was requisitioned and the Club returned to play on the Cape Hill ground for the period.

The League record partnership created by Harry Kirton and R.A.D. Wyatt was scored at Portland Road.

In 1959 Jack Bannister, formerly with Mitchells and Butlers, took 10–41 for Warwickshire v Combined Services on the ground. The best bowling figures in an innings in First Class cricket by a Warwickshire bowler.

Moseley

Until Moseley moved to their present ground they had shared facilities with rugby and soccer clubs.

Their first League ground at the Reddings was shared with Moseley Rugby Club. In the early part of each season there is reference to the poor state of the outfield, although spectators benefited from the grandstand erected for the rugby supporters. In 1902, when the Rugby Club were making improvements, Moseley played games at the County Ground, Edgbaston, and again in 1911 the Moseley Second Eleven had to play all their games at Barnt Green C.C.

The Rugby Club gave the cricket club notice of termination of tenure in 1924 but as a result of representations by the League, cricket continued there until 1930.

Cricket then joined up with soccer and Moor Green F.C. at the Moorlands. This ground was more spacious than the Reddings and again there was ample covered accommodation for spectators.

In 1938, Alec Hastilow presented the Club with a scoreboard to mark his retirement from League cricket.

With the onset of the war in 1939 there was not sufficient funds to maintain the ground in a fit condition for play and Moseley played all games from 1940 until 1946 away from home.

In 1953, Moor Green F.C. served notice on the cricket club and at the end of the season the black, green and silver Moseley flag, which had flown in the summer time, was hauled down after 23 years. Then followed a bizarre ceremony, the funeral of the 'Clonking Stick', a bat which had been used by Norman Parker for twenty years. Preceded by a tolling bell, a procession moved out of the pavilion to the wicket, headed by 'Rusty' Scorer, with Cecil Addleman and Peter Cranmer acting as pall-bearers carrying the bat on a bier draped with Club Flag. Behind walked the chief mourner, Norman Parker, and the bat was ceremoniously buried in a hole dug by Peter Horne. Later Norman returned, dug the bat up, and used it the following season!

The Club then moved to the Robin Hood Stadium where they had their own cricket facilities alongside another soccer club, Jack Mould's Athletic. The pavilion and scoreboard were moved from Moorlands to the new ground. By 1957 the ground had been taken over for development as a crematorium and for one season the club played on a wicket on the football pitch bound with cow dung!, until their present ground was ready for use in 1959.

1959 saw the start of a new era for the club at the present ground, where the club have developed excellent cricket facilities and a flourishing social membership.

Old Hill

The Old Hill ground with its grassy tree-lined slopes set next to Haden Hill Park must be one of the prettiest in the country. When the Club joined the League in 1920 the ground was basin-shaped with a pronounced slope. Measures were taken in 1923 to level off the playing area and a scoreboard and press box were presented by Mr. G.F. Sykes. In those days crowds of 4,000 covered the slopes to see the League games and a similar number turned up in 1976 when the great West Indies side played in a benefit match for Ron Headley.

In 1925, the Club voted against Bank Holiday fixtures because a 'right of way' was used for visitors to the fete in the Park.

The ground was originally held on lease. In 1934 the Club raised £3,000 in ten weeks to buy the ground and a tablet was unveiled in 1938 in the pavilion recording the names of donors and the celebration in 1935 of the Silver Jubilee of King George V and Queen Mary. The ground was levelled off and enlarged to its present state for the 1947 season.

The refreshment building was erected in 1950 as a memorial to W.L. Edwards, late player and President of the Club, who, with Major G.H. Green was instrumental in obtaining the purchase of the ground. The building was extended in 1977.

Smethwick

The ground is situated in Broomfields, Smethwick. Part of the ground was originally Glebe Land attached to Smethwick Old Church. It was purchased by Mr. Henry Mitchell who let it to the club at peppercorn rent under the Harry Mitchell Trust. The area to be used by an official Smethwick Cricket and Athletic Club comprising at least 20 members.

An old pavilion, built in 1903, originally stood at the lower end of the ground, to be replaced later by the present pavilion. The present bar was opened in 1959.

In 1926 it was recorded that new seating had been installed and the ground layout altered to give parking for motor cars.

The scoreboard was a gift of Cyril Goodway and first used in 1934. It was damaged by vandals in 1986 but soon brought back into use.

There are frequent references in early years to the batting of players such as Geoffrey Tomkinson, Kidderminster, and Wally Hatfield, Mitchells and Butlers, whose big hits cleared the Drill Hall adjoining the ground and scattered the troops and horses on the parade ground.

Stourbridge

The ground on High Street, Amblecote, is owned by Dudley Town Council and leased to the club. The lease was handed over to the Club by the Mayor of Stourbridge on the occasion of the opening of the pavilion in 1928. The pavilion was donated by Mr. Ernest Stevens, a local philanthropist, who also furnished the rooms. New turnstiles were added in 1932 and an old racing track was removed, although the gravel was not grassed over until 1980.

During the 1939—1945 war, the pavilion was commandeered for use by American forces and the cricketers changed in an old wooden football pavilion. In 1952, the electric light replaced the gas lighting in the pavilion and in 1958 the supporters' club built the scoreboard. The pavilion was extended in the 1970's and was completely renovated in 1987.

The record tenth wicket stand in English County Cricket was

established on the ground in 1909 when F.E. Woolley, 185 and A. Fielder, 112 not out, added 235 for Kent in their match v Worcestershire. Over sixty First Class games have been staged on the enclosure.

No visit to the Club in recent years would have been complete without a chat with Norman Pearson, 'Uncle Pete', a player and administrator of the Club for over 55 years.

Walsall

Walsall originally played on the 'Chuckery'. This ground belonged to the Earl of Bradford and was formerly part of a large sports complex on which Walsall Town F.C. and Walsall Swifts F.C. played. The ground was the scene of a number of visits from the All England Elevens. On their last visit, in 1883, they lost to a Walsall and District Twenty Two.

With building development encroaching upon the ground the Club endeavoured to purchase the land but negotiations failed and the present ground in Gorway Road was purchased for use from 1909. The ground known as 'Gorway' was formerly surrounded by golf links, and many of the young cricket supporters went home with a stray golf ball as a trophy. Although good crowds were reported, the Club had difficulty in maintaining the ground and, in 1930, sold it for £1,500 to the Town Council from whom the Club now rent the ground.

A scoreboard was presented to the Club in 1934 by Mr. S.N. Jones, and the present scorebox erected in the 1950's.

In 1945 an appeal was launched to replace the old pavilion which had been moved from the Chuckery and was then eighty years old. In 1963 improvements were made in the Gorway Club Rooms and bar and in 1971 as a result of a fresh appeal and initial finance from the Gorway Club, the present pavilion was officially opened on 11th July. The concrete terracing in front of the pavilion and tea rooms was laid in 1948.

West Bromwich Dartmouth

The original ground at Four Acres lay about one mile west of the present ground and was rented from the Earl of Dartmouth. It was also used by West Bromwich Albion from 1882–85. The first pavilion was a tool shed and the visitors changed in the horses' stable which was cleaned out each Saturday. The playing area was described as being confined, with an incline from side to side. The enclosure was bounded by brick walls with a school on one side and cottages at one end, white-washed to form a sight-screen. A pavilion was built in 1900 and transferred later to the Sandwell Park ground in 1920.

When play restarted after the Great War, the long grass on Four Acres was burnt off and it was reported that it was difficult to determine where the pitch was! The site was sold for development in 1920 and play has since continued at Sandwell Park.

The Sandwell ground was initially rented from the Earl of Dartmouth, then in 1933, he offered the site to the club on generous terms and the Club celebrated the centenary year by completing the purchase. In 1947, the scoreboard was presented by Mr. H.H. Hackett and a new tea room built.

The present splendid pavilion, dressing rooms and grounds-man's house were opened in 1968. The cost was met by voluntary donations and fund raising events initiated in the 1950's by Jim Gaunt followed in succeeding years by club members led by Clive James and Jack Williams.

In 1984, the Club staged the Minor Counties v West Indies match — the first such match by a touring side on a Birmingham League ground.

Worcester City

The ground in Evendine Close was taken on lease from the Dean and Chapter of Worcester Cathedral in 1968.

Warwickshire

Warwickshire play all their First Division games on the famous Edgbaston County Ground, except when staging of Test matches causes a re-arrangement of League fixtures, when the home game is played on the opponents' ground.

The side in the Second Division play on a small Colts' ground adjoining the main ground. With its small boundaries behind each wicket the high netting does not always prevent lusty hits clearing for a six.

Aldridge

Aldridge own their ground at The Green, Aldridge, and have played there for over a century. The third team matches are played on ground behind the Club House. The Club have a long lease on this additional ground.

Moseley

CHARITY AND BENEVOLENCE

The League promoted a new Competition in 1894, a League Charity Shield Competition with the object of raising funds for donation to charities. A trophy which had been presented originally to the Birmingham Cricket Association by Mr. Henry Mitchell was, with his approval, to be awarded to the winners to be held for one season and not won outright.

The Trophy was initially competed for each season by the top four clubs in the League during the previous season. In 1897 it was decided that the clubs competing should be drawn from the top four, as before, except that, if the cup holders were not one of the four, it should be that club plus the top three. This created a problem in the season, for Stourbridge, the holders, were not in the top four and Handsworth Wood and Moseley had tied for third place. Handsworth Wood were nominated because Moseley's match the previous year had made a financial loss!

The Competition did not prove successful. Games were played mid week under normal League Rules — no overs matches then! The Clubs found it difficult to raise sides or spectator support. The proceeds of the games did not justify the effort and the Competition was abandoned after the 1897 season. In that year Aston Unity and Handsworth Wood shared the trophy after two replays failed to bring a decision, yet the profit from the 'gate' was only £2.8s.0d.

With the consent of Mr. Mitchell, the Trophy was allocated from 1899 to be presented to the Division Two Champions. The League was to donate five guineas to a charity nominated by the winning club. The Trophy, a large shield, is still an imposing feature at League Presentation evenings.

In 1898, the League made another endeavour to promote a match to raise money for charity by arranging for a League 15 to play Warwickshire at Edgbaston. This match was rained off so Warwickshire and the League shared the expenses, each club in the League having to pay 7s.6d.

Following the lack of success of this latter venture the League arranged that each year there should be a levy on the Clubs to build up a Charity and Benevolent Fund. The object of the fund was to provide assistance for League players, umpires or officials, or their close relatives who were in financial difficulty due to illness, injury or bereavement. As a further source of income, the First Division Champions v The Rest was arranged from season 1906 to 1975 with a similar arrangement for the Second Division from 1922 to 1966.

The Charity and Benevolent Fund received a fresh stimulus

in 1923 when the Handsworth Wood Cricket Club closed and donated to the League their remaining cash balance of £82.11s.1d. Conditions agreed were that the League Benevolence should cover old Handsworth members and that if the Champions v Rest did not raise £10 per annum then the League should make good the shortfall.   In practice, the sum and more was generally reached since, in addition to the proceeds of the match, the participating finalists often made additional donations to the Fund to mark their success.   Following the donation by Handsworth, the Fund was placed in an independent account with the appointment of Trustees nominated initially by the League and Handsworth Wood and subsequently by the League.   In 1980, at the instigation of the League Treasurer, Mac White, a Trust Deed was drawn up to ensure that the investment income of the Fund would be exempt from tax.

In connection with this Fund, it is worth recalling that before the Government National Insurance legislation in 1911 workers often received no help towards expenses of sickness and no wages or sick pay during illness, so families could suffer great hardships. The League have made numerous grants and, although in the early 1900's the sums seem a trifle by today's standards, for example £5 to an umpire to be paid at 5/- per week, the letters of appreciation received by the League Secretary show just how welcome this aid has been.

In addition to grants from the Benevolent Fund, the League also fielded League representative sides to play Clubs raising funds to assist their members.   As mentioned in the Chapter dealing with the period 1939—1945, the League promoted a number of matches in aid of war time charities.

In 1930, when Gordon Field died, his family was left in straightened circumstances.   Gordon had been a fine captain and for 25 years a League player.   The League contributed towards the admission of his two sons to the Royal Orphanage at Wolverhampton.   This was to mark the start of annual donations to the School.   In 1934, the Orphanage accepted the sons of J. Sparkes, also of West Bromwich Dartmouth, the League then doubling its annual contributions.   Whilst the lads were in his care, the Principal of the Orphanage sent to the League regular bulletins on their progress and the League, as a sponsor to the Charity, was entitled to vote on applications for admission.   The Orphanage eventually became the Royal Wolverhampton School and it is pleasing to record that the League still makes an annual contribution to the Orphans of the School.

The Clubs still make donations to the Fund which in the 1986 Report, stands at a healthy £2361, the investment income from which enables the present day members to continue the ideals of the Founder Members.

Winners of Charity Shield

> 1894 Aston Unity
> 1895 Walsall
> 1896 Stourbridge
> 1897 Aston Unity   )
>   Handsworth Wood) Joint Holders
> Highest Score 218—6 Dudley v Aston Unity 1895
> Lowest Score 42 Dudley v Aston Unity 1894

Highest Individual Score 113 n.o. G.F. Wheldon Dudley v Aston Unity 1895

Best Bowling:- 8—47 J. Barton Handsworth Wood v Walsall 1897.

Match Double:- H.B.G. Hill 71 and 7 wickets for Handsworth Wood v Walsall, 1895.

Kidderminster

THE CHALLENGE CUP

With the introduction in the 1930's of evening 20 over knock out competitions, suggestions were made that the League should promote such a competition. It was not until 1957 that a Kidderminster proposal received support and a competition was inaugurated in 1958 to compete for a cup presented by Mr. C.H. James:- 'The Birmingham and District League Challenge Cup'. The first set of Rules is given in the Appendix, the principal changes since then being: —

* Dates for rounds fixed (1959)
* Clubs invited from outside the League to widen scope of competition (1964) when 6 Clubs were to be nominated by Midlands Club Cricket Conference and (1978) when Clubs to be decided by Management Committee.
* Teams allowed to play a professional, providing he received no fee (1959)
* 1958—1963 games were 18 — 6 ball overs thereafter 16 —8 ball overs.
* No player to bowl more than 4 overs in any one innings (1968)
* 1964 Club scorers allowed to score in Final
* From 1968, proceeds of each match divided by the two contesting clubs.
* 1965 Neutral umpires to be appointed for all rounds — until then umpires had been appointed for the Final only.
* 1986 Competition for 2nd Division Knock Out Cup inaugurated, Shield presented by Dudley. Runners-up Cup by West Bromwich Dartmouth.

No non League side has won the Challenge Cup. In 1968 Bridgnorth C.C. became the first non-League side to reach the Final, followed by Wolverhampton C.C. in 1972, Harborne C.C. in 1985.

The Birmingham and District League Challenge Cup

	Winners	Runners Up
1958	Moseley I	Stourbridge II
1959	Old Hill I	Moseley II
1960	Walsall I	Moseley I
1961 +	Moseley II	West Bromwich Dartmouth II
1962	Moseley	Mitchells and Butlers
1963	Old Hill	Walsall
1964*	Dudley	Old Hill
1965	Old Hill	Moseley
1966@	Kidderminster	Old Hill
1967	Kidderminster	Dudley
1968	Aston Unity	Bridgnorth
1969	West Brom. Dartmouth	Moseley
1970	West Brom. Dartmouth	Kidderminster

1971	Kidderminster	Stourbridge
1972	West Brom. Dartmouth	Wolverhampton
1973	Walsall	Stourbridge
1974	Walsall	Moseley
1975	Smethwick	Old Hill
1976	Smethwick	Mitchells and Butlers
1977	Kidderminster	Old Hill
1978	Old Hill	West Bromwich Dartmouth
1979	Aston Unity	West Bromwich Dartmouth
1980	Kidderminster	Aston Unity
1981	Mitchells and Butlers	Smethwick
1982	Kidderminster	Stourbridge
1983	% Old Hill	Walsall
1984	Old Hill	Moseley
1985	Old Hill	Harborne
1986	Old Hill	Moseley
1987	Coventry & Nth.Warks.	West Bromwich Dartmouth

2nd Division Knock Out Cup

	Winners	Runners Up
1986	Stourbridge	Moseley
1987	Walsall	Kidderminster

+ In 1961 Moseley also won the Championship of both First and Second Divisions

@ In 1966 Kidderminster were also joint Champions with Walsall of the First Division

% In 1983 Old Hill were Champions of First Division

* Prior to 1964 League Clubs were permitted to enter two sides.

Edgbaston

REPRESENTATIVE MATCHES

Apart from the sides raised for the Champions v The Rest matches and matches in support of Clubs or players benefits the League fielded one Representative side in the period before 1914. This was a League XI v Rest of Warwickshire and was played in September 1892.

League XI 1st Innings — 144 Hawke out 'handled the ball' 39
2nd Innings — 126 J.E. Hill absent 0
Rest of Warwickshire 1st Innings 117 H.B.G. Hill 5 wickets, Colston 5 wickets Quaife 40 Richards 32. 2nd Innings 24—1
Match drawn.

Many of the players in the Rest of Warwickshire side were also League players.

A match in 1898 Warwickshire C.C. v A League Fifteen was rained off.

In 1920 a League eleven met Old Hill in aid of the benefit of the Old Hill professional Meunier.

In 1924 and 1929 the League inaugurated matches against Coventry and District League and The South Wales and Monmouth Cricket Association, the latter fixtures being two day games. Eric Perry showed his talent in a game versus South Wales and Monmouth played in 1931 at Portland Road.

League XI 414 E. Perry 110 G.S. Tomkinson 98 R.I. Scorer 62 L.E. Gale 56
South Wales and Monmouth Cricket Association First Innings 200 Second Innings 99 E. Perry 4—0

Eric Cross, the Moseley wicket-keeper, took three catches in the first innings and had five catches and a stumping in the second innings.

R.I. Scorer took a side of League players to Nottingham in 1934 to play a two day game against Sir Julian Cahn's XI.

League XI First Innings 182 H. Kirton 73, E. Perry 51. Second Innings 135—8 E. Perry 35, N.L. Mathews 39 n.o.
Sir Julian Cahn's XI 378 F. Gross 5—101.

Caps were awarded to the players, an innovation which met with general approval.

In the succeeding years prior to 1939, games were also played against North Staffordshire League.

After the 1939—45 war, the League fielded sides for games against Aston Unity, in 1947, and Halesowen, in 1949, to mark the opening of their new grounds. League clubs voted in 1951 to revive the practice of playing other Cricket Leagues and Associations.

In 1951 the League fielded a side at Dudley against a West Indies Eleven in aid of George Headley's benefit. The West Indies were captained by Learie Constantine and a crowd of over 10,000 attended.

League XI 258—7 R. Dovey 61, B. Rowley 72
West Indies XI 225 E. Weekes 101, R. Dovey 4—17.

Annual pre-season 'warm up' games versus Warwickshire County Cricket Club were inaugurated in 1953. In the first match the League side fell to defeat at the hands of Eric Hollies, on a wicket that suited his talents. The League was due to receive 40% of gross receipts but made a loss of £7. In 1955 Under 21 games against a Warwickshire Nursery XI was added to the fixture list — the summary record of the first game included some names of interest:—

League Junior XI 148—7 P. Booton 33, R.G.A. Headley 44, W.B. Bridge 3—34
Warwickshire Colts 90—4 D.P. Ratcliffe 18, M.L. Simms 22 n.o.

In 1956, the League Senior XI came close to beating the County in a closely fought two-day game.

League XI 1st Innings 140 I. King 43 n.o. N.H. Whiting 37
2nd Innings 162 R.W. Powell 40 C.W. Grove 33
Warwickshire C.C.C. 1st Innings 202 C.W. Grove 5—61 B. Shardlow 3—62. 2nd Innings 86—7 C.W. Grove 3—28 B. Shardlow 4—42

The Under 21 side recorded a good win against the Warwickshire Nursery on May 21st 1960 scoring 202—5 in reply to the Nursery's 201—6, Les Rolinson 118 n.o. and Ken Porter 65 were the League's batting stars.

In 1963 the League agreed that players who appeared in the League Representative side could purchase a League Cap and after three appearances, a tie would be awarded.

The 1964 Warwickshire match was reduced to a one day game by rain. David Ratcliffe scored the first century by a League player in the fixture, the League having the better of the game.

League XI 244—7 D.P. Ratcliffe 115 B. Rowley 42 n.o. D.M.W. Heath 38
Warwickshire C.C.C. 167—8 R.B. Abell 3—29 B. Rowley 2—62 P.J. Robinson 2—12

In 1966, it was arranged with Warwickshire to play two knock-out games instead of a two day game. Bernard Rowley became the second League player to score a century when, on the first day, he scored 102 in a League total of 215—9 with Warwickshire responding with 217—6. The League lost 153—9 to 154—3 on the second day but Bernard again performed well with the bat, scoring 40. Colin Price took advantage of the good Edgbaston wicket to score a century, 101 n.o., in 1968 but the County side won the game by 6 wickets. In 1970 the two day matches v Warwickshire were discontinued and a single day substituted.

1973 and 1974 were to see further centuries against the County side and 1974 a splendid win.

1973 League XI 197—5 (50 Overs) D.N.F. Slade 125 T. Pearsall 25 C.L. Price 20
Warwickshire 161—2 (27.5 overs) rain stopped play

1974 Warwickshire C.C.C. 239 (50 Overs)
League XI 244—4 (43.3 Overs) J.F. Taylor 102 n.o. T. Pearsall 31

With the entry of Warwickshire into the League in 1975 the League Junior XI versus Warwickshire Nursery matches were discontinued.

Doug Slade recorded his second century against the County in 1975.

Warwickshire 276—6 (45 Overs) D.L. Amiss 98 J.A. Jameson 64
League XI 223—4 (45 Overs) D.N.F. Slade 117 J.F. Taylor 45 T. Pearsall 34

League Representative side cricket received a fresh impetus in 1965 when the League Cricket Conference, which had been formed in 1962, promoted an Inter-League Knock Out Competition. The League had joined the Conference in 1963 and, in 1965, decided to enter the Inter-League Competition which was then sponsored by Rothmans.

In their first venture, the League side lost against the North Staffs and Cheshire League but had the later consolation of knowing that they had lost to the eventual winners. In 1967, the League side won through to the Final, losing a close game against the Lincolnshire League. In the semi-final against old opponents North Staffs and Cheshire League the League side batting second scored 242—8 to win in 44.2 overs. David Kench scoring 100.

The side reached the Final again in 1970 but once more the Lincolnshire League side came out victors. Success was to be achieved in 1972 when the League won the Trophy beating the North Yorkshire and South Durham League in an exciting finish. First 3 overs to go and 30 runs needed, then 1 over and 10 runs required. With 2 balls left, the scores were level and after careful field placing the bowler bowled a 'No-Ball'! Scores in this successful run were as follows:—

Round 1 v North Staffs & District Cricket League (at Kidderminster)
Birmingham League 165 all out (43.5 overs) J.B. Sedgley 40 I. Watson 33
North Staffs & District Cricket League 87 (29.1 overs) W.A. Bourne 3—14 R.B. Abell 3—25

Round 2 v North Warwickshire League (at Bedworth) North Warwickshire League 163—6 (45 overs)
Birmingham League 66—3 (after 25 overs)Rain stopped play. Round awarded to Birmingham League by default.

Round 3 v Bassetlaw League (at Worksop)
Birmingham League 201—7 (45 overs) D.N.F. Slade 85
Bassetlaw League 124 all out (42.3 overs) D.N.F. Slade 3—20 W.A. Bourne 3—24

Semi-Final v Central Lancashire League (at Sandwell Park)
Birmingham League 245—8 (45 overs) D.N.F. Slade 74 R.N. Abberley 53
Central Lancashire League 164 all out (43.3 overs) D.N.F. Slade 4—39 J.D. Inchmore 2—18

Final v North Yorkshire and South Durham League (at Sandwell Park)
North Yorks & South Durham League 170—9 (45 overs) D.N.F.

Slade 4—51 H.J. Latham 3—30
Birmingham League 174—8 (44.4 overs) G.S. Warner 58 n.o. D.N.F.
Slade 25 R.N. Abberley 25 H.J. Latham 21 T. Hawkes 18 n.o.

The Inter League Competition had no sponsor in this winning
season but the Warwickshire Supporters' Club presented £100 in
appreciation of the League's success and this cancelled out the
financial loss sustained by the League.

In 1984, 46 year old Peter Goodwin the Chairman of the
League Selection Committee had to turn out in one game as a late
replacement when Ricardo Elcock dropped out through injury. The
League side won through to the Final in that season but lost on
scoring rate in a rain affected game.

The League side were losing finalists in 1981 when they lost
to the Western League in the last over of the game, and again in
1983 when they lost to Durham County in a game reduced to 30
overs and yet again in 1985 the victors this time being the Bassetlaw
District League, who won a rain restricted game on a faster scoring
rate.

After a number of changes in sponsorship the Competition was
unable to attract a sponsor from 1983.   The League reluctantly
withdrew from the Competition in 1986, not only because of the
cost but also because of the difficulty in raising a strong, representative side, owing to the plethora of competitions to which clubs are
now committed.

1975 saw the introduction of representative games versus the
Midland Cricket Club Conference and 1977 an Under 21 Competition against Coventry and District Cricket League.   1983 started
pre-season games against Worcestershire County Club.   The League
has also fielded Representative sides against touring sides from
Australia and an Ireland Under 23 side, but probably the most
pleasant occasion in recent years was a game against West Bromwich
Dartmouth in 1983 as part of the club's 150 years' celebrations.

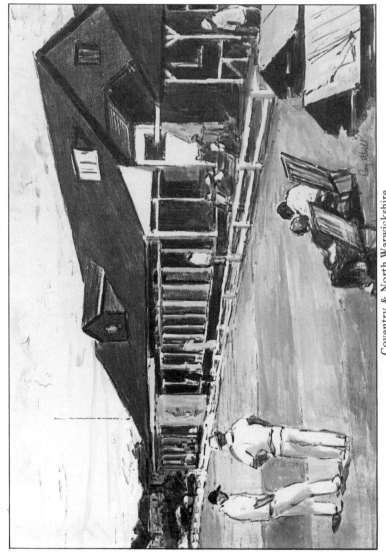

Coventry & North Warwickshire

UMPIRES AND SCORERS

Umpires, scorers and scoreboard operators form the unobtrusive third team in each game. Generally it is only when there is an incident that they get a mention in match accounts. It is a tribute to the members of this third team that such incidents have occurred infrequently and highlighting them can only emphasise their singularity.

Umpires

The appointment of neutral umpires for club games was a new and significant measure introduced by the League at its formation. The first umpires had to be recruited from the clubs who nominated candidates they considered suitable, such nominees being precluded from umpiring games in which their Clubs were engaged. Umpires' Associations, Instructions to Umpires and training courses were then unknown, so such candidates would have been cricket enthusiasts of mixed ability. It is noticeable that, as Associations and training have developed, the accounts of incidents have changed their nature from umpires' lack of knowledge of Laws to authorititive interpretation of Laws or League Rules. Two instances to illustrate: —

(1) In 1900 the Rev. W.L. Thomas (Walsall) was incorrectly given out when, after a hit, the ball lodged in his pad and was retrieved by a fielder. The M.C.C. had ruled, in 1899, that the ball was 'dead' in that situation.

(2) In 1982 when Moseley met Mitchells and Butlers in a rain curtailed match Moseley decared thinking that Mitchells would only be able to receive 19 overs and thus no bonus point would be awarded, since 20 overs were needed to be bowled for a bonus point to be gained. The umpires, however, pointed out that 20 overs could in fact be bowled and Mitchells were able to ensure their scoring rate would obtain the bonus.

The M.C.C. issued the first version of 'Instructions to Umpires' in 1892 and the League referred umpires to these as applicable until 1896 when the first issue of the League's own 'Instructions to Umpires' was sent out with the League Rules. A copy of these is included in the Appendices.

The Umpires' appointments were arranged by the Honorary Secretary and each year the umpires' list was reviewed at the League A.G.M., incompetent umpires being 'struck off'. In 1895, the umpires requested a meeting with the League to discuss the system of appointments. The League agreed provided the umpires would agree to discuss fitness!. Minutes of League meetings of this period refer to an umpire drawing stumps early, apologising to the League, and resigning, whilst another Minute recommends an umpire be given a 'rest'. The umpires fee was then 7/6 plus expenses. In 1904 when an umpire reported a player for 'unbecoming conduct, inciting the crowd and personal verbal attack', — the League commended the umpire and expressed confidence in his ability.

A pleasant event took place in 1909 when the League umpires entertained the retiring League Secretary H.B.G. Hill at a Smoking Concert and presented him with a smoking cabinet. By 1910, a Secretary to represent the umpires had been appointed, Mr. E.V. Coe, who drew attention to the bad state of the umpires' coats which were then provided by clubs. In the years prior to the 1914 war, the umpires unsuccessfully campaigned for a rise in fee but the League agreed to keep a short list so that the umpires would have more matches!

When play was resumed in 1919, the League found it necessary to advertise for umpires and an umpires' sub-committee was formed to vet applications but no umpire served on the sub-committee. In 1923 umpires were urged to study the Laws before taking League games. This followed an incident in a game when Spring, the West Bromwich Dartmouth professional, was 'no-balled' because he delivered the ball with both feet behind the bowling crease — the player protested and after conference between umpires and captains the no ball was cancelled.

1925 marked an important development when the 'Birmingham and District Cricket Umpires Association' was formed, the first such organisation in the area. Two League umpires, W.J. Lawday and J. Horne, were prominent figures in the new Association. W.J. Lawday had been appointed to the Minor Counties' panel in that year. The new Association was soon to become effective with the introduction of an 'Umpires Corner' in the 'Sports Argus', and a talk to umpires by 'Tiger' Smith, who recommended that the Association should develop training and promote examinations for umpiring candidates. The Association tried to follow up his suggestion in 1928 but the initial response from umpires was poor and it was the early 1930's before courses and examinations became a feature in training. In this period the title of the Association was changed to 'The Midland Counties Cricket Umpires Association'.

In 1926 A. Steward, the Kidderminster professional, was bowling left arm over the wicket when the batsman complained he was damaging the pitch. The umpire asked Steward to bowl round the wicket and the bowler complied — an early illustration of the 'danger area' and a novel solution.

1931 saw an umpire informed that he was out of order in discussing his decisions with the crowd! Then in 1936, umpires were advised to say 'Over' and not 'Keep it' or similar wording, after a dispute in a game about whether the ball was 'dead'.

The League moved into closer co-operation with the 'Midland Counties Cricket Umpires Association' in 1937 when the Association was given a seat on the League umpires' sub-committee. At the same time the Association arranged for League representatives to be members of the examination board, to appoint a delegate to the Council and also nominated the League President as a Vice President of the Association. The League umpires sub-committee at this time comprised three or four regular players and a past player. Mr. W.J. Phair and Mr. C.A.F. Hastilow are recorded as having given excellent service.

On 6th May 1939 West Bromwich Dartmouth dismissed Smethwick for 45. When the Dartmouth had scored 47—0 tea was taken.

During tea the umpires ascertained that a ball hit by G. Dodd, Dartmouth, had not crossed the boundary although signalled as a 4. The batsmen had not crossed so the Dartmouth score was reduced to 43 and the winning runs scored after tea! Following a misunderstanding about a winning hit in an Old Hill v Smethwick match in 1944, umpires were instructed to obtain a signal from the scorers immediately a winning hit was made. This has not always been complied with, and similar misunderstandings have arisen since then. On one occasion, the score of the team batting first had been altered by children and on another occasion the score on the board at the completion of an innings had been incorrect.

From 1947 to 1949, the League arranged a dinner for the umpires with an address by 'Tiger' Smith and in 1949 umpires with five year's service were awarded a 'Complimentary Pass' to all grounds and after 21 years one for life, although the latter was not likely to be claimed very often.

The composition of the League umpires' sub-committee was changed in 1953 to comprise captains of Club elevens of both Divisions One and Two but the weekly appointments were still made by the League Secretary and arranged through the Assistant Secretary who acted as Hon. Secretary of the sub-committee.

The pavilion clock was designated the official time piece from 1956 and all clubs were instructed to make sure this was working correctly. Reference to 'the Pavilion Clock' was then included in the Instructions to Umpires and not deleted until 1983.

Since 1960, the Honorary Secretary of the umpires' sub-committee has been a member of the Midland Counties Cricket Umpires Association, the first holder of the post being Lewis Sutcliffe followed by Norman Cook and the present incumbent, George Wenman. These three have done outstanding work in arranging umpires appointments and have received help from members of the Association to supplement the regular panel when necessary. By 1960 new umpires appointed to the League Panel had to hold an examination qualification issued either by the Association or by the Association of Cricket Umpires which had been formed in 1953. In 1960 the League introduced a system of captains awarding points to umpires at the conclusion of each game and it is pleasing to note that a yearly report of average marks obtained are in the region of 7 out of 10, which indicates general satisfaction with the umpires ability.

Norman Cook has had a long association with the League. He joined Kidderminster in 1920, took up wicket-keeping and had spells with Stourbridge, Old Hill and Aston Unity before leaving the League to play for Halesowen C.C. He then served on the League Umpires' panel and has taken a leading role in both the Midland Counties Cricket Umpires Association and the Association of Cricket Umpires. He has been Secretary of the Warwickshire Cricket Association since its formation and was elected President of the League in 1983.

In 1980, Peter Stevens, a League Umpire became only the third non-county player in recent years to be appointed to the list of First Class Umpires.

A unique umpiring event took place on 10th May 1975, when official umpires appointed for the Old Hill v Smethwick game were the two Club Presidents, Jack Wakeman, Old Hill, and Norman

Downes, Smethwick, — the game was drawn and the marks given to the umpires have not been divulged!

Umpires' names have been included in the League Handbooks since 1962 and from these the following is a list of umpires who have given ten or more years service to the League since then: —

+	Bonham R.W.		Johnson A.
+†	Burrows R.	+	Jones D.B.
	Chapman F.H.	+	Judd W.P.
†	Cook H.N.		Law F.
+	Court B.	+	Lewis J.E.
	Cowles H.A.		Ogden P.D.
	Crowther F.		Penny K.
	Dark G.		Rhodes O.
	Dibnah G.		Riley A.
†	Downes N.C.A.		Sheldon W.M.
+	Dwyers J.A.	+	Stevens P.
	Fennell N.J.	+	Turner B.
†	Grainger S.	†	Wakeman J.
	Hall J.E.	+	Walker J.A.
	Harper D.		Watts T.S.
+	Harvey W.	+†	Wenman G.
	Howard M.S.		

+ On 1987 list
† Played in the League

Other Umpires in 1987

		1st Year
	Brampton B.H.	1982
	Clarke W.	1982
	Brown S.	1987
	Farrah A.	1979
	Fradgley S.	1981
	Lewis P.	1987
†	Moore G.	1979
	Potts J.A.	1981
	Turner K.	1983
†	Woolley B.D.A.	1982
	Bentley B.F.G.	1982
	Hall R.	1982
	Berry B.A.	1984
	Holmes N.V.	1985
	Hughes W.B.	1985
	Keeling J.C.	1985
	Little K.A.	1985
	Bolger J.	1986
	Hamlett B.	1986

† Played in the League

Scorers

Scorers receive even less publicity than umpires but it is their dedicated work that records the matches and scores so that even one hundred years later we can follow the performances of clubs and individuals. Examination of old League club books shows that there has been little change in format. In some clubs there was a record written up from the book used on the day. Another practice was for the fielding side scorer only to record each ball in the bowlers analysis, the batting side scorer just entering the analysis. This could mean that the continuous check and balance with each other made by present day scorers was not carried out and could account for one newspaper match report in 1911 which said 'The captain refused to give the bowling analysis because it did not correspond with the score'! The importance of accurate scoring was illustrated in 1921 when Aston Unity and Mitchells and Butlers tied a game with 128 runs each. Looking in a scorebook after the game it was found that a six signalled by the umpires had been entered as a four. Mitchells and Butlers' captain is reported to have said that his club would not appeal. In a Division Two game, in 1929, Walsall and West Bromwich Dartmouth tied but at the close the umpires found a wide had not been recorded and the match was awarded to West Bromwich Dartmouth, which suggests that perhaps the signalling and acknowledgement procedure broke down.

In 1933 'The Smethwick Telephone' contained an article in praise of scorers which is worth quoting:— "Talking of records gives an opportunity to set forth an expression of appreciation to the scorers who, with the persistent and maybe sometimes too inquisitive newspaper men around them contrive to keep their figures true and their mouth from speaking guile. Local clubs were served by Percy Boneham for Smethwick and Percy Reed Mitchells and Butlers — masters in their craft. Mr. Boneham has completed his 40th season at Broomfield".

Percy Reed was to continue to score games for Mitchells and Butlers until 1975 and completed fifty seven years of meticulous service to the club, a record which is unlikely to be surpassed in the annals of the League. Percy's long service meant that Reg Stimpson, the Mitchells Second XI scorer, could not gain promotion although he is recorded in 1960 as having completed twenty years scoring.

In 1933, a newspaper cartoon recorded the only lady scorer in the League, Miss I.J. Sanders for Aston Unity, and warned umpires that it may be their turn next! a fortaste of today's equal rights! Miss Sanders was not, however, the first lady scorer the 'History of Walsall Cricket Club' for 1894 includes reference to a gift of a gold pencil case to Miss Ada Newman, as a mark of esteem and appreciation of her services. Miss Newman was often assisted by her sister, Emily. In recent years, many wives, girl friends and daughters have given their services. Warwickshire's Second Division side has had lady scorers since their entry into the League, in 1975, the first Mrs. Christine Davis, wife of the author, followed in 1983, by Mrs. Peggy Lloyd.

In 1987, the scorer with the longest service is Donald Parkes of Moseley in his twenty ninth season, closely followed by Mike Rowley of Stourbridge, twenty seven years, Brian Oakley, Walsall twenty six years and Peter Tyzzer, Kidderminster, 14 years.

Other present day scorers are Ken Hayes, Mitchells and Butlers, Stan Cresswell, Smethwick, Gordon McKenzie, West Bromwich Dartmouth, Roy Bent, Worcester City, Chris Cowdell, Old Hill, Dave Shilton, Coventry and North Warwickshire, and the author Alex Davis, for Warwickshire.

Tom Rider, West Bromwich Dartmouth, retired in 1986 to become League Results Secretary after over twenty years service and Fred Freeman gave up his pencil in 1980, after scoring for Smethwick for 35 years.   In the Second Division Barry Thompson continues long service with Smethwick and Mike Brady with Moseley.   Tom Wilde who served Kidderminster for many years died in 1987 whilst preparing to go to a game.   Brian Oakley took over as scorer for the League Representative side on the retirement of Percy Reed.

Whilst all scorers are dedicated to their job, none can be more so than Mike Rowley, whose life is cricket and the Stourbridge Club. This dedication made newspaper headlines and television news when his wife applied for a divorce.   Mike could not be at the Hearing or be interviewed because he was on tour and scoring with a Club side.

Worcester

TEAS, TELEPHONES AND TRANSPORT

Tea Interval

In 1889, there was no specific provision made for a tea interval. The only interval permitted was ten minutes between innings. It is interesting to note that a letter to the editor of the 'Birmingham Post' in that year complained about the practice of teams at Edgbaston going into the pavilion for tea, arguing that it disrupted the continuity of play and concentration of batsmen. The letter went on to ask why could not cups of tea be taken out to players as at Lords and the Oval!

In a Second Division game in 1898 the report states that shortly before 7.00 p.m., the game between Dudley and Mitchells was stopped and there was an adjournment for tea. The batsman dropped his bat, took off his gloves and 'scooted' to the tea tent. Others followed him and the game was suspended for a quarter of an hour, much to the disgust of the Dudley spectators who were not used to that sort of amateur cricket.

It was not until 1943, that the interval between innings was increased from 10 to 15 minutes and twenty years later the present day interval of 20 minutes was introduced.

The work of the tea-makers must receive an appreciative mention. Mrs. Gethin and Mrs. Glover at Kidderminster 1909—1949, Mrs. Ingram at Aston Unity in the period 1947—1983 and Joyce and Ben Green at Stourbridge are a representative few of many who have served Clubs and donated profits to the club funds.

Telephone

With the present day facility of contact by telephone it is easy to forget the problems of communication in early days. Selected players had to be notified by post or by team sheets posted in pavilions and as publicity for the League grew names of players in teams began to be printed in the local newspapers.

At the end of the season, when championship deciders were being played at different venues, sides had to await the arrival of a telegraph boy to confirm whether they had won the title. Contrast this with the situation in 1985 when the local radio broadcast commentaries on deciding games being played at Worcester and Moseley.

When Aston Unity moved to their Hillcourt ground in 1947 they had no telephone but their own pigeon post. Jimmy Lee took a pigeon to away games so that the score could be sent back to the club.

Transport

In 1889 there was an extensive local rail network with reasonably frequent services which enabled teams to reach Dudley and Walsall and Handsworth, albeit usually with a change en-route. When Kidderminster and Stourbridge joined the League, travel to those towns was also by train and Old Hill was a busy railway junction.

In the city, public transport was by steam trams or horse drawn trams and later by cable cars and electric trams.

In 1890, an advertisement for transport to the County Ground at Edgbaston read:—

Fares per person	Hansom	4 Wheeler
Stephenson Place		
to Constance Road	1/4	1/—

Most players worked until 12.30 and then had to rush to make the start but in later years fewer players worked on Saturday mornings and many had their own cars.

Even when motor cars and motor buses became more common -place after 1919, they were subject to mechanical failures so journeys could be fraught with difficulty.

It is not surprising to find numerous accounts of transport delays.   In 1899 the Dudley conveyance on the way to Handsworth Wood broke down at Great Bridge and the team had to walk to West Bromwich to obtain another brake.   They arrived late and were dismissed for 69 H.B.G. Hill, 8—35, and lost by nine wickets. A Walsall side on the way to Handsworth Wood might find them-selves having to walk up Hamstead Hill if the horses could not manage the load.

Kidderminster, or their visitors, were regularly subject to late starts due to breakdowns or trains missing connections.   In 1921, when the Kidderminster side were on the way to Aston Unity, their motor caught fire and the journey was completed in a furniture van! The game started two hours late and Kidderminster, batting first, were all out in eighty minutes for 65.

Even travel in the city was not without its problems for the trams were heavily loaded and players with large cricket bags were not popular with tram conductors, who sometimes refused to accept the heavily laden passenger.

As private cars became more in evidence it was not unknown for a player to be selected on the merit of his passenger availability! Kidderminster probably enjoyed the most luxurious travel, in the Tomkinsons' Rolls Royce.

Wartime travel in 1940—1945 had its problems with reduced rail services and limited petrol.   On one occasion, Smethwick hired taxis to travel to Stourbridge only to be turned out at Lye because the driver had reached the limit of the radius he was allowed to carry a fare.   The side set off to walk but Cyril Goodway somehow managed a fresh booking and saved his legs.

Reports of late arrivals are now infrequent but as West Brom-wich Dartmouth found in 1976, on their way to Walsall, even motor-way links can prove unreliable.

Umpires were often faced with more travelling problems than players for players could make team arrangements.   In 1903, captains were advised that, although games had to be played out to the agreed time for drawing stumps, the umpires could be allowed to leave if a result had been achieved. Forty years later clubs were asked to ensure umpires were not kept waiting for their fee as umpires complained they were missing their trains and buses. Until an all-in fee was agreed in 1940 umpires were exhorted to take advantage of cheap fares to keep expenses to a minimum.

Transport services on conclusion of the game were less frequent than at the lunch time and so on return journeys a mid-night arrival at home was commonplace.

With all the problems of transport it says much for the enthusiasm of the players that fixtures were honoured and that the League's aim to provide ordered cricket has been sustained over the years.

PAST, PRESENT AND FUTURE

This history has been but a resume of the many summers when the League has brought the enjoyment of good class, competitive cricket to lovers of the game in the Midlands. Perhaps this book will stimulate the Clubs to write up their own histories and provide a useful source of social history in the locality in which they have played.

The Founders of the League would no doubt be delighted to know that their ideals and aims are still being followed after 100 years. Indeed, if the Founders were to have returned on Friday, 7th August 1987, to read the fixtures for the next day, they could almost have imagined that it was 7th August 1896 such is the resemblance between the two sets of fixtures.

Fixtures for Saturday August 8th

1896		1987	
Kidderminster v Stourbridge		Kidderminster v	Coventry & Nth. Warwicks.
Mitchells	v Handsworth Wood	Old Hill v	Smethwick
Smethwick	v Dudley	Stourbridge v	Walsall
Walsall	v Moseley	Warwickshire v	Mitchells & Butlers
West Brom. Dartmouth	v Aston Unity	West Brom. Dartmouth v	Aston Unity
		Worcester City v	Moseley

The Founders would no doubt be pleased to see that eight of the Clubs who played in the early years are still carrying on the traditional annual competition for honours and that they have been rejoined by the County Club, and by the old established clubs, Old Hill and Coventry and North Warwickshire, and representatives from Worcester. The absence of Handsworth Wood and Dudley due to loss of their grounds would be regretted but on visiting other grounds the Founders would surely be delighted to see the immaculate playing surfaces and excellent Club facilities the Clubs now enjoy.

The absence of a large crowd of supporters might cause the Founders some concern as to the state of the finances but the large social gathering enjoying the bar and the 'one-armed bandits' would supply the answer.

On the playing side there would surely be misgivings about the need to make games more lively and competitive by introducing limited overs, a points system differentiating between winning and losing draws and penalty points for slow over rates. These misgivings would, however, be mollified by the good order of the games and the enthusiasm with which they are played.

178

Coaching at West Bromwich Dartmouth with Alan Neal and Doug Slade.

The substitution of helmets for colourful caps would be a surprise and the absence of gaily coloured blazers would be noticed but the immaculate turn out of the umpires and their exemplary officiating would be sure to evoke favourable comment.

As they recalled the years and the great players, with the old supporters on the boundary, Founders would be pleased to hear that the League had been the nursery in which many Test and County players had first had experience of highly competitive cricket and that one of the original objects of the League had been fulfilled.

At the close of play, as players and spectators replay the game, just as they have through the years, the Founders would be satisfied that the game of cricket they knew is still a sport much to be enjoyed.

What of the Future?   With the excellent facilities at their disposal, the result of dedicated work by club members over the years, the present members of clubs have a splendid opportunity to ensure the continuing development of interest in the game.

Already League clubs are promoting youth coaching schemes making up in good measure for the reduction in school cricket. This move should, in the long term, be beneficial to the Clubs, leading to greater support of clubs from the youngsters and their families.

The entry of League Clubs into other leagues for Sunday play may pose a threat to the future status of the League, particularly with growth of sponsorship, which may make some leagues more financially appealing than others.   With the rising cost of the sport, the attraction of sponsorship is strong but it would be a pity if financial support rather than the standard of play, were to be the deciding factor in the League's standing.

The need to ensure a closely fought high standard competition may revive suggestions, mooted some years ago, of introducing more clubs so as to form two Divisions, with promotion and relegation between the Divisions.   The excellent network of motorways in the Midlands presents possibilities of enlarging the sphere over which the League could draw its support, just as the growth of the railway system did in the latter part of the 19th Century.

These factors and many others will no doubt be given serious thought by the League as the League progresses into its second century.   May the decisions taken ensure that the League flourishes as it has in the past and that it will continue to hold its place as 'First in the Field!'

APPENDICES

Playing statistics extracted from match reports by John Reeves, Aston Unity C.C.

Notes

Playing records relate to First Division games unless otherwise stated.

Prior to 1945 sides 'Batted On' after winning so bowling and batting records before 1945 may not be truly comparable with those from 1945.

8 + wickets refers to 8 or more wickets in an innings.

Records have been compiled from information found or made available by September 1987. Results of all matches played since 1889 have been collected but a few match reports and averages in the early years have not been traced.

LEAGUE OFFICERS

Honorary Secretary

The League has been extremely well served by it's Honorary Secretaries the present holder of the post David Bryant being only the sixth in the hundred years of the League.

H.B. Grosvenor Hill 1888 to 1909

One of the League's founders. A solicitor, played for Handsworth Wood until 1909. He was an opening bowler with his left arm deliveries, taking more than 60 wickets in each of five seasons including 85 victims in 1902 and scoring useful runs batting right handed. He played five games with Warwickshire 1894-1900.

Sir C. Herbert Smith 1910 to 1919

Head of a large firm of Chartered Accountants he was a well known figure in Birmingham. Knighted in 1938 for his philanthropic and business acumen. C.H. Smith played for Moseley in the First Division of the League from the 1894 season for fifteen years as an all-rounder bowling slow leg breaks. He was President of the League from 1935-1936 and also served on the Warwickshire Committee.

J.A. Lones 1920 to 1949

Chief Engineer with Mitchells and Butlers he played for the sports club in the League, mainly in the Second Division captaining the side in 1921. In 1922 he scored 157 v West Bromwich Dartmouth Second Eleven to win a bat awarded by the Sunday Mercury. He was honoured with the Presidency of the League in 1932-34, 1945 and 1951. In 1945 he was given a presentation to mark his 25 years as Hon. Secretary and Treasurer when reference was made to his courtesy and genial personality, his knowledge and love of cricket and above all his sense of fairness being an inspiration to all. He was assisted during his term of office by W.T. Clarke.

K. Spooner 1950 to 1963

Ken Spooner was an accountant, who loving cricket and finding himself with no playing ability, turned his interest to the administrative side. He served as Treasurer and then as Honorary Secretary of Moseley, and then until his untimely death in 1963, devoted his leisure hours to League affairs. He did play for Moseley on one occasion, in 1936, when Moseley Second Eleven only had nine men and Ken moved from the scorers chair to play.

LEAGUE OFFICERS

David Heath
1988 President

David Bryant
Hon. Secretary

sharing enjoyment of success with Ron Headley (Dudley C.C.)
and Leslie Deakins, President in 1982.

H.B.G. Hill
First League Secretary

J.A. Williams
Secretary 1963-1977
President 1970

J.A. Williams, JP. 1963 to 1977

Jack Williams, a metal merchant, started his life in cricket administra-
by becoming Match and Fixture Secretary of West Bromwich Dartmouth Non
League XI at the age of 15.

He played for, and captained, the Dartmouth Second Eleven for over
thirty years during which time he also turned out for the First Eleven. In his
final appearance for the Second XI he hit 115 not out in 65 minutes against
Old Hill. He became President of West Bromwich Dartmouth and was
President of the League in 1970 having served on the Umpires Sub-Committee
and Advisory Committee. He has also been active in local affairs being Mayor
of West Bromwich, 1971/2, and was elected an Alderman.

David C. Bryant 1978 to date.

An Architectural Technician, he has devoted his leisure interests to
Smethwick and the League. He played for Smethwick Second XI for over
fifteen years. He served as Secretary of Smethwick for over 20 years, took
up the post of Secretary to the League having previously served as Assistant
Hon. Secretary from 1970 to 1975. He was elected President in 1985. He
also serves on the Committee of the Warwickshire C.C.C.

1988 President Elect D.M.W. Heath

Past Presidents

1888-1930	F.T. Cozens J.P.
1931	W.J. Phair
1932-1934	J.A. Lones
1935-1936	Sir C. Herbert Smith
1937	W. Eve
1938	W.G. Gethin
1939-1940	W.L. Edwards
1941	W. Preston J.P.
1942	W.L. Edwards
1943	G.T. Ryder, O.B.E., J.P.
1944	B. Evans
1945	J.A. Lones
1946	J.H. Greenaway
1947	W.H. Thursfield J.P.
1948	R.I. Scorer, M.C., J.P.
1949	A.E. Morgan
1950	H.W. Homer
1951	J.A. Lones
1952	H.E. Mitchell, M.B.E.
1953	R.I. Scorer, M.C., J.P.
1954	Sir Geoffrey Tomkinson, O.B.E. M.C., J.P.
1955	W.H. Thursfield J.P.
1956	J.A. Hight
1957	A.E. Morgan
1958	G.H. Humphries
1959	H.W. Homer
1960	K. Spooner
1961	C.C. Goodway
1962	F.H. Hunt
1963	R.I. Scorer, M.C., J.P.
1964	W.H. Edwards
1965	A.D. Hayes
1966	H. Maynard Mitchell, D.F.C.
1967	G.H. Piddock, D.F.C., M.A.
1968	F.W. Berry

1969	J.J. Hossell
1970	J.A. Williams J.P.
1971	J.A. Hight
1972	R.I. Scorer, M.C. J.P.,
1973	M.F. White, M.A.
1974	J.R. Oldham
1975	A.F. Brown
1976	G.H. Humphries
1977	H.M.F. Hughes
1978	R. Smith
1979	D.M.W. Heath
1980	C.J. Sanders
1981	J. Wakeman
1982	L.T. Deakins, M.B.E.
1983	H.N. Cook
1984	J. Richardson
1985	D.C. Bryant
1986	H.J. Latham
1987	S.A. Neal

Honorary Treasurer

1888-1964	Honorary Secretary
1965-1981	M.F. White, M.A.
1982-	D.M. Cowin

Honorary Assistant Secretary

1920-1949	W.T. Clarke
1950-1954	J.W. Gaunt
1955-1969	No appointment
1970-1975	D.C. Bryant
1976-1978	J.L. Tewson

Hon.Sec. Umpires Sub-Committee

1920-1949	W.T. Clarke
1950-1960	J.W. Gaunt
1961-1966	L. Sutcliffe
1967-1980	H.N. Cook
1981-	G. Wenman

Publicity Officer

1983-	J.A. Allen

Results Secretary

1986-	T.E. Rider

Advisory Committee

1948-77	R.I. Scorer, (Chairman)
1948-60	C.C. Goodway
1948-56	H.F. Hill
1948	H.W. Homer
1950-58	H.W. Homer
1961-70	H.W. Homer
1948-49	G.S. Tomkinson
1949	W.H. Thursfield
1957-70	J.A. Williams
1959-77	G.H. Humphries
1961-77	J.J. Hossell
1966-68	P.G. Heard
1970-77	H.J. Latham

Management Committee

1978-	D.M.W. Heath
1978-	S.A. Neal
1978-	B.A. Middleton
1978	J.A. Williams
1978-82	J. Wakeman
1978-80	M. Hill
1979-82	R. Smith
1981-	J. Huband
1983-5	P. Goodwin
1983-	D. Johnston
1987-	G. Smith

Honorary Auditor

1952-67	S. Cox
1968-78	K.J.W. Bamford
1979-80	I. Littlehales
1981	D.M. Cowin
1982-	R.A.B. Viner

RULES (1889)

Objects of League

The objects of this League shall be to promote the best interests of Local Cricket and Club Matches, consistent with loyal support to County Cricket.

1. That a Committee comprising one representative of each Club forming the League — who shall select two of their body to act as Chairman and Hon. Secretary respectively — shall transact all necessary business.

2. That the Annual Meeting be held in or about the month of November in each year, to receive reports, make all necessary elections, alterations of rules and arrange fixtures for the ensuing season.

3. That the Subscription be Five Shillings per annum subject to further call if necessary.

4. That the Clubs forming the League shall arrange Home and Away Fixtures with each other, the matches to be played between the first Saturday in May and the first Saturday in September; each to faithfully carry out its matches with its best available eleven. The Home Team in each case shall take the gate money and pay all expenses incurred.

5. The matches shall commence not later than 2.45 prompt stumps being drawn at 7.30 p.m.

6. Neutral Umpires approved by the League shall be appointed to each match, such Umpires to be paid by the Home Club. Five Shillings and Third Class Railway Fare. No umpire shall act in a match in which the Club nominating him is interested.

7. Only bona-fide members shall take part in matches and these must not be members regularly playing with some Club outside the League and therefore being available for one or two League matches only. Professionals must have recognised connection with the Clubs for whom they play. No club to engage to play in League matches more than three professionals whose names shall be submitted to and approved by the League prior to the start of the season. The words 'recognised connection' are intended to mean that the Club playing that man must have first call on the professional's services, subject only to calls for County matches.

8.   A match won shall count two points and drawn games one point. The Club gaining the highest number of points to be adjudged the Champions of the League.

9.   Any dispute having reference to the interpretation of the Laws of Cricket shall be referred to the M.C.C. for settlement, but in other matters the decision of the League shall be final.

(N.B. No original copy of the Rules has been traced but the above has been deduced from 1900 rules and Minutes of Meetings.)

INSTRUCTIONS TO UMPIRES
(First Issued 1896)

1.   When appointed to officiate in a match and you are unable to do so, reply immediately to the Hon. Sec. stating your inability to stand. This enables him to provide a substitute.

2.   Arrive punctually on the ground at 2 or 2.30 as the case may be and having measured and pitched the wickets and compared watches arrange boundaries with the other umpire.

3.   If a Club be late and unable to start by 2.15 or 2.45 as the case may be, make a note of the fact and carefully carry out the provisions of Rule 5*. If the captain of the punctual Club notifies his readiness to commence by 2.15 or 2.45 and later on appeals for extra time, order play to continue for another quarter of an hour if the weather and light are favourable.

4.   The Umpires shall decide on extra time, after appeal for unpunctuality, light, weather, fitness of wicket for play after rain and all other points — entirely without molestation from Captains, players or supporters. An appeal for light can only be entertained when made by a batsman.

5.   If an Umpire shall be unfairly treated or molested in any way by any player or spectator, or shall be subjected to any threats abuse or unfair pressure, he shall immediately report the affair to the Hon. Sec. of the League, who will at once have the matter brought before and dealt with by the League.

6.   Umpires must see that on conclusion of an innings the game is resumed punctually within ten minutes.

7.   These Rules shall be read in conjunction with the Instructions to County Umpires drawn up by the M.C.C. and if there shall be any variance or inconsistency between them, the provisions of these Rules shall prevail.

* By 1896 Rule 5 had been amended from that given in 1889.

THE BIRMINGHAM & DISTRICT LEAGUE CHALLENGE CUP

1.—The Competition shall be called "The Birmingham and District League Challenge Cup."

2.—The Competition to be limited to all League Clubs, First and Second Divisions.

3.—Round 1 (20 teams).
Four matches (8 teams) and 12 byes through to Round 2. The games to be played in the evening on the Home Ground of the first drawn Club, and completed by 31st May—the dates to be arranged between the opposing teams.

4.—Round 2 (16 teams), Round 3 (8 teams) and Round 4 (semi-final).
The Matches to be played in the evening on the Home Ground of the first drawn Club, and completed by 14th June, 28th June and 12th July respectively.

5.—Round 5 (Final).
The Final to be played home and away on the grounds of, and on a date and time to be mutually agreed between, the finalists, but on or before 26th July if played in the evening, otherwise before 31st August, the aggregate score to determine the winner, and the team batting second in the first match to have the choice of innings in the second match.

6.—The entrance fee for each first and second team to be ONE POUND, to be paid to the League Hon. Treasurer on or before 1st April. This money to be devoted to the purchase of awards for individual members of the two teams competing in the Final.

7.—Only bona fide Club players to be eligible to participate in the Competition, and a player may play with either the First or Second team, but not both, in any one season.

8.—Teams are not to be allowed to play a Professional.

9.—In Rounds 1, 2, 3 and 4, and in the Final, which should commence promptly not later than 6.45 p.m., 18 complete overs batting to be allowed each side, though all the 10 wickets may not have fallen.
The side scoring most runs wins.
Should any side be dismissed in less than 18 overs, their batting is to be considered at an end.
The opposing side would still be entitled to bat for 18 overs if necessary, provided all the 10 wickets had not fallen.
There will be a break of 10 minutes between innings, during which time the wicket may be rolled for seven minutes.

10.—All matches must begin punctually, even if all the players are not present. If a team is unable to start at the appointed time, it shall forfeit the right to toss for innings.

11.—In Rounds 1, 2, 3 and 4, each Club to provide an Umpire and Scorer. In the Final, League Umpires and independent Scorers to be appointed.

12.—The number of overs bowled to be clearly and promptly recorded on the scoreboard for the benefit of players and spectators.

13.—In Rounds 1, 2, 3 and 4, used balls of a similar condition to be provided by the Home Club. In the Final, a new ball to be provided for each innings.

14.—In the event of a tie, the side losing the lesser number of wickets to be declared the winners. Should this still be equal, the side with the lesser number of extras to be the winners.
Should a match be abandoned owing to rain or unfitness of the wicket, at any stage, the game to be replayed in its entirety on a date to be fixed by mutual agreement between the two teams, providing such date conforms with Rule 3, 4 or 5.

15.—The results of all matches to be forwarded to the League Secretary within three days.

16.—The winners to hold the trophy (which will remain the property of the B. & D. C.L.) until 30th April next year. The trophy holders to be responsible for the safe keeping and insurance a st damage and/or loss of the same.

17.—The decision on any point arising in connection with the Competition to rest with the League Committee, and this decision shall be final.

18.—After deduction of actual match expenses, one-half of the proceeds of each match to be equally divided between the two contesting teams, and one-half to be forwarded to the League Secretary.
The total funds to the League from the whole Competition to be equally divided amongst the 10 participating League Clubs.

19.—Admission charges shall be as in League matches.

Extracts from
Birmingham & District Cricket League
Rules, Fixtures & Instructions to Umpires 1958

TEST PLAYERS WHO HAVE PLAYED BIRMINGHAM LEAGUE CRICKET

England

Amiss D.L. (Smeth., Warw.)
Arnold E.G. (Stour.)
Barnes S.F. (Smeth.)
Barnett C.J. (M & B)
Brown D.J. (Wal.)
Calthorpe Hon. F.S.G. (H. Wood)
Clark E.W. (W.B.D.)
Cook G. (Wal.)
Cook N.G.B. (W.B.D.)
De Freitas P.A.J. (Stour.)
D'Oliveira B.L. (Kid.)
Dollery H.E. (Smeth.)
Flavell J.A. (Stour. Wal.)
Foster F.R. (Mos.)
Foster R.E. (Stour.)
Freeman A.P. (Wal.)
Gifford N. (Dud.)
Goddard T.W.J. (Kid.)
Gover A.R. (W.B.D.)
Graveney T.W. (Dud.)
Hemmings E.E. (Warw.)
Hobbs R.N.S. (Dup.)
Hollies W.E. (O.H., W.B.D., M & B)
Horton M.J. (Stour.)
Howell H. (A.U.)
Howorth R. (Wal., Stour., O.H.)
Hutchings K.L. (A.U., Dud.)
Jameson J.A. (Smeth.)
Jenkins R.O. (W.B.D., Stour.)
Jones A.O. (Dud.)
Kenyon D. (Stour.)
Kinneir S. (H. Wood)
Larter J.D.F. (Stour.)
Larkins W. (Wal.)
Lilley A.F.A. (H. Wood)
Lloyd T.A. (Wark., Worc. C.C.C.)
McConnon J.E. (Wal., Mos.)
Nichols M.S. (A.U.)
Oakman A.S.M. (Wark.)
Paine G.A.E.(Smeth. Mos. Wal. Kid.)
Palmer C.H. (O.H.)
Perks R.T.D. (W.B.D., Dud., Kid.)
Pollard R. (A.U.)
Quaife W.G. (Mos., Stour.)
Richardson D.W. (Stour., O.H.)
Richardson P.E. (Stour.)
Root C.F. (Dud.)
Rumsey F.E. (Kid.)
Smailes T.F. (Wal.)
Small G.C. (Wark.)
Smith T.P.B. (W.B.D.)
Steele D.S. (W.B.D.)
Tate M.W. (Wal.)
Tattersall R. (Kid.)
Taylor L.B. (W.B.D.)
Waddington A. (W.B.D.)
Wellard A.W. (Kid.)
White D.W. (A.U.)
Willis R.G.D. (Wark.)
Wyatt R.E.S. (Mos.)

Australia

Matthews G.R.J. (O.H.)
O'Donnell S.P. (Stour.)
Yallop G.N. (Wal.)

New Zealand

Dempster C.S. (Smeth.)
Donnelly M.P. (Smeth.)
Lees W.K. (Worc. C.C.C.)
Merritt W.E. (Dud.)
Patel D.N. (WBD. Worc. C.C.C.)
Parker J.M. (Kid.)
Sinclair B.W. (M & B)
Taylor D.D. (O.H., W.B.D.)
Turner G.M. (Stour.)

Pakistan

Imran Khan (Stour.)
Mushtaq Mohammad (Wal., O.H.)
Sadiq Mohammad (Wal.)

South Africa

Carlstein P.R. (O.H.)
Fellows-Smith J.P. (W.B.D.)
Pegler S.J. (A.U.)
Taylor H.W. (A.U.)

Sri Lanka

De Silva D.S. (W.B.D.)

West Indies

Croft C.E.H. (Smeth.)
Headley G.A. (Dud.)
Headley R.G.A. (Dud., O.H.)
Holder V.A. (W.B.D.)
King F.M. (W.B.D.)
Scott A.P.H. (W.B.D.)
Valentine A.L. (Wal.)

India

Doshi D.R. (Wal.)
Amar Singh (Mos.)

One Day Internationals

Humpage G.W. (Wark.) – England
Ramanyake C.F. (W.B.D.) – Sri Lanka

South African Unofficial Tests

Donald A.A. (Wark.)
McMillan B.M. (Mos., Wark.)
Page H.A. (Mos.)

South African One Day Internationals

Ferreira A.M. (Wark.)
Pienaar R.F. (Kid.)

West Indies XI v South Africa XI

Alleyne H.L. (Dud.)

D.H. Robins XI v South Africa XI

Lee P.G. (Dud.)
Rouse S.J. (Mos., Wark.)

Victory Tests England v Australia Services

Roberts T.W. (W.B.D.) — England
Stephenson J.W.A. (Kid.) — England
Workman J.A. (W.B.D.) — Australia

Commonwealth XI v India (Unofficial Test)

Livingston L. (Stour.)

New Zealand XI v Sir Julian Cahn's XI

Pritchard T.L. (Smeth., Mos., W.B.D.)

Sri Lanka v England 'B'

Ranatunga D. (A.U.)

FIRST DIVISION
League Records

Number of Matches in a Season

1889-90	1891	1892-3	1894	1895	1896-1974	1975- to date
12	14	16	18	16	18	22

Most Wins — 14 — Old Hill 1921; Walsall 1937; Warwickshire II 1978.

Fewest Defeats — 0 — Kidderminster 1967, 1969; Mitchells & Butlers 1923, 1925, 1954, 1961, 1971; Moseley 1895, 1908, 1967, 1969; Old Hill 1941; Walsall 1912; West Bromwich Dartmouth 1932, 1945, 1963, 1974; Warwickshire II 1980.

Most Defeats — 15 — Aston Unity 1983; West Bromwich Dartmouth 1919.

Fewest Draws — 0 — Aston Unity 1919, 1937; Walsall 1919, 1938.

Most Draws — 17 — Kidderminster 1969; Warwickshire II 1980.

CUMULATIVE LEAGUE TABLE — 1889 — 1987

	P	W	D	L	% Points obtained	Champions*
Coventry & North Warwickshire	44	15	23	6	55.45	—
Salters	12	4	5	3	54.17	—
Handsworth Wood	464	180	148	136	52.31	5
Warwickshire II & Club & Ground	304	103	144	57	51.19	2
Moseley	1740	583	719	438	48.07	21
West Bromwich Dartmouth	1740	576	647	517	47.09	17
Old Hill	1276	378	580	318	44.76	4
Walsall	1740	563	626	551	44.54	14
Kidderminster	1652	521	683	448	44.26	11
Mitchells & Butlers	1674	497	801	376	43.80	10
Dudley	1642	465	622	555	41.61	5
Smethwick	1716	495	659	562	41.15	2
Worcester City	132	40	46	46	39.20	—
Stourbridge	1670	376	733	561	38.58	2
Aston Unity	1740	478	653	609	35.79	12
Worcestershire II	44	8	20	16	34.09	—
Wednesbury	58	11	17	30	31.90	—
Small Heath	50	9	12	29	28.00	—
Duport	110	5	56	49	18.80	—

* Some championships shared

HIGHEST AND LOWEST TEAM SCORES

For	Against	Aston Unity	Dudley	Handsworth Wood	Kidderminster	Mitchells & Butlers	Moseley	Old Hill	Smethwick	Stourbridge	Walsall	Warwickshire	West Bromwich Dartmouth
Aston Unity	H		304-7 1896	236-8 1911	262-7 1901	293-8 1900	268-4 1913 / 268 1911	309-5 1939	300 1913	285-2 1923	272-6 1926	260-3 1977	375-3 1907
	L		43 1926	31 1894	19 1952	23 1924	39 1893	44 1940	20 1923	43 1953	38 1912	46 1978	35 1945
Dudley	H	264 1921 / 264-0 1932		284-7 1906	301-5 1940	262-6 1964	283 1906	262 1939	306-7 1940	332-5 1921	334-8 1905	223-7 1977	262-2 1983
	L	43 1928		32 1902	44 1897	32 1896	49 1936	37 1924	29 1965	42 1920	12 1919	96 1979	30 1945
Handsworth Wood	H	264-9 1913	333-5 1896		274 1903	280-6 1907	285 1913		244-4 1896	241-3 1909	295-5 1897	123-3 1894	279-5 1894
	L	22 1890	25 1889		51 1907	33 1890	27 1919		43 1907	49 1919	39 1899	104 1894	44 1891
Kidderminster	H	263-4 1911	293-3 1910	255-5 1904		315-1 1940	309-4 1984	281-5 1930	295 1940	271-8 1928	279-4 1903	265-7 1978	300-9 1913
	L	27 1927	23 1898	38 1901		46 1911	43 1902	63 1926	24 1919	42 1921	42 1920	78 1981 / 78 1983	16 1945
Mitchells & Butlers	H	321 1908	307-9 1921	303-1 1911	295-4 1984		301-5 1913	297-5 1929	299-7 1921	382-9 1912	279-8 1982	279-8 1982	302-4 1914
	L	41 1890	22 1898	26 1892	49 1899		47 1914	49 1943	48 1945	46 1942	45 1979	80 1984	43 1890
Moseley	H	309-9 1910	354-3 1912	330 1911	310-4 1895	310 1911		307-4 1925	283-9 1984	350-6 1908	329-5 1919	270-4 1981	405-8 1908
	L	37 1958	39 1970	41 1890	25 1899	48 1941		33 1945	34 1935	31 1942	20 1912	74 1985	23 1941
Old Hill	H	413-6 1931	283-8 1928			301-5 1930	278-6 1946		298-6 1927 / 298-5 1930	269-4 1951	271 1938	271-3 1978	299-6 1983
	L	54 1935	37 1942			75 1925	61 1986		49 1927	49 1963	43 1922	69 1987	33 1934
Smethwick	H	352-6 1911	269-9 1938	253-8 1908	410-5 1922	285-9 1920	301 1911	315-5 1928		280-3 1977	270-9 1926	260-6 1981	265-7 1913
	L	33 1896	43 1935	29 1903	25 1905 / 25 1936	32 1900	40 1954	67 1933		49 1904	36 1920	127 1984	45 1939
Stourbridge	H	279 1902	289 1908	242 1908	268-4 1983	295-8 1930	266 1921	272-9 1925	273-8 1922		255-2 1897	230-5 1987	271-6 1906
	L	42 1944	37 1896	18 1906	13 1899	28 1899	30 1967	21 1926	31 1908		35 1965	47 1976	25 1961
Walsall	H	261 1937	280-8 1930	314-8 1896	282 1905	311-4 1924	330-8 1919	265-7 1939	377 1896	310-4 1895		242-3 1981	326-9 1908
	L	38 1932	33 1940	47 1894	40 1899 / 40 1921	19 1943	29 1899	19 1925	47 1906	40 1932		56 1977	24 1890
Warwickshire	H	269-4 1985	301-3 1894	203-4 1894	314-7 1982	285-5 1982	287-6 1984	315-6 1985	285-2 1977	279-4 1982	369-5 1984		300-3 1983
	L	37 1894	145 1982	95 1894	117 1979	114 1976	147 1977	93 1975	118-9 1981	49 1979	70 1977		73 1975
West Bromwich Dartmouth	H	283-4 1987	309-7 1934 / 309-3 1930	301-6 1909	269-3 1981	267-8 1909	298-4 1942	298-6 1933	305-8 1923	272-5 1909	323-5 1931	268-9 1982	
	L	27 1920	25 1891	31 1893	37 1919	49 1919	20 1897	56 1924	31 1905	45 1903 / 45 1919	38 1954	97 1979	

Highest Team Score

					Since 1945			
413-6	O.H.	v	A.U.	1931	369-5 Warw.		v Wal.	1984
410-5	Smeth.	v	Kid.	1922	315-6 Warw.		v O.H.	1985
405-8	Mos.	v	W.B.D.	1908	314-7 Warw.		v Kid.	1982
					312-4 Worc.C.		v Mos.	1982
					309-4 Kid.		v Mos.	1984

Lowest Team Score

					Since 1945			
12	Dud.	v	Wal.	1919	16 Kid.	v	W.B.D.	1945
13	Stour	v	Kid.	1913	19 A.U.	v	Kid.	1952

Highest Individual Scores

200*	Stephens F.G.	Mos.	v	Stour	1913
197	Merritt W.E.	Dud.	v	Smeth	1940
189	Kirton H.O.	M&B	v	W.B.D.	1939
185	Wilkinson W.H.	M&B	v	Stour	1912
183	Bainbridge H.W.	Warw.	v	Dud.	1894

Since 1945

182*	Hick G.A.	Kid.	v	Mos.	1984
169*	Headley G.A.	Dud	v	M&B	1952
162*	Wilkinson K.W.	O.H.	v	M&B	1977
159	Wootton S.H.	Warw.	v	Kid.	1982
159	Stokes I.W.E.	Mos.	v	W.B.D.	1987

10 Wickets in an Innings

Breedon F., Latham H.J. (2) — Moseley
Hill H.B.G. — Handsworth Wood
Lockett A., Hollies W.E., Howorth R., — Old Hill
Smith D., Wellard A.W. — Kidderminster
Backhouse E.N. (2), Freeman A.P. — Walsall
Snow R. — Stourbridge
Miller R. — West Bromwich Dartmouth
Stringer T., Merritt W.E., — Dudley
Stevenson T. — Mitchells and Butlers

50 runs and 5 wickets in a match

12 times	Wilkinson W.H. 10 (M & B) and 2 (Wal)
11	Merritt W.E. Dud.
9	Slade D.N.F. 6 (W.B.D.) and 3 (Worc. City)

High Wicket Partnerships

1	288	M&B	v	W.B.D.	Kirton H.O.	189	Wyatt R.A.D.	87*	1939
2	254*	Warw	v	Smeth.	Abberley R.N.	146*	Jones A.K.C.	103*	1975
3	234	O.H.	v	A.U.	Homer H.W.	170*	Eley J.B.	82	1931
4	214	Smeth	v	O.H.	Haines W.H.	80	Mathews N.L.	140	1938
5	225*	W.B.D.	v	O.H.	Clift P.B.	102*	Edmundson M.	130*	1975
6	161*	Smeth	v	O.H.	Neale A.J.L.	108*	Haines W.H.	100*	1935
7	170	Kid	v	Dud.	Tomkinson G.S.	101	Thorp P.	75	1929
8	195*	Mos.	v	H.Wood	Stephens G.W.	161*	Cooper J.H.	56*	1910
9	140*	Mos.	v	Wal.	Jenkins J.A.	55*	Smith A.	62*	1890
10	102	A.U.	v	Mos.	Whitehead J.E.	90*	Ingram N.F.	10	1932

Most Runs in a Season

1407	Slade D.N.F.	W.B.D.	1978
1236	Stokes I.W.E.	Moseley	1984
1234	Hick G.A.	Kidderminster	1984
1152	Yallop G.N.	Walsall	1975
1102	Townsend A.	M & B	1961
1093	Price C.L.	A.U.	1975
1008	Townsend A.	M & B	1970

Most Centuries in League

32	Kirton H.O.	M & B
16	Perry E.	W.B.D.
14	Devey J.H.G.	A.U.
	Stevenson J.F.	M & B
	Warner G.S.	Smethwick (1) M & B (13)
	Wilkes W.H.W.	Kidderminster

Most 500 + Runs in a Season

15	Kirton H.O.	M & B
14	Warner G.S.	M & B
12	Fletcher A.E.	M & B (11) Walsall (1)
11	Harris P.M.	Kidderminster

500 + Runs and 50 + Wickets in a Season

567 runs	65 wkts	Nichols J.E.	Stourbridge	1904
528	51	Wilkinson W.H.	M & B	1911
793	63	Wilkinson W.H.	M & B	1919
538	54	Lee W.	O.H.	1938
687	60	Howorth R.	Walsall	1940
878	80	Merritt W.E.	Dudley	1940
508	56	Paine G.A.E.	Kidderminster	1943*
508	57	Paine G.A.E.	Kidderminster	1945*
529	50	Rowley B.	Smethwick	1960

* in 1944 G.A.E. Paine scored 498 runs and took 70 wickets

Most Wickets in a Season

99	Hollies W.E.	O.H.	1940
98	Freeman A.P.	Walsall	1937
95	Backhouse E.N.	Walsall	1935

50 + Wickets in a Season

10 times	Brammer W.	Walsall
9	Hollies W.E.	W.B.D.(7) O.H. (2)
8	Hill H.B.G.	Handsworth Wood

4 Wickets in 4 Balls

Bird A.	Walsall	v	W.B.D.	1893
Bird A.	Walsall	v	W.B.D.	1896
Brammer W.	Walsall	v	M & B	1907
Lockett A.	O.H.	v	Stourbridge	1926
Merritt W.E.	Dudley	v	Aston Unity	1948
Rea G.W.	A.U.	v	W.B.D.	1909

Youngest Players to score a Century in the First Division

Kenyon D.	Age 16yrs. 80 days	103 for Stourbridge 1940
Hutchings I.D.	Age 16yrs. 343 days	100* for A.U. 1982
Humphries N.M.	Age 17yrs. 42 days	105* for Kidderminster 1934
Hick G.A.	Age 17yrs 355 days	182* for Kidderminster 1984

ASTON UNITY CRICKET CLUB
Club formed 1868

Members of League: — First Division 1889 to date — Founder Members
Second Division 1893 to date — (Did not compete in 1945)

1987 Secretary: — N.F. Ingram (1948—52, 1968 to date)

Highest Team Score   Since 1945

375-3	v	W.B.D.	1907	269-5	v	Stour.	1984
311	v	W.B.D.	1913	260-3	v	Warw.	1977
309-5	v	O.H.	1939	257-9	v	Dudley	1959

Lowest Team Score: —   19 v Kidderminster 1952

Highest Individual Scores   Since 1945

174 Ogden S	v	Stour	1923	138 Cook M.S. v O.H.		1965
147* Devey J.H.G.	v	Stour	1907	130 Kennedy J.M. v M&B		1959
145 Devey J.H.G.	v	Smeth.	1904	129*Gough J.H. v Warw.		1977

Nine Wickets in an Innings

9—23	Leake E.J.	v K.Heath	1899	9—61 Heywood E.	v Dudley	1931
9—?	Leake E.J.	v Wed.	1891	9—48 Nichols M.S.	v Smeth.	1949
9—19	Pallett H.J.	v Moseley	1891	9—52 Eames E.A.	v Moseley	1950
9—103	Edden E.T.	v M & B	1922	9—42 Harrys G.	v Walsall	1981

Highest Wicket Partnerships

2.	209	v Moseley	Davies B.N. 103	Burgoyne F.	114		1913
4.	193*	v M & B	Davies B.N. 90*	George W.G.	109*		1913

Most Runs in a Season

1093	Price C.L.	1975
813	Devey J.H.G.	1907
792	Devey J.H.G.	1904
724	Yarnold H.	1975
703	Hutchings I.D.	1984

Most Centuries for Club

14	Devey J.H.G.
7	Price C.L.
4	Hossell J.J., Riley T.M.N.

500 + Runs in a Season

9	Price C.L.
4	Devey J.H.G.
2	Devey A.
1	Cook M.S., Gough J.H., Hutchings I.D., Kennedy J.M., King I., Ogden S., Ranatunga D., Woodroffe A., Yarnold H.

Most Wickets in a Season

71	Howell H.L.	1927
69	Nichols M.S.	1949
67	Edden E.T.	1906
59	Edden E.T.	1910
59	Howell H.L.	1929

50 + Wickets in a Season

4	Edden E.T.
2	Howell H., Jackson G.K., Leake E.J., Pollard R., Rea G.W., Thomas A.E. A.E.
1	Eames E.A., Junkin P., Meunier J.B., Nichols M.S., Simms H.L.

Most 8 + Wickets

3	Bird W., Howell H., Leake E.J., Pallett H.J.

COVENTRY & NORTH WARWICKSHIRE CRICKET CLUB
Club Formed 1851

Members of League:— First and Second Divisions 1986 to date

1987 Secretary:— E.L. Shilton

Highest Team Scores:—

285-6	v	Kidderminster	1987
262-5	v	Old Hill	1987
242-9	v	Moseley	1987

Lowest Team Score

58   v   Worcester City   1986
(Coventry & Nth. Warwickshire then dismissed Worcester City for 32)

Highest Individual Scores

127	Carew M.	v	Old Hill	1987
123*	Grant A.	v	West Brom. Dartmouth	1986
121	Matthews W.P.	v	Kidderminster	1987

Best Bowling in an Innings

8—12   Ogrizovic S v   Worcester City 1986

Highest Wicket Partnership

1   144   v   Kidderminster. Eames M. 67   Grant A 77   1986

Most Runs and 500 + in a Season

595	Matthews W.P.	1987
585	Grant A.	1986
567	Eames M.	1986

Most Centuries for the Club

2	Carew M.
1	Davies G., Eames M., Grant A., Matthews W.P.

Most Wickets in a Season

55	Grant R.	1987
38	Edmunds G.S.	1986
30	Ogrizovic S.	1986

DUDLEY CRICKET CLUB
Club formed 1840

Members of League:— First Division 1893 to 1985
Second Division 1893 to 1985
Secretary:— 1983-85 W. Probert.   Long Serving Secretary H.R. Winchurch
1929-1944, 1968-1978

Highest Team Score			Since 1945		
334-8	v Wal.	1905	262-2 v W.B.D.	1983	
332-5	v Stour.	1921	262-6 v M & B	1964	
332	v S.Heath	1894	260-6 v Smeth.	1971	

Lowest Team Score			Since 1945		
12	v	Wal.	1919	29 v Smeth.	1965

Highest Individual Scores				Others Since 1945	
197	Merritt W.E.	v Smeth.	1940	141 Headley G.A. v Kid.	1953
169	Headley G.A.	v M & B	1952	139 Headley G.A. v Kid.	1952
162	Root C.F.	v Stour.	1921	139 Headley R.G.A. v Stour.	1959

Best Bowling

10-48	Stringer T	v	Smeth.	1906	9-51	Haycock E.	v Wal.	1932
10-59	Merritt W.E.	v	A.U.	1940	9-6	Sheffield E.J.	v M & B.	1934
9-26	Davidson F.	v	W.B.D.	1897	9-20	Sheffield E.J.	v A.U.	1936
9-22	Stringer T.	v M & B.		1908	9-53	Merritt W.E.	v M & B.	1940
9-29	Root C.F.	v M & B.		1920	9-63	Merritt W.E.	v Smeth.	1946
9-29	Root C.F.	v Mos.		1920	9-69	Merritt W.E.	v Stour.	1947

Highest Wicket Partnerships

| 1. | 264* v A.U. | Gale L.E. | 150* | Bull C.H. | 107* | 1932 |
| 2. | 241* v M & B. | Headley G.A. 169* | | Thomas H.A. 74 | | 1952 |

Most Runs in a Season

922	Headley G.A.	1951
878	Merritt W.E.	1940
834	Gale L.E.	1932
765	Headley G.A.	1953
744	Fox W.V.	1925

500 + Runs in a Season

5	Headley R.G.A.
3	Grimshaw C.H. Headley G.A.
2	Dews G, Thomas H.A.
1	Barker A.R., Bull C.H., Fox W.V., Gale L.E., Green C., Hutchings W.E.C., Kimber S.J.S., Merritt W.E., Pearson A., Richardson A., Wrightson J.

Most Centuries for the Club

12	Gale L.E.
7	Headley G.A., Headley R.G.A.
6	Grimshaw C.H, Merritt W.E.
4	Sedgley J.B.
3	Barker A.R., Dews G, Palmer T., Thomas H.A.

Most Wickets in a Season

90	Stringer T.	1908
85	Stringer T.	1906
82	Stringer T.	1907
80	Merritt W.E.	1940
77	Merritt W.E.	1948

50 + Wickets in a Season

5	Merritt W.E.
4	Stringer T.
3	Root C.F.
2	Perks R.T.D., Sheffield E.J., Thomas T.O.
1	Baker H.F., Bateman J., Forrester T., Kelleher H.R.A., Lavender H.A. . Moseley M., Smith G., Trees W.P.

Most 8 + Wickets

5	Merritt W.E.
4	Stringer T.
3	Thomas T.O.
2	Forrester T, Root C.F., Sheffield E.J., Smith G.

KIDDERMINSTER CRICKET CLUB
Club formed 1850

Members of League: – First and Second Divisions 1895 to date
1987 Secretary G. Capper (Long Serving Secretary J. Sewter 1968-1977)

Highest Team Score   Others Since 1945

315-1	v	M & B	1940	267-4 v Smeth. 1962
309-4	v	Moseley	1984	265-7 v Warw. 1978
302-6	v	Moseley	1929	264-5 v M & B. 1986

Lowest Team Score   Since 1945

16   v   W.B.D.   1945   24 v Dudley   1968

Highest Individual Scores   Others since 1945

182*	Hick G.A. v Mos.	1984	151 Hick G.A. v Smeth. 1984
158*	Humphries C.A. v M & B.	1940	138 Harris P.M. v Smeth. 1966
151	Dalloe H. v Mos.	1933	138 Watson F.P. v A.U. 1982

Most Wickets in an Innings

10-33	Wellard A.W. v Stour.	1950	9-37 Perry E.H. v Mos. 1935
10-18	Smith D. v Stour.	1968	9-55 Perks R.T.D. v Dudley 1942
9-31	Wilson G.A. v Stour.	1897	9-43 Wellard A.W. v O.H. 1950
9-47	Bowles J.J. v Mos.	1925	9-80 Wellard A.W. v Mos. 1951
9-30	Gethin W.G. v A.U.	1921	9-41 Hemsley C.R. v M&B 1976
9-32	Hutchinson E. v Mos.	1932	

Highest Wicket Partnerships

2.	231* v M & B Humphries C.A. 158* Moule H.G. 113*		1940
1.	216 v Dud. Moule H.G. 119 Wyers A. 92*		1950

Most Runs in a Season

1234	Hick G.A.	1984
867	Harris P.M.	1967
800	Lamb G.	1986
763	Harris P.M.	1966
733	Gethin S.J.	1909
730	Lamb G.	1985

Most Centuries for the Club

14	Wilkes W.H.W.
11	Harris P.M.
10	Gethin S.J.
9	Wyers A.
8	Hick G.A.
7	Moule H.G.

500 + Runs in a Season

11	Harris P.M.
5	Lamb G
4	Wyers A.
3	Heard P.G.
2	Gethin S.J., Johnson J.S., Paine G.A.E., Wilkes W.H.W.
1	Blakey G.M., Bradby H, Barker A.R., D'Oliveira B.L., Hick G.A., Humphries C.A., Humphries G.H., Moule H.G., Sedgley M., Thorp P., Tomkinson F.M., Watson F.P.

Most Wickets in a Season

89	Bowles J.J.	1925
86	Perry E.H.	1938
85	Perks R.T.D.	1942
83	Bowles J.J.	1924
83	Perry E.H.	1937
80	Brook G.W.	1929

50 + Wickets in a Season

4   Skelding A, Wilson H.
3   Paine G.A.E.
2   Bowles J.J., Gethin S.J. Goddard T.W., Holroyd J., Perry E.H., Sanders
     C.J., Thomas A.E., Wellard A.W.
1   Brook G.W. Brooker M.E.W., Gethin W.G., Hutchinson E., Crosskill H.O.
     Perks R.T.D., Wilson G.A.

Most 8 + Wickets

4   Sanders C.J., Wilson G.A.
3   Gethin W.G., Perry E.H., Perks R.T.D., Thomas A.E., Wellard A.W.

MITCHELLS & BUTLERS CRICKET CLUB

Club Formed — Circa 1879 — Mitchells C.C. became Mitchells &
Butlers in 1898

Members of League: — First Division 1889-1892 - Founder Members
First and Second Divisions 1896 to date

1987 Secretary M. Ralphs.   Long serving Secretaries F.C. Smith 1938-59,
T.G. Elias 1966-78

Highest Team Score   Since 1945

382-9   v   Stour.   1912   295-4   v   Kidd.   1984
321   v   A.U.   1908   279-8   v   Wal.   1982
307-9   v   Dud.   1921   270-5   v   Dud.   1950

Lowest Team Score   Since 1945

22   v   Dud.   1898   45   v   A.U.   1978
                                   45   v   Wal.   1979

Highest Individual Scores   Since 1945

189 Kirton H.O.   v W.B.D. 1939   152 Watts E.A. v Dud.   1950
185 Wilkinson W.H. v Stour. 1912   150 Masood A. v Warw.   1976
168 Wilkinson W.H. v A.U.   1919   136* Townsend A. v Smeth. 1969
                                      136* Warner G.S. v Stour. 1973

Most Wickets in an Innings

10-61 Stevenson T. v Dud.   1902 9-56 Gross F.A. v Mos.   1944
 9-29 Horton J.   v W.B.D. 1892 9-67 Patel K.   v Kid.   1983
 9-61 Wilkinson W.H. v Smeth 1923

Highest Wicket Parnerships

1.   288   v W.B.D. Kirton H.O. 189 Wyatt R.A.D.   87* 1939
2.   223   v Kid.   Warner G.S. 105 Moore N.   126 1984

Most Runs in a Season

1102   Townsend A.   1961
1008   Townsend A.   1970
 881   Moore N.   1984
 878   Kirton H.O.   1935
 831   Fereday J.B.   1906
 810   Kirton H.O.   1939
 803   Kirton H.O.   1933

Most Centuries for the Club

32   Kirton H.O.
14   Stevenson J.F.
13   Fletcher A.E., Townsend A., Warner G.S.
12   Fereday J.B.
11   Wilkinson W.H.

500+ Runs in a Season

15   Kirton H.O.
14   Warner G.S.
11   Fletcher A.E.
 8   Wilkinson W.H.
 7   Fereday J.B.
 5   Townsend A.
 4   Stevenson J.F.
 3   Watts E.A.
 2   Lumb J, Porter K.C., Thomas G.P.
 1   Green M., Harvey W., Holloway A., Howard W., Malhotra C.L., Masood A.,
     Moore N., Powell G.H.J., Williams J., Workman S.F.

Most Wickets in a Season

86   Gross F.A.   1934
65   Gross F.A.   1930, 1940
64   Stevenson T.   1900
63   Wilkinson W.H.   1919
60   Gross F.A.   1935
60   Pope A.V.   1947

50 + Wickets in a Season

7   Gross F.A.
4   Wilkinson W.H.
3   Fereday J.B.
2   Melley A., Pope A.V.
1   Nutter A.E., Stevenson T.

Most 8 + Wickets

9   Gross F.A.
4   Stevenson T., Wilkinson W.H.
3   Fereday J.B.
2   Nutter A.E.
1   Pope A.V.

MOSELEY CRICKET CLUB

Club formed 1855 (exact date uncertain)

Members of League: – First Division 1889 to date – Founder Members
          (Titled Kings Heath C.C. in 1889 season)
                    Second Division 1893 to date (did not compete in
1945 & 1946)

1987 Secretary: – J.F. Taylor, Long Serving Secretaries G.W. Horlick 1950-
1964, A.F. Brown 1965-1975

Highest Team Score				Since 1945			
405-8	v	W.B.D.	1908	283-9	v	Smeth.	1984
354-3	v	Dud.	1912	278-5	v	W.B.D.	1984
350-6	v	Stour.	1908	275-5	v	M & B.	1984

Lowest Team Score				Since 1945			
20	v	Wal.	1912	36		v W.B.D.	1958

Highest Individual Scores   Since 1945

200* Stephens F.G. v Stour	1913	159*	Stokes I.W.E. v W.B.D.	1987
170 Stephens G.W. v O.H.	1920	142	Heath D.M.W. v Dud.	1959
166 Stephens G.W. v W.B.D.	1912	140	Watts J.M. v Smeth.	1983

Most Wickets in an Innings

10-? Breedon F	v Smeth.	1892	9-51 Morter F.W. v W.B.D.	1925
10-37 Latham H.J.	v Kid.	1954	9-40 Hastilow C.A.F. v Dud.	1929
10-29 Latham H.J.	v Kid.	1957	9-70 Davis P. v Kid.	1982

Highest Wicket Partnerships

2. 222 v Dud. Heath D.M.W. 142 Malhotra C.L. 82 1959
8. 195* v H.Wood Stephens G.W. 161* Cooper J.H. 56* 1910

Most Runs in a Season

1236	Stokes I.W.E.	1984
727	Moles A.J.	1984
722	Heath D.M.W.	1959
718	Taylor J.F.	1975
710	Everitt R.S.	1908

Most Centuries for the Club

13 Stephens F.G.
11 Stephens G.W.
 8 Taylor J.F.
 7 Stokes I.W.E.
 6 Heath D.M.W.

500 + Runs in a Season

6 Heath D.M.W.
5 Taylor J.F.
4 Moles A.J., Watts J.M.
2 Milne R.B., Stephens F.G., Stephens G.W., Stokes I.W.E., Wright M.
1 Abberley R.N., Baines W., Bird R.E., Byrne J.F., Chase R., Cheslin M.W., Everitt R.S., Fletcher B.E., Gough J.H., Turner H.T., Santall F.R., Wyatt R.E.S.

Most Wickets in a Season

63	Hastilow C.A.F.	1935
62	Riley W.	1925
61	Morter F.W.	1900
58	Latham H.J.	1964
57	Abell R.B.	1960
57	McMillan B.M.	1985

50 + Wickets in a Season

6 Riley W.
4 Latham H.J.
2 Abell R.B., Hastilow C.A.F.
1 Cook D.S., Loveridge F., McMillan B.M., Morter F.W., Smith A.W., Watts S.

Most 8 + Wickets

4 Riley W.
3 Latham H.J., Smith A.W.
2 Morter F.W., Hastilow C.A.F.

OLD HILL CRICKET CLUB

Club formed 1884

Member of League:– First and Second Divisions 1920 to date

1987 Secretary:– E. Willetts (1980 to date)
Long Serving Secretary:– B.G. Forrest (8 + years)

Highest Team Score				Since 1945			
413-6	v	A.U.	1931	299-6	v	W.B.D.	1983
301-5	v	M & B	1930	278-6	v	Mos.	1946
				276-6	v	Mos.	1984
				275-4	v	Smeth.	1951

Lowest Team Score

	Since 1945
33 v W.B.D. 1934	42 v W.B.D. 1951

Highest Individual Scores

Others since 1945

170 Homer H.W. v A.U.	1931	145 Matthews G.R.J. v Kid. 1984
162*Wilkinson K.W. v M&B	1977	142 Lord G.J. v M & B 1987
		138* Edwards J.B. v Smeth. 1951
		138 Weston M. v Worcs.C. 1982

Most Wickets in an Innings

10-14	Lockett A	v Stour	1926	9-52 Warne F v Dud.	1934
10-38	Howorth R	v Smeth.	1933	9-26 Hollies W.E. v Dud.	1940
10-21	Hollies W.E.	v M & B.	1940	9-45 Lee W. v M & B.	1945
9-35	Platt G.W.	v Dud.	1922	9-38 Dovey H. v Kid.	1960
9-44	Lockett A.	v Kid.	1926	9-63 Watts P. v Stour.	1968
9-44	Howorth R.	v Stour.	1933	9-19 Bagley P. v W.B.D.	1983

Highest Wicket Partnership

3.	234	v A.U.	Homer H.W.	170* Eley J.B. 82	1931
1.	199	v Warw,	Hemsley C.R.	117* Watson F.P. 111	1985

Most Runs in a Season

937	Matthews G.R.J.	1983
866	Headley R.G.A.	1978
864	Wilkinson K.W.	1978
854	Homer H.W.	1927

Most Centuries for the Club

10	Edwards H.C.
7	Homer H.W.
6	Wilkinson K.W.
5	Headley R.G.A., Matthews G.R.J.
4	Oliver P.R.
3	Dovey R., Mohammad M., Moule H.G. Weston M.J.

500 + Runs in a Season

6	Wilkinson K.W.
4	Mohammad M., Headley R.G.A.
3	Edwards H.C., Pearsall T.
2	Dovey R., Hemsley C.R., Homer H.W., Lee W., Moule H.G., Oliver P.R., Weston M.J., Watson F.P.
1	Edwards J.D.B., Lea A.E., Matthews G.R.J., Palmer C.H., Sedgley J.B. Woodhouse F.

Most Wickets in a Season

99	Hollies W.E.	1940
82	Lee W.	1937
78	Hollies W.E.	1941
74	Howorth R.	1933
74	Mantle J.	1921

50 + Wickets in a Season

7	Lee W.
5	Thomas A.E.
4	Platt G.W.
3	Lockett A.
2	Hollies W.E., Howorth R., Kelleher H.R.A.
1	Bowles J.J., Jackson P.F., Mantle J., Warne F.

Most 8 + Wickets

7	Lee W.
5	Hollies W.E.

SMETHWICK CRICKET & ATHLETIC CLUB

Club formed 1880

Member of League: — First Division 1891 to date
Second Division 1893 to date

1987 Secretary: — J. Cooper. Long Serving Secretary D.C. Bryant 1959-1975

Highest Team Score   Since 1945

410-5	v	Kid.	1922	280-3	v Stour.	1977
352-6	v	A.U.	1911	260-6	v Warw.	1981
315-5	v	O.H.	1928	257-6	v M & B	1981
				257-8	v Mos.	1983

Lowest Team Score   Since 1945

25	v	Kid.	1905 and 1936	43 v	M & B	1972

Highest Individual Scores   Since 1945

154	Neale A.J.L.	v Wal.	1926	150	Moore N	v Stour.	1979
145	Shipman W.	v Kid.	1921	141*	Moore N	v O.H.	1977
				135*	Smith K.D. v	O.H.	1987
				127*	Rowley B. v	Kid.	1961

Nine Wickets in an Innings

9-46 Rollings T.	v Warw.	1894	9-29 Durnell T.W.	v W.B.D.	1931
9-44 Bucknell A.	v W.B.D.	1912	9-40 Barnes S.F.	v Dud.	1935
9-47 Bucknell A.	v W.B.D.	1914	9-20 Durnell T.W.	v Wal.	1938

Highest Wicket Partnerships

2.	235* v M & B.	Neale A.J.L. 102*	Ellerker W.H. 136*		1929
4.	214 v O.H.	Haines W.H. 80	Mathews N.L. 140		1938

Most Runs in a Season

739	Moore N.	1978
701	Smith K.D.	1987
666	Binks T.	1977
657	Rowley B.	1957
649	McHenry R.	1960

Most Centuries for the Club

7	Ellerker W.H., Neale A.J.L.
5	Mathews N.L., Moore N.
4	Burgoyne F., Rowley B.
3	Pearson R.M.

500 + Runs in a Season

6	Binks T., Rowley B.
5	Moore N.
2	McHenry R., Thompson G.
1	Amiss D.L., Mathews N.L., Conway P., Ellerker W.H., Kallicharran D.I., Kaypee A., Mohammad Shadid, Pearson R.M., Pigott J., Smith K.D., Woodhouse F.

Most Wickets in a Season

85	Paine G.A.E.	1940
78	Booth A.	1952
77	Cowley	1901
75	Barnes S.F.	1935
71	Eden E.	1930
70	Boneham A.W.M.	1905

50 + Wickets in a Season

5	Boneham A.W.M.
4	Bucknell A.

3	Booth A., Shipman W.
2	Cowley, Durnell T.W., Oldham J.R., Paine G.A.E.
1	Armstrong T.R., Barnes S.F., Bird W., Downes N.C., Eden E., Pritchard T.L., Rowley B., Tucker C.

Most 8 + Wickets

5	Shipman W.
4	Bucknell A.
3	Boneham A.W.M., Durnell T.W.
2	Barnes S.F., Cowley., Paine G.A.E., Pallett H.J., Oldham J.R.

STOURBRIDGE CRICKET CLUB
Club formed 1860
(A Club is known to have existed and played on the present ground in 1857)

Member of League:- First and Second Divisions 1894 to date

1987 Secretary:- D. Collins. Long Serving Secretary J. Huband 1974-1982

Highest Team Score

Since 1945

295-8	v	M & B	1930	271-5	v	A.U.	1984
289	v	Dud.	1908	268-4	v	Kid.	1983
286-8	v	M & B	1927	255-4	v	W.B.D.	1987

Lowest Team Score

Since 1945

13	v	Kid.	1899	25	v	W.B.D.	1961

Highest Individual Scores

Since 1945

151*	Quaife W.G.	v	M & B	1897	146 Wright J.P. v M & B	1984
147	Burrows R.D.	v	Warw.	1894	140* Wright J.P. v O.H.	1985
					123* Richardson P.E. v M&B	1950
					123 Wright J.P. v M & B	1986

Most Wickets in an Innings

10-41	Snow R.	v	A.U.	1966
9-?	Burrows R.D.	v	A.U.	1894
9-40	Hickton W.H.	v	M & B	1907

Highest Wicket Partnerships

2.	223	v M & B	Wright J.P. 146	Banks D.A.	74*	1984
1.	201*	v Mos.	Horton M.J. 116*	Whiting N.H.	74*	1954

Most Runs in a Season

877	Wilkinson K.W.	1976
817	Livingston L.	1958
765	Wright J.P.	1985
752	Livingston L.	1959
748	Clare T.	1911

Most Centuries for the Club

9	Clare T.
5	Richardson P.E.
4	Bloomer J., Hill M., Kenyon D.
3	Banks D.A., Patel H., Quaife W.G., Wootton S.H., Wright J.P.

500 + Runs in a Season

6	Hill H.
3	Banks D.A.
2	Clare T., Livingston L., Wright J.P.
1	Bird R.E., Burchill S., Elliott C.S., Fitton G.A., Nichols J.E., Patel H., Quaife W.G., Richardson P.E., Robinson A.W., Stewart D.E.R., Walker D., Wootton S.H.

Most Wickets in a Season

75	Hickton W.H.	1907
71	Andrews W.H.R.	1948
70	Howorth R.	1952
69	Andrews W.H.R.	1949

50 + Wickets in a Season

4 Shepherd S.G.
3 Nichols J.E.
2 Andrews W.H.R., Hickton W.H., Howorth R.
1 Allchurch T., Grainger S., Mobberley C., Perry H., Smith G., Tilt J.D.

Most 8 + Wickets

2 Allchurch T., Hickton W.H.

WALSALL CRICKET CLUB
Club formed 1815

Member of League:- First Division 1889 to date — Founder Members
Second Division 1893 to date

1987 Secretary:- B.A. Middleton (1975 to date)

Highest Team Score   Since 1945

377	v	Smeth.	1896	265-6	v	M & B	1982
330-8	v	Mos.	1919	255-4	v	W.B.D.	1986
326-9	v	W.B.D.	1908	255-5	v	Worcs C.	1983

Lowest Team Score   Since 1945

19	v	O.H.	1925	39	v	Mos.	1965
19	v	M & B	1943				

Highest Individual Score   Since 1945

175 Taylor L.F.   v Smeth. 1914   129 Smailes T.F. v M & B   1950
168*Ashwell J.   v M & B. 1929   126 Paine G.A.E. v Mos.   1947
                                      124*Virgin R.T. v Warw.   1983
                                      118 Bender R. v W.B.D.   1972

Most Wickets in an Innings

10-37 Backhouse E.N. v Stour 1934   9-21 Freeman A.P. v Mos.   1937
10-34 Backhouse E.N. v W.B.D. 1935 9-65 Partridge N.E. v M & B 1937
10-44 Freeman A.P.   v Dud. 1937   9-25 Mayer J.H.   v M & B   1943
 9-20 Bird A.   v W.B.D. 1894 9-20 Aldridge K.J. v A.U.   1961

Highest Wicket Partnerships

2.   225* v M & B Ashwell J. 168* Wilkinson W.H. 60*   1929
1.   191   v M & B Brammer W.105   Preston W.   74   1910

Most Runs in a Season

1152	Yallop G.N.	1975
851	Virgin R.T.	1980
807	Mohammad Sadiq	1983
756	Archer N.J.	1984
729	Virgin R.T.	1981

Most Centuries for the Club

5 Virgin R.T.
4 Smith A
3 Foster M.K.

500 + Runs in a Season

5	Virgin R.T.
3	Archer N.J., Smith L.K., Taylor L.F.,
2	Cox D.F., Hewson N.P., Pearsall T.
1	Fletcher A.E., Foster M.K., Howorth R., Lowbridge G.R., Marsh N. Mohammad M., Mohammad S., Moore J.D., Parsons A.B.D., Patterson R.S., Smailes T.F.

Most Wickets in a Season

98	Freeman A.P.	1937
95	Backhouse E.N.	1935
85	Sedgwick H.A.	1922
80	Brammer W.	1908

50 + Wickets in a Season

10	Brammer W.
4	Sedgwick H.A.
3	Backhouse E.N., Doshi D.R., Durose A.J., Gregory G.J., Mayer J.H. Valentine A.L.
2	Bailey F., Bird A., Churm J., Freeman A.P., Partridge N.E.
1	Aldridge K.J., Bucknell A., Colston R., Dewsbery D., Hawley G., Howorth R., Mohammad M., Paine G.A.E., Smailes T.F., Soult., Wardrop J., Wilkinson W.H.

Most 8 + Wickets

10	Brammer
4	Backhouse E.N., Freeman A.P., Sedgwick H.A.
3	Mayer J.H., Partridge N.E.
2	Aldridge K.J., Bird A., Boothroyd R., Gregory G.J.

WARWICKSHIRE COUNTY CRICKET CLUB
Club formed 1882

Members of League:- 1894 One Season Club and Ground Side - First Division
1975 to date First and Second Divisions

1987 Secretary for League Side:- A.S.M. Oakman (Served 1978 to date)

Highest Team Score   Lowest Team Score

369-5	v	Wal.	1984	37	v	A.U. 1894 (Club & Ground)	
315-6	v	O.H.	1985	49	v	Stour. 1979	
314-7	v	Kid.	1982				

Highest Individual Scores

183*	Bainbridge H.W.	v	Dud.	1894 (Club & Ground)
159	Wootton S.H.	v	Kid.	1982
153	Lord G.J.	v	Wal.	1984
149	Lloyd T.A.	v	Kid.	1978

Most Wickets in an Innings

9-32 Pallett H.J.	v	Smeth.	1894	7-46 Morton W.	v	A.U.	1984	
7-16 Smith D.M.	v	Kid.	1983	7-48 Smith D.M.	v	Dup.	1981	
7-19 Pierson A.R.K.	v	A.U.	1986	7-55 Lord G.J.	v	Stour.	1979	
7-34 Ferreira A.M.	v	C&NW	1986					

Highest Wicket Partnerships

1.	266*	v Smeth.	Thomas G.P.	117*	Asif Din M.	139*	1979
2.	254*	v Smeth.	Abberley R.N.	146*	Jones A.K.C.	103*	1975

Most Runs in a Season

834	Jones A.K.C.	1975
770	Lord G.J.	1985
770	Thomas G.P.	1979

Most Centuries for Club

8	Asif Din M.
6	Lord G.J.
5	Lloyd T.A.
4	Wootton S.H.

500 + Runs in a Season

3	Lord G.J., Thomas G.P.
2	Asif Din M.
1	Abberley R.N., Jones A.K.C., Lloyd T.A., Percival D.C., Ratcliffe J.D., Tedstone G.A., Wootton S.H.

Most Wickets in a Season

51	Smith D.M.	1982
36	Hopkins D.C.	1977
35	Hopkins D.C.	1976
33	Smith D.M.	1981
33	Weir R.S.	1987

50 Runs and 5 wkts. in a Match

2	Lord G.J.

WEST BROMWICH DARTMOUTH CRICKET CLUB
Club formed 1834

Member of League:- First Division 1889 to date — Founder Member
Second Division 1893 to date

1987 Secretary:- M.K. Cooper, Long Serving Secretary H.E. Mitchell 1930 approx — 1957

Highest Team Score   Since 1945

323-5	v	Wal.	1931		283-4	v	A.U.	1987
309-3	v	Dud.	1930		275-4	v	O.H.	1975
309-7	v	Dud.	1934		269-3	v	Kid.	1981

Lowest Team Score   Since 1945

20	v	Mos.	1897		33	v	Smeth. 1954

Highest Individual Scores   Since 1945

176	Perry E.	v	Dud.	1930	155	Perry E.	v	A.U. 1948
153	Spring A.W.	v	Smeth.	1923	130*	Edmundson M. v		O.H. 1975
					127*	Williams R.	v	O.H. 1965
					126*	Perry E.	v	Mos. 1948

Most Wickets in an Innings

10-47	Miller R.	v	A.U.	1968	9-58	Perks R.T.D.	v	Stour. 1940
9-?	Treadwell W.	v	Stour.	1894	9-52	Hollies W.E.	v	Dud. 1943
9-56	Pallett H.J.	v	M&B	1901	9-62	Hollies W.E.	v	Wal. 1945
9-34	Mitchell H.E.	v	Dud.	1908	9-25	Hollies W.E.	v	Smeth.1945
9-55	Langwell W.W.	v	Kid.	1914	9-39	Allen F.	v	Mos. 1946
9-43	Waddington A.	v	A.U.	1928	9-30	Shardlow B.	v	Kid. 1955
9-31	Tate C.F.	v	Smeth.	1936	9-32	Bradley P.	v	A.U. 1974

Highest Wicket Partnerships

1.	228	v	Dud.	Stimpson P.	108	Slade D.N.F. 114*	1973
5.	225*	v	O.H.	Clift P.B.	102*	Edmundson M. 130*	1975

Most Runs in a Season

1407	Slade D.N.F.	1978		746	Slade D.N.F.	1973
908	Slade D.N.F.	1979		706	Perry E.	1934
780	Perry E.	1930		701	Slade D.N.F.	1977

Most Centuries for the Club

16   Perry E.
11   Jones W
10   Slade D.N.F.
 6   Williams R.
 4   Fellows-Smith J.P., Neal S.A.

500 + Runs in a Season

8   Slade D.N.F.
7   Perry E.
6   Neal S.A.
5   Williams R.
4   Patel H.V.
3   Croom L.C.B.
2   Humphries A.P.
1   Abel B., Babar A., Brown T., Clift P.B., Din A., Edmundson M., Fellows-Smith J.P., Holloway A., Humphries D.J., Hunt P.J., Jackson S., Jones W.E., Morton A., Patel K., Stanley T.H.

Most Wickets in a Season

94   Perks R.T.D.   1940
91   Shardlow B   1955
90   Hollies W.E.   1945
89   Gover A.R.   1948
81   Hollies W.E.   1944

Most 8 + Wickets

7   Tate C.F.
6   Hollies W.E.
4   Shardlow B.
3   Pallett H.J.

WORCESTER CITY CRICKET CLUB
Club formed 1919

Member of League:-   1982 to date

1987 Secretary:-   I.C. Pugh

Highest Team Score

312-4   v   Mos.   1982
293-5   v   W.B.D.   1982
279-5   v   M & B   1984

Lowest Team Score

32   v   C & N.W.   1986

Highest Individual Score

128   Slade D.N.F. v M & B.   1982
120*   Henderson S. v Stour.   1982
113*   Hounsell P.   v M & B.   1984

Best Bowling in an Innings

8-47 D'Oliveira D.B. v Wal.   1983

Highest Wicket Partnerships

2.   140   v   O.H.   Scott M.   79*   Watkins S.G.   68   1984
3.   117   v   W.B.D. D'Oliveira D.B. 75   Walker D.J.   63   1982

Most Runs in a Season and 500 +

849 Slade D.N.F.   1982   638 D'Oliveira D.B.   1982
834 Hounsell P.   1984   516 Walker D.J.   1983
793 Walker D.J.   1982

Most Centuries for Club

2   Hounsell P.
1   Henderson S., Slade D.N.F.

Most Wickets and 50 + in a Season

55   McEwan S.M.   1984

Eric Lawday, still scoring for the Second Eleven in 1987, was present at the meeting when the Club was founded.

DUPORT CRICKET CLUB

Club formed 1940 — Closed 1981

Members of League:- First Division 1977–1981
                           Second Division 1975–1981

Secretary:- W. Probert.

Highest Team Score: 278-8   v   Kid.   1978

Lowest Team Score: 54   v   Wal.   1980

Highest Individual Score: 124   Jones K.V. v Kid.   1978

Best Bowling: 7-29 Buttress J. v   Mos.   1980

Highest Wicket Partnership:
1.   128 v Kid. Barker A.R. 77 Wilcock H.G. 69 1977

Most Runs and 500 + in a Season: 519 Hemsley C.R.   1978

Most Centuries for Club: 2   Wilcock H.G.

Most Wickets in a Season

32   Hobbs R.N.S.   1977
32   Wilson N.   1978
28   Jones P.H.   1978

WORCESTERSHIRE COUNTY CRICKET CLUB

Club Formed 1865

Members of League:- First Division 1975–1976

Secretary:- M.D. Vockins

Highest Team Score: 248-2   v   Stour   1975

Lowest Team Score: 79   v   Kid.   1976

Highest Individual Score

152*   Wilkinson K.W. v   Stour.   1975
146*   Neal P.A.   v   Mos.   1975

Best Bowling in an Innings: 7-53 Roberts C.P. v Smeth. 1975

Highest Wicket Parnerships

1.   119   v   A.U. Wilkinson K.W. 77* Bates C 50   1975
2.   182   v   Mos. Bates C. 71 Hemsley E.J.O. 102 1975

Most Runs and 500 + in a Season: 556 Wilkinson K.W.   1975

Most Wickets in a Season

29   Roberts C.P.   1975
27   Pridgeon A.P.   1975
27   Senghera R.   1975

SALTERS CRICKET CLUB

Members of League:- First Division 1889 — Founder Member

Highest Team Score: 229-5   v   Kings Heath

Lowest Team Score: 57   v   H. Wood

Highest Individual Score: 115* Richards W.   v   Kings Heath

Best Bowling in an Innings: 9-19 Horton J. v   Wal.

SMALL HEATH CRICKET CLUB

Members of League:- First Division 1892—1894
Second Division 1893—1894

Highest Team Score: 221   v   Smeth.   1893

Lowest Team Score: 20   v   Stour.   1894

Highest Individual Score: 104* Gibbons J.   v   W.B.D.   1894

Best Bowling: 8-24 Whitehead J.   v   Mos.   1893

50 + Wickets in a Season: 54 Whitehead J.   1893

HANDSWORTH WOOD CRICKET CLUB

Club Formed 1877 closed 1920

Members of League:- First Division 1889 to 1919 — Founder Members
Second Division 1893 to 1919

Highest Team Score : 333-5   v   Dudley   1896

Lowest Team Score: 22   v   A.U.   1890

Most Wickets in an Innings

10-11	Hill H.B.G. v	M & B	1905	9-74 Hill H.B.G.	v	A.U.	1896
9-?	Hill H.B.G v	A.U.	1890	9-63 Hill H.B.G.	v	Kid.	1907
9-19	Hill H.B.G. v	W.B.D	1892	9-49 Evans R.	v	Wal.	1911

Highest Wicket Partnerships

1.   226 v Kid. Manton J. 170 Wigley E.H. 54   1908
2.   187* v Wal. Hill J.E.   101* Everett R.S.100*   1893

Most Runs and 500 + in a Season

689 Hill J.E.   1897
547 Fereday J.B.   1913
522 Hill J.E.   1893
514 Hill J.E.   1892

Most Centuries for Club

9   Hill J.E.
6   Everett R.S.
4   Quaife W.
2   Fereday J.B.

Most Wickets in a Season

83   Hill H.B.G.   1902

50 + Wickets in a Season

8   Hill H.B.G.
1   Barton J.

8 + Wickets

15   Hill H.B.G.
 4   Barton J.

WEDNESBURY CRICKET CLUB
Club Formed 1875

Members of League:- First Division 1890 to 1893
Second Division 1893

Highest Team Score:	158-5	v	W.B.D.	1892
Lowest Team Score:	14	v	W.B.D.	1892
50 + Wickets in a Season:		63 Flowers J.		1891

HOLY TRINITY CRICKET CLUB
Club Formed 1923 at Holy Trinity Church, Smethwick

Members of League:- Third Division 1980 to 1981

Long Serving Secretary:-   R. Lowe 1948–1986.

ALDRIDGE CRICKET CLUB
Club Formed 1853

Members of League:- Third Division 1983 to date.

1987 Secretary:-   M. Cooper.

DIVISION TWO

Championships

21	Mitchells and Butlers	5	Smethwick
15	Moseley	4	Dudley
11	Walsall	4	Kidderminster
10	Aston Unity	3	Handsworth Wood
8	West Bromwich Dartmouth	3	Stourbridge
6	Old Hill		

Highest Team Scores

A.U.	338-9	v	Moseley	1913
		v	Smethwick	1913
C & N.W.	236-5	v	Kidderminster	1987
Dudley	305	v	H. Wood	1910
H.Wood	334-9	v	Moseley	1898
Kid.	300-8	v	M & B	1923
M & B	367-4	v	Walsall	1924
Moseley	349-6	v	Walsall	1924
O.H.	398-6	v	Smethwick	1928
Smeth.	329-2	v	Moseley	1929
Stour.	289-9	v	M & B	1909
Walsall	357	v	Stour.	1898
Warw.	348-1	v	Duport	1978
W.B.D.	343-8	v	Kidd.	1905
Worc. C.	268-6	v	O.H.	1983

Lowest Team Scores

A.U.	25	v	Dudley	1966
C & N.W.	85	v	M & B	1987
Dudley	23	v	H.Wood	1903

H.Wood	22	v	W.B.D.		1894
Kidd.	23	v	H. Wood		1899
M & B	34	v	W.B.D.		1920
		v	Moseley		1922
Moseley	9	v	S. Heath		1893
O.H.	13	v	W.B.D.		1948
Smeth.	17	v	Moseley		1893
Stour.	14	v	Smethwick		1938
Walsall	20	v	Stourbridge		1930
Warw.	46	v	Stourbridge		1985
W.B.D.	16	v	H. Wood.		1900
Worc. C.	60	v	O.H.		1982

Highest Individual Innings

	A.U.	128	Ingram R.N.	v	Kid.		1982
	C & N.W.	110*	Robinson D.	v	W.B.D.		1986
	Dudley	202*	Willetts N.	v	Moseley		1984
	H. Wood	161	Mottershead T.	v	Kid.		1903
	Kid.	200	Tomkinson G.S.	v	Stour.		1934
	M & B	225*	Ogle W.	v	Walsall		1924
	Moseley	163	Thompson R.	v	Stour.		1959
+	O.H.	243*	Forrest B.G.	v	Walsall		1931
	Smeth.	170*	Bayley T.E.	v	Moseley		1929
	Stour.	147*	Perry H.	v	Kid.		1922
	Walsall	176*	Thacker H.D.	v	M & B		1930
	Warw.	155*	Wootton S.H.	v	Duport		1978
	W.B.D.	130	Hodgson A.	v	Moseley		1967
	Worc. C.	127	Cairney S.	v	M & B		1984

+ 243* is the Highest in any Division

E. Hadley of M & B also topped 200 with 221 v Walsall 1906.

Best Bowling in an Innings

A.U.	9-24	Mortimore H.L.	v	Walsall		1906
C & N.W.	7-59	King M.	v	A.U.		1987
Dudley	9-15	Haycock E.	v	W.B.D.		1930
H.Wood	9-?	Ward R.T.	v	Kidd.		1911
Kidd.	10-38	Weston P.	v	O.H.		1983
M & B	10-18	Fereday H.	v	Walsall		1932
Moseley	9-22	Morgan P.	v	Walsall		1973
O.H.	9-35	Cresswell A.	v	Dudley		1983
Smeth.	9-40	Wheldon C.	v	M & B		1920
Stour.	9-10	Bidmead P.	v	Moseley		1897
Walsall	9-9	Colston R.	v	M & B		1898
Walsall	9-9	Gilbert C.H.	v	Moseley		1900
Warw.	9-25	Khan H.	v	A.U.		1979
W.B.D.	9-21	Kenway	v	H. Wood		1894
Worc. C.	8-47	Instan C.	v	Kidd.		1982

100 Runs and 5 Wickets in a match

Rea G.W.	108	and	5-18	A.U.	v	Moseley	1925
Hastilow C.A.F.	100		6-16	Moseley	v	W.B.D.	1926
Broadbent F.	124*		7-?	M & B	v	Stour.	1928
Woodroffe A.	103*		7-37	A.U.	v	Stour.	1936
Clements V.	100		6-67	Warw.	v	Dudley	1980

4 Wickets in 4 Balls

Martin H.	W.B.D.	v	Smethwick	1895
Stanley E.	O.H.	v	Stourbridge	1938

LEAGUE PERSONALITIES

Alan Townsend
M & B

C.L. Price
Aston Unity

A.E. Fletcher
M & B, Walsall

Norman Downes
Smethwick

Eric Perry
West Bromwich
Dartmouth

G.A.E. Paine
Smethwick, Kidderminster,
Walsall, Moseley

G.S. Tomkinson
Kidderminster

W.H. Wilkes
Kidderminster

B. Rowley
Smethwick, Old Hill

211

CHRONOLOGICAL TABLE

League	General Cricket	General Events
	1880 Birmingham and District Cricket Association formed.	
		1887 Queen Victoria's Diamond Jubilee.
1888 Birmingham and District Cricket League formed		1888 Birmingham became a County Borough
	1889 'Lords' Pavilion built	1889 Birmingham became a City
1890 Wednesbury C.C. replaced Salters C.C.		
1891 Smethwick C.C. joined League		
1892 Small Heath C.C. joined League F. Breedon (Moseley) takes 10w v Smethwick	1892 'Instructions to Umpires' issued by M.C.C.	
1893 Dudley C.C. replaced Mitchells C.C. Second Division formed Moseley 2nd XI out for 9 v Small Heath.		
1894 Wednesbury C.C. resigned Stourbridge C.C. and Warwickshire Club and Ground joined. Charity Cup inaugurated.	1894 Warwickshire, Derbyshire, Essex and Leicestershire recognised as 'First Class Counties'.	
1895 Warwickshire Club & Ground and Small Heath C.C. resigned Kidderminster C.C. joined.	1895 First visit of English team to West Indies	
1896 'Instructions to Umpires' issued by League. All Hits to or over boundary to be 4's. 2 Professionals instead of 3 per Club. 1896 Mitchells C.C. rejoined.		1896 Power driven vehicles allowed on roads without a man in front with red flag.
1898 Mitchells C.C. became Mitchells and Butlers C.C.		

League	General Cricket	General Events
1899 Charity Cup Competition discontinued. 1 Professional instead of 2 per club. Stourbridge C.C. all out for 13 v Kidderminster.	1899 Worcestershire elected to 'First Class County' status	1899 Boer War started
1900 6 ball overs adopted.	1900 6 ball overs (instead of 5) introduced.	1900 Birmingham University Incorporated
		1901 Queen Victoria died. Edward VIIth became King.
	1902 First Test Match at Edgbaston (v Australians.) Bowling crease widened from 3ft to 4ft on either side of wicket.	1902 Boer War ends.
	1903 RV. Ryder succeeded W. Ansell as Secretary of Warwickshire.	
1909 Walsall C.C. moved to 'Gorway'.	1909 Imperial Cricket Conference instituted.	1909 First Air crossing of English Channel (by Bleriot)
1910 Adopt hits dropping over boundary to count 6. C.H. Smith succeeded H.B.G. Hill as Hon. Secretary. 3 points for win instead of 2.	1910 Hits dropping over boundary to count 6.	1910 King Edward VII died King George V became King.
	1911 Warwickshire County Champions for first time.	1911 Greater Birmingham established.
1915-1918 No Cricket.		1914-1918 Great War.
1919 League Cricket resumed. 3 May Dudley 12 all out v Walsall. 9 Aug. Aggregate runs 659 Moseley v Walsall. Stourbridge win Championship for first time.		1919 First Airship, R34 crossed Atlantic.

League	General Cricket	General Events
1920 Handsworth Wood left League — Old Hill joined. W.B. Dartmouth moved to Sandwell Park. Kidderminster bought Chester Road ground. J.A. Lones appointed Hon. Sec.		1920 First Traffic Islands in Birmingham.
	1921 Glamorgan last County to be admitted to County Championship..	
1922 Smethwick scored 410-6 v Kidderminster.	1922 Warwickshire dismissed Hampshire for 15 — Hampshire won!	1922 BBC started daily broadcasts from London. Austin 7 launched at cost of £165.
1924 Moseley survived special General meeting to consider disbanding.		1924 First Crossword published in British newspaper.
1925 Kidderminster opened new pavilion.	1925 8 ball overs used in M.C.C. tour of Australia. Local cricket umpires Association formed.	
1926 First League Handbook issued.	1926 'Umpires Corner' started in Sports Argus.	1926 General Strike 3rd — 13th. May.
	1927 First radio commentary on a game — Essex v New Zealand.	
1928 Stourbridge opened new pavilion.	1928 Examination for Umpires started by Midland Counties U.A.	
		1929 First radio commentary on F.A. Cup Final. First Traffic Lights in Birmingham.
1930 F.T. Cozens — President for 42 years retired. First grant from Benevolent Fund to Royal Orphanage Wolverhampton. Mitchells & Butlers opened ground at Portland Road.		1930 R101 Airship disaster.

League	General Cricket	General Events
1931 Moseley moved to Moorlands. Walsall sold 'Gorway' to the Corporation. May - B.G. Forrest Old Hill 2nd's scored 243 n.o. v Walsall. Aug. - Old Hill scored 413-6 after Aston Unity dismissed for 82.	1931 Wicket height and width increased to 28" and 9".	
1932 L.E. Gale and C.H. Bull of Dudley scored 264 unbroken for first wicket v Aston Unity.	1932 P. Holmes and H. Sutcliffe record partnership of 555. Bodyline controversey in Australia.	
1935 West Bromwich Dartmouth and Old Hill purchased their grounds. Walsall's team dubbed as 'Preston's Circus.' Sydney Barnes returned at the age of 62 to play for Smethwick.		1935 Silver Jubilee of King George V and Queen Mary.
	1936 Lbw law extended to cover ball pitched on offside of wicket.	1936 King George V died – Edward VIII became King but Abdicated and in December George VI became King. Spanish Civil War started. BBC Television Service opened.
		1937 Thousands attempting to visit Dudley Zoo were locked out due to large attendance.
1938 C.H. Smith - former League Secretary received Knighthood.	1938 First television broadcast of a Test Match.	
1939 H.O. Kirton and R.A.D. Wyatt (M&B) scored 288 for first wicket v W.B. Dartmouth.		1939 3rd September Great Britain declared war on Germany. Elmdon airport opened.
1940 League continued but one Division only. Eric Hollies took 99 wickets.	1940 First Class Cricket in England discontinued.	
1941 Aston Unity and Moseley play all away games. Mitchells and Butlers play war-time games at Cape Hill.		

League	General Cricket	General Events
	1942-44 Birmingham Cricket Festivals at Edgbaston.	
1944 From 1945 Score books to be closed when game won.	1944 Mr. L.T. Deakins appointed Secretary of Warwickshire C.C.	
1945 Restart Div. 2.		1945 8th May V.E.Day 14th August VJ Day.
1946 Aston Unity loaned ground in Erdington.		1946 National Health Service created.
1947 Aston Unity moved to 'Hillcourt'.	1947 Laws of Cricket Revised.	
1948 League Advisory Committee formed.	1948 Last appearance in England of Donald Bradman - bowled by Eric Hollies.	
1949 League Rules revised.		
1950 Ken Spooner appointed Hon. Secretary.		
1951 Smethwick win Championship for first time. League 'Consider' writing of League History.	1951 Warwickshire win County Championship.	1951 Festival of Britain
		1952 King George VI died Elizabeth II became Queen.
1953 Pre-season games v Warwickshire C.C.C. inaugurated.	1953 Len Hutton first Professional to Captain England in modern times.	
1954 Moseley to Robin Hood Stadium.		
		1955 I.T.V. broadcasting service started.
	1956 Jim Laker 9-37 and 10-53 v Australians at Old Trafford.	1956 Suez Crisis.
1958 Challenge Cup Inaugurated.		
1959 Moseley moved to 'Scorers'.	1959 Second Eleven County Competition Inaugurated.	
1962 Bonus point system introduced for faster scoring rate.	1962 League Cricket Conference formed.	

League	General Cricket	General Events
1963 J.A. Williams appointed Hon. Secretary.	1963 'Gillette Cup' introduced. Distinction between Amateur & Professional discontinued.	
	1964 Worcestershire won County Championship.	1964 Birmingham 'Bull Ring' Shopping Centre opened.
	1965 Worcestershire won County Championship.	1965 Winston Churchill died.
	1966 Warwickshire won Gillette Cup.	1966 Aston College became Aston University. England won Soccers' 'World Cup'.
		1967 Modernised Birmingham New Street Railway station opened.
	1968 Basil D'Oliveira not allowed on Tour of South Africa. Tour cancelled. Warwickshire Cricket Association formed. Warwickshire won Gillette Cup.	
1969 Maximum overs for side batting first to be 60.	1969 John Player League introduced.	1969 M6 Spaghetti Junction opened.
	1970 '20 overs' minimum in last hour of match introduced. South African Tour of England cancelled.	
	1971 Worcestershire won John Player League.	1971 Decimal currency introduced.
1972 League won League Cricket Conference Trophy. Maximum overs for side batting first to be 55. Presentation to 'Rusty' Scorer on his 80th. birthday.	1972 Benson & Hedges Trophy introduced. Warwickshire won County Championship.	1972 Britain joined Common Market. 1972 Snow Hill Railway Station, Birmingham closed.
1973 Aston Unity move to Coppice Lane.		
	1974 Worcestershire win County Championship. Warwickshire's John Jameson 240 and Rohan Kanhai 213 scored world record 2nd wicket partnership of 465 unbroken.	1974 I.R.A. bombs at Rotunda Birmingham.

League	General Cricket	General Events
1975 League increased from 10 to 12 Clubs with entry of Warwickshire Div 1 and 2, Worcestershire Div 1 and Duport Div.2.	1975 First Cricket World Cup in England.	
	1976 Alan C. Smith appointed Secretary of Warwickshire C.C.C.	1976 National Exhibition Centre opened by H.M. Queen Elizabeth II.
1977 Duport replaced Worcestershire in Div.1. League Management Committee replaced Advisory Committee. Third Division formed.	1977 Geoff Boycott scored 100th First Class Century.	1977 Queen Elizabeth II's Silver Jubilee.
1978 D.C. Bryant appointed Hon. Secretary. League Rules revised.	1978 Dennis Amiss introduced helmets for batsmen.	
	1979 Association of Cricket Umpires formed.	
1980 Moseley win National Cricket Association Trophy at Lords (John Haig Trophy)	1980 Laws of Cricket revised - introduced new dismissal 'Timed Out'. Warwickshire win John Player League.	
1981 Points system changed to 5 for a win.		
1982 Worcester City replaced Duport.	1982 Warwickshire C.C.C.'s Centenary.	1982 Falklands War.
1983 50 over matches introduced. 10 points for Win 6 for Winning Draw 2 for Losing Draw.		
1984 Old Hill win National Cricket Association Trophy at Lords (Wm. Younger Cup). Radio West Midlands gave commentaries on games. Penalty points for slow over rates introduced.		
1985 Dudley ground closed by subsidence. Old Hill win National Cricket Association Trophy at Lords (Wm. Younger Cup).	1985 Penalty runs for No Balls and Wides to count against bowlers analysis.	

1986 Coventry and
North Warwickshire
replaced Dudley.
Stourbridge win
National Cricket
Association Trophy at
Lords (Wm.Younger
Cup).
2nd Division Challenge
Cup Inaugurated.

1986 David Heath
appointed Secretary of
Warwickshire C.C.C.
Dennis Amiss scored his
100th First Class Century.
Norman Gifford took his
2000th First Class wicket.

1987 Old Hill win
National Cricket
Association Trophy at
Lords ('Cockspur Cup').

1987 Worcestershire won
Refuge Assurance League.

1987 Snow Hill Rail-
way Station Birming-
ham re-opened.

INDEX

*:- League Player who has played in First Class Cricket —

a:- Reference in Appendix.

Grace, A. 104, 130
Grace, W.G. 148
Grainger, S. 68, 69, 85, 171, a
Grainger, T. 87, 104
Grant, A. 134, 139, a
Grant, E.T. 2, 5
Grant, R. 134, 139, a
* Graveney, T.W. 104, a
Green, B. 175
Green, Carlton. 128, 144
Green, Chris. 130, 138, a
Green, D. 84
Green, F.G. 27
Green, G.H. 152
Green, M. 119, 128, 136-8, a
Green, Mel. 104, 130
Green, Mrs. J. 175
Greenaway, J.H. a
Greenhough, M. 106-7, 121
Greenwood, J. 150
Greenwood, L.H. 39
* Greenwood, P. 77
Gregory, G.J. 78, 92, 106, a
Grew, -. 15
* Griffiths, K. 102
* Grimshaw, C.H. 24, 26, 29, a
Grimshaw, J.A. 137
* Gross, F.A. 57, 62, 63, 69, 71, 76,
163, a
Grosvenor, D. 122, 143
* Grove, C.W. 64, 69, 85, 164
* Groves, C. 132-4
Groves, H.G. 89
Guest, D. 106

Hackett, H.H. 153
Hackett, N. 125
Hadley, E. 33, 49, a
* Hagan, D. 134
Hagger, T. 130
Haines, W.H. 59, 68, a
Hall, J.E. 171
Hall, D. 104, 106
Hall, R. 171
Hamilton-Brown, R. 113
Hamlett, B. 171
Hammonds, C. 78
Hampton, G. 103-4
Harbage, C.B. 41, 49, 57, 62, 69
Hardwick, S. 143
Hardy, -. 15
Hargreaves, R. 101, 122, 136
Harmer, W.A. 57
Harold, -. 5
Harper, D. 171
Harper, G. 85
Harper, L. 85
Harris, Dan. 37
Harris, D. 58, 88
* Harris, D.F. 75, 83
* Harris, E.J. 128, 131, 143
Harris, P.M. 75, 88, 99, 102-4, 112,
118-19, 132, a
Harris, W.H. 37

Harrison, C.S. 75, 83, 87
Harrison, W.K. 24
Harrys, G. 98, 129, 130-1, 138, 142,
a
Hartill, N. 55
Hartley, W.H. 26
Hartwell, C.H. 18
Harvatt, M. 59
Harvey, W. a
Harvey, W.H. 171
* Hastilow, C.A.F. 37-8, 48, 58, 151,
169, a
Haswell, T.H. 23
Hatfield, B. 93
Hatfield, W.E. 24-5, 38, 41, 45, 152
Hawke, A.H. 20, 29
Hawkes, T. 103-4, 126, 128, 166
Hawkins, -. 27, 32
Hawkins, T. 2
Hawley, G. 37, a
Haycock, E. 55, a
Hayes, A.D. a
Hayes, G. 119, 129
Hayes, K. 173
Haynes, G. 122, 123
Head, A. 106, 110
* Headley, G.A. 79, 80, 84, 89, 92,
164, a
* Headley, R.G.A. 74, 79, 81, 93, 124,
125, 130, 141, 152, 164, a
Headley, S. 100
Headley, S.A.E. 143
Heard, P.G. 75, 102, 104, 106, a
* Heath, D.M.W. 76, 79, 81, 88, 90,
92-3, 96, 97, 98, 100, 112, 130, 142,
164, a
Heath, J. 87, 113
Heath, M. 142, 144
Heath, N. 139
Hedges, T. 25
Hemmings, B. 89
* Hemmings, E.E. a
Hemsley, C.R. 118-9, 124, 125, 132,
135, 137, 139, 142, a
* Hemsley, E.J.O. a
* Henderson, S.P. 130, a
Herbert, E.J. 75
Hewson, N.P. 20, 26, 37, 39, a
Heywood, E. 43, 57, 63, a
* Hick, G.A. 117-9, 141, a
Hickin L.B. 87
Hicklin, W. 75, 79, 89, 130
Hickman, J. 89
* Hickton, W.H. 26, a
* Higginson, J.D. 37
Hight, J.A. 54, 78, 103, a
Hill, A.O. 75, 83
* Hill, H.B.G. 3, 5, 7, 15-16, 23, 27, 29,
32, 59, 158, 163, 169, 176, a
Hill, H.F. 73, 147
* Hill, J.E. 15, 16, 23, 29, 163, a
Hill, M. 101, 106, 112, 122, a
Hill, T.E. 15

224

226

227

INDEX OF ILLUSTRATIONS